FRINGES

LIFE ON THE EDGE OF PROFESSIONAL RUGBY

BEN MERCER

OUTLIER PRESS

INTRODUCTION

Athletes, maybe even more than other people, depend on the myths they can tell about themselves

— BENJAMIN MARKOVITZ

We all tell our own story. Look at a block of flats and you'll see 1000 souls all starring in their own drama, telling and retelling their own lives.

I moved to France to continue my professional rugby story. I'd given England a bash and hadn't made the top division. This was a bit of a last go, a chance to do something different, live somewhere I'd always wanted to live.

French rugby always held a romantic appeal for me. The *laissez-faire* approach to life, learning the language and the thrill of *'joue'* when everything comes off miraculously.

Famous French wins against the All Blacks in 1999 or even heroic defeats like the World Cup Final in 2011, the European dominance of the swashbuckling Stade Toulousain in the 2000s with homegrown players slinging the ball everywhere, their insouciance combined with the sheer joy of playing so expressively.

My years there did give me these experiences. I learned the language, threw the ball around and lived with a degree of insouciance for a while. Later things began to rub against me, shaking me out of my complacency and I began to question what I was doing there. The team began to think the same thing.

This story is about the things I learned or didn't learn during my career. How professional rugby works. And what you do when you realise that what you're doing isn't enough for you anymore.

What I'll tell you about in this book is not necessarily right and others who were there could disagree. The events I describe are true to the best of my recollection and how I feel about these things may be tempered by time and perspective, a gradual shaping of my own history. I'm now retired from playing and don't necessarily miss it.

I'm not beholden to sensitivity or reputation in the way that a higher profile player is, although I will withhold some details to save potential embarrassment or just to do right by some of my former teammates. My gay teammate doesn't need outing by me, even if he was happy for everyone at the club to know about him. My teammates taking drugs don't need naming, even if they may not still be playing. To know that these things happen in the context of professional sport is insight enough.

Some of the insights may be easy to dismiss as things that only happen at a lower level, not at the more rarefied echelons of the game. I can tell you that many of these things are universal and that money doesn't make people essentially different. It just gives them greater resources to indulge their similar impulses.

Where top players vary from the likes of me is in the diversity of their experiences. They play the same teams every year. They visit the same stadiums every year. They play against the same guys by and large every year. A guy like me has a far more diverse range of rugby experiences and in this book, I'll attempt to communicate them to you.

I gained an English Literature degree before embarking on my professional rugby career proper and have always fancied the idea of writing a book. Infrequent attempts at writing things up to this point have been me paying lip service to this idea but perhaps not really believing in it. The pages of a book are an easy place to fail and I became someone scared to fail, both on the field and away from it.

Simultaneously I've regarded myself as something of a scholar athlete, finishing my studies and continuing to learn while I've been playing, most notably by learning French. This book is partly me justifying my self-proclaimed status as a Platonic scholar athlete, partly a way of showing you what's behind the curtain of professional rugby in another country.

Stories can keep us alive and moving forward, even as they exert a pull back into the past. In sport you're always looking back at where you've come from, what you've just done and at what's coming next weekend, but you never feel more alive than you do in the moment, on the field, where you can forget about everything else. That's why we all play.

Crafting our own story is something we do every day, with everything we do. Here I'm writing my own history. Moving to France wasn't an attempt at writing history; I just didn't have a job and felt that this could be my next adventure. That adventure became something unique and special, being a part of building a new bastion of rugby in a non-traditional rugby region. Now, that adventure is over but I get to tell my version of it here. I hope you enjoy it.

1

YEAR ONE - CROSSING THE CHANNEL

WHEN THE BALL I PASSED HIT MY WINGER IN THE FACE, KNOCKING him over and halting the session, I looked around at the desolate training pitch in the French public park, at my motley collection of new teammates in a random array of training attire and thought I'd made a big mistake.

I'd signed for a year at Stade Rouennais; a project team with wealthy owners and lofty ambitions in the north of France. The aim was to create a new rugby power in the non-traditional rugby region of Normandy. Judging by our first session, this aim was not a realistic one.

Realism was something that was beginning to permeate my view of rugby as a career path. I'd spent a couple of seasons as a second division player for Plymouth Albion in the RFU Championship, the second tier of English rugby, taking a short break in Sydney before pitching up at the Cornish Pirates, and was now beginning to take stock of my options.

I'd been an ambitious young player, deferring my plans to pursue professional rugby to attend university and get the security that came with a degree. The utility of my English Literature degree is up for debate but credentialism and the need to justify my decent school grades played their part, as well as my desire to leave home and experience the university lifestyle.

Upon graduation, I immediately decamped to Plymouth for two seasons, fabricating a holiday so I could spend a week in the gym sweating out my final university excesses before arriving for preseason. After two years in Devon, I headed to Australia for a couple of months, which turned into almost a year, before heading back to the UK where I saw the Pirates as an opportunity to restate my claims of being a good enough player to reach the Premiership.

Rugby is not a good option as a career path. Even if you avoid serious injury, your career will be over in your thirties and the average Premiership salary is about £150,000 a year. There are only 500 or so of these contracts, making getting one extremely competitive, and I'd wager that this average salary is heavily skewed by the top end of the market where some guys will be receiving up to half a million pounds per season for their efforts. A select few are now getting more than that.

There is also the matter of your position. If each team had 4 players in each position then you need to be in the top 50 players in yours to get a deal. With hundreds of thousands of registered players in the UK, as well as talented foreign players being readily available, the odds are not in your favour.

The Championship is far less well remunerated while offering you little to no job security. Most deals are one year long and are liable to be snatched away from you if injury suddenly makes you unavailable for any substantial length of time. As an outside back in my mid twenties, I was no longer a 'young' player but almost a mid-career professional and unless something changed for me quickly, my youthful dreams of the top level of the sport would remain just that.

Demographics are against you in rugby and securing a contract in the Championship that pays you a liveable wage is no mean feat.

Extending the statistics quoted above means that you're probably in the top 100 players in your position in the country if you're playing in the Championship, yet this is not enough to guarantee a living. Many contracts are less than £20,000 a year while some are as little as £6,000. You can be in the top 100 in your profession and feel like a failure. I'd tended to earn reasonably in the Championship through incentivised contracts and keeping my living costs down but I by no means felt like I'd 'made it'; to me that meant getting to and staying in the top division, with all the advantages that brings.

I'd not enjoyed my time at the Pirates; accumulated fatigue and a raft of players and coaches moving on had disrupted one of the more exciting teams to play for over the previous few seasons. This French offer had come out of the blue, when I'd been seriously questioning for the first time whether professional rugby was a sensible choice for me anymore.

Essentially my options were go to France, find another RFU Championship contract or consider whether playing rugby any longer was a sustainable option.

Choosing to take a leap into the unknown, I packed two bags, made sure I had my boots and gum shield and caught a flight to Paris.

We were quickly thrown into training and I'd just knocked over this poor chap with my pass. I'd pitched up at far flung rugby clubs before but this was an offsetting experience, testing my capacity for optimism. Limited funding and poor facilities were par for the course at Cornish Pirates but the paucity of this first training session, in amenities and quality, was a shock.

When arriving anywhere new you are always a little wary, expecting surprises and trying to keep an open mind. What awaited me in France was not quite what I had imagined and keeping an open mind was harder than I'd thought.

For this session we had made our way to some playing fields opposite the football stadium, situated on the outskirts of the city but easy to find from our accommodation. France is replete with *les stades*, ranging from an actual stadium like the Stade de France to public facilities all over the country. Most of them are open to *le public* who can come and use the facilities and we would often have people running around the athletics track that surrounded the playing surface at our home ground. The *stade* hosting this training session was at the lower end of the sophistication scale.

The training session was also at the lower end of this scale consisting of a melange of A and B team players. The winger who tried to catch my pass with his face was nicknamed 'Lapinau' owing to his physical resemblance to a startled bunny. He went down like he'd been shot after letting the spinning ball fly right between his hands.

I hadn't been expecting to find Toulouse quality players and facilities but this first training session was really quite something. Beyond the football stadium lay the motorway which would take you to Paris. I did briefly consider continuing on after training and going home but that moment of darkness passed.

The football stadium itself had a melancholic air; Le Stade Robert Diochon seats around 12,000 people with one large stand on the west side of the field reaching up and up, giving a good view of the field and accommodating a reasonable number of corporate boxes, a necessity in modern day professional sport. The other sides of the ground are smaller but probably closer to the field, which is surrounded by the metal cage typical of many European sports grounds.

FC Rouen were once a reasonable side, spending much of their professional history in what is now Ligue 2. To cut a long story short they made it back to Ligue 2 after a period in the lower divisions before getting relegated and suffering serious financial trouble, casting the club to the nether regions of French football where they currently reside. At the time of our arrival the stadium was locked up and not used, the football club playing their matches on what would once have been an adjacent training pitch.

We didn't even train on these, instead crossing the road to the public *stade* and setting up a session where the quality was frankly embarrassing.

I really thought I'd made a bad call.

2

WHAT WAS I THINKING? THE ALLURE OF FRENCH RUGBY

THE FIRST GAME OF RUGBY I EVER WENT TO WATCH WAS BATH VS Toulouse at the Rec, under lights on a Friday night in the Heineken Cup. Bath were recently the European champions while Toulouse were soon to begin their dominance of the competition.

Émile Ntamack , only remembered by a later generation of fans for being smashed by Jonny Wilkinson, scored a hat trick as Toulouse put on a show. I can't remember much of the game but they were exotic, Peugeot emblazoned across the front of their long-sleeved cotton jerseys and playing alien rugby. Their backs were aligned incredibly deep, the openside winger having to run about 20 metres before he caught the ball.

I was a Bath fan, born in the area and playing my junior rugby for Bath. Later I became an academy player and wore the shirt proudly, even if I never made a competitive appearance for the first team.

Even with my blue, black and white fandom, Toulouse were the team I found truly exciting. They became the best team in Europe, based around a core of homegrown players and supplemented by the odd foreign import. They were full of handsome mavericks like Frédéric

Michalak and Clément Poitrenaud who enjoyed a glamorous image not previously associated with rugby, posing for photoshoots, wearing diamond earrings and playing courageous rugby full of soul and self-belief.

I watched all the games that I could on television, even the away games in Europe where they weren't necessarily too concerned with the result. I remember them outscoring Llanelli at Stradey Park where they basically decided not to bother defending, inviting the Scarlets to engage them in a shootout. My brother and I went to the 2008 final in Cardiff where they narrowly lost to Munster, Cédric Heymans setting up a wonder try in defeat.

They embodied what was best about rugby for me, playing attacking rugby without compromise, even in the face of adverse weather conditions or a mountain of accumulating evidence that they should change their approach. They believed in themselves and their abilities and every game there would be a small moment that no other team could have pulled off.

Poitrenaud was the ultimate expression of their philosophy and he is the man who defined the line between their genius and madness when he famously failed to touch down the ball over his own line in the dying minutes of the Heineken Cup final, seeing Rob Howley snatch the ball away from him and score the game winning try in one diving motion.

It will be what he's remembered for, even with his raft of caps and medals, but I remember a European group stage game away at Northampton when he stepped past three defenders to escape his own corner and hare away up field when putting the ball straight out would have been the orthodox option. He continued to back himself throughout his career, despite having committed one of rugby's greatest ever cockups and for that, I loved watching him play. Seeing him inculcate a new generation of Toulouse players with the same ethos in his new capacity as a coach and precipitating their recent revival is a small joy.

They made me set playing in France as a faraway goal. A pipe dream to pursue one day. I even uncharacteristically boldly sent a video to their club email address when I was at a loose end, hoping that I could get a junior contract or a trial. I didn't.

Nevertheless, I always thought that I would go to France one day and could exercise my desires to play rugby in that off the cuff way. The free way. The French way.

I did get there in the end. It wasn't glamorous like Toulouse. Rouen had no reputation to speak of and no players that I had ever heard of. They were based in the rugby oblivious north rather than the hotbed that is the south and had no idea who we were or why they should care. They were unprofessional, unprepared for what was ahead for them and unexpectant of success.

How did we end up there? Through an old contact, former Bath and England scrum half Richard Hill. He'd accepted the job at Rouen and phoned me out of the blue.

'What are you up to at the minute Ben?'

I'd recently trained at Bedford for two weeks having left Cornish Pirates and was seriously considering whether playing rugby was still the best use of my time. The only other interest I had was from London Welsh and although I was keen on the idea of moving to London and seeing more of my mates, Welsh was not a very stable place and neither was their interest.

'Not much Richard.'

'That's what I wanted to hear!'

He explained his proposal; a year in northern France at this new team before trying to then move southwards to a more established club. I was all ears, partly because it sounded fun, albeit a little risky, partly because I could also use this interest to potentially push Welsh along a bit.

Part of the risk was that a year playing in the French 4th division, even though some of the games would be against fully professional teams, would essentially signal the end of my time in England as a serious rugby player. Ambitions of achieving future rugby excellence would rely on a good year in France and a quick move to a more storied French team. To be fair though, hitching to the Richard Hill bandwagon would be the best way for me to do this, his prospects of swift upward mobility being much more likely than my own.

My relationship with Richard goes back a long way. He is a big figure in the game having captained the national team in the early 1990s and was an integral part of the Bath side that dominated English rugby in that period. He was known as a tough player, a nasty little chap who would stamp on his own forwards if he felt that they were obstructing the ball from coming out, using his fast pass to get the Bath backs moving.

The reason I knew him was because his son Josh was in the same year as me at school. Josh played school rugby with us and was an outrageous physical specimen due to his ability as a gymnast; I once saw him flagpole off the side of a school minibus at the age of about 13 while we were waiting to go to some athletics meet. At a predominantly academic school, this was not commonplace.

Josh and I both played junior rugby for Bath and Richard used to come and help the assigned coaches for the age group we were in. They were incredibly fortunate to be able to learn from a rugby man of his experience and he was coaching professionally the entire time that I knew him. When I first met him he was coaching Ebbw Vale in Wales, coming to our games on top of Lansdown on Sunday mornings and taking Josh for a warm up of hundreds of passes. My mum's abiding memory of him is him taking notes on our U14s rugby matches, standing there with fingerless gloves and a beanie to both avoid the cold and be able to write down stats for our players. Even at that level of rugby he was always assiduous and meticulously prepared as well as being very fit for an older chap, banging out press ups between drills at our training sessions.

In my very limited experience of high level rugby and coaching, it seems that the actual coaching of players takes a back seat to the mental and social side of management. Good players don't have that much more to learn and even if they do, many think that they don't. I listened to a podcast with Paul Clement, a trusted assistant manager for Carlo Ancelotti at PSG, Chelsea, Bayern Munich and Real Madrid where he coached several great players. He said that training sessions tended to be 'one for them, one for us', meaning that for every tactical session working on team shape or organisation, they would have a session where they would basically just play games or compete in some way.

This is obviously at the top level of a sport and some of the best work a coach can do, the sort of work that can make their reputation, is to take a smaller team with a lower budget and a less talented squad and get them to achieve above their assumed capacity. Memorable instances include Jose Mourinho winning the Champions League with Porto or the rise and rise of Exeter Chiefs in English rugby.

Hilly had done something similar with Bristol and although the team he put together that made the Heineken Cup knockouts had some great players in it, he had spotted and signed them before others had. He'd then managed Worcester for several years and had left before signing to come to Rouen.

Hilly is an intelligent guy and spoke fluent French already having learned it in his youth. This wasn't his first job in France, having spent a year or so coaching a lower division French team previously, meaning that he had an existing knowledge of the French rugby landscape and the potential pitfalls involved in working there. The reason he was moving to Rouen was partly that he fancied it and that it was a project with potential but also, crucially, it was the only offer that he'd received to oversee another team.

He'd been at Worcester in the Premiership and had come to Fédérale 2 in France. Something often overlooked is that although being a top professional player is very competitive, there are probably 500 or so contracts spread across the 12 Premiership teams, it's even more competitive to be a Director of Rugby. There are only 12 of those jobs. These jobs are not limited by age like that of a player and don't often open up. He needed a job and ended up in Rouen, bringing us, equally unable to find an attractive gig at a better level, along for the ride.

This shared reason for coming kept us close in the first season and meant that the relationship we had with him was closer and more relaxed than it would have been with another coach. He'd often come out to eat with us and our families and it was fun to see his own family when they came to visit.

Being an RFU Level 5 coach means that in some respects he's a Jedi level trainer and you could see from his use of training aids that he had a love and compulsion for detail; we'd come out to train and find a smorgasbord of cones, colour coordinated and carefully placed all around the field, waiting for us. He was very detailed and would typically analyse the games himself on the bus back, doing statistics and planning the coming week's training. His work ethic was above and beyond what was expected of him from the presidents as he became an evangelist for the project, spending his evenings educating coaches and presenting to potential sponsors, all the while availing himself of the opportunity to eat around the region. He certainly compared well to the previous coach who apparently would turn up right before training was due to start and leave immediately afterwards.

Hilly's contacts also meant we had an array of guest coaches come to visit, often taking sessions or even whole weeks of training. Phil Greening abused us with 'collision fitness', Jon Callard came to improve our kicking game along with a selection of less heralded but no less useful other coaches, including a procession of Frenchmen we'd never heard of. He'd also commit to his own education by travelling around France to observe other teams, bringing back drills and technical pointers to integrate into our sessions, not always successfully due to the discrepancies in technical quality between us and the likes of Racing Metro.

London Welsh weren't moved to make me a concrete offer by my tale of French interest. Instead they advised me to take it. I struck out for Europe where players and coach were in the same boat; somewhat unwanted back in England and embarking on an adventure in a foreign land where they did not know our game or our names. The seeds of all this were sown watching *les Rouges et Noirs* play that Friday night game all those years before.

3

WELCOME TO STADE ROUENNAIS RUGBY

STADE ROUENNAIS RUGBY WAS A NEW TEAM, FORMED FROM THE ashes of the former Rugby Club de Rouen after their dissolution due to financial issues. The club had been purchased and rebranded by a pair of local businessmen who became co-presidents with the aim of creating a new rugby bastion in the north of France.

The team was based at an old *stade* right at the edge of the city and had been promoted the previous year from Fédérale 3, our arrival coinciding with preparations for Fédérale 2. This is technically the fourth tier of French rugby.

The league is amateur in theory but contained a wide variety of expectations. There were teams with full time players, aiming to move up the divisions and there were resolutely amateur outfits that were just concerned with having a good runaround and a pleasant time. The recruitment of an English coach and some foreign players was a move designed to help Stade Rouennais bridge the gap between these alternatives. The resistance or otherwise of the existing squad would be crucial to the success of the plan.

Hilly took us out for pizza the night of our arrival, eaten outside one of the cafes in the old town centre before dropping us at our accommodation on the other side of the river in the depths of Rive Gauche. Our flat was sparse and bare, a tiled floor paved the way into the living area giving it an additional coldness, although this was of some succour to me when my flatmate Luke cooked some prawns purchased at the wrong time of the week, causing me to spend a night using our floor as a way to keep cool in between bouts of vomiting. We then learned to heed what day the catch of fresh fish came in (Friday).

Initially we did not have a cooker, the kitchenette equipped only with two electric hobs, making mealtimes somewhat basic until our peti-tions for something more versatile were listened to. The apartment was kitted out with proper shutters, giving the gift of absolute dark-ness for afternoon siestas and helping to keep some of the noise from the busy crossroads outside at bay.

The beds were ok, with cheap mattresses from Ikea having been purchased for our arrival and Richard had bought us some bedding emblazoned with Union Jacks in a thoughtful and tasteless nod to home. I had brought some more to my liking with me but the Union Jacks did get the odd outing if guests came to stay, us rigging up a spare bed in the living room.

We were part of a small core of full time professionals, the majority being part time and working jobs in the day. We would meet for weights in the mornings which was usually followed by skills train-ing. Anyone else that could come would be included and we would also work coaching some of the younger French guys. The level of these sessions was not great but it was another area where we could potentially have a big impact.

Hilly would stress we be collectively conscious that the existing way of doing things had to be both respected and adjusted, not discarding their rhythms and inclinations but placing greater emphasis on skills, detail and speeding up the sessions which could contain a lot of talk-ing. Some of the habits around training, including diet and lifestyle preferences, would take longer to adjust.

Weights sessions in particular were not well attended and we would frequently be the only squad members participating, quite a departure from a full-time rugby environment where you are all there jostling for space. We trained in a well-appointed public gym which didn't open before 9am, giving our mornings a leisurely air. Sometimes Olivier Barthaux, the team's conditioner, would arrive late, leaving us sat around stretching, waiting for the day to begin. The lack of full time players and the late opening time of the gym meant that we were often some of the only people in there, training alone, at a total remove from both normal society and the rugby environments we'd previously belonged to.

A big part of our own adjustment would be learning the language. It was in our interest, and that of the team, to learn as quickly as we possibly could and one of the presidents told us this almost immediately upon meeting us, saying that we should be fluent by Christmas. This was ridiculously hyperbolic and did not come to pass but we were certainly under no illusions regarding the necessity of learning the lingo. Without it, we were in for a lonely time out there.

There were five English playing arrivals at the club including myself. Two of the guys, Ed Carne and Pierre Alex-Clark were already fluent in French having spent several years playing in France and, in Pierre's case, having a French mother. Both Pierre and Ed had a great breadth of knowledge regarding France and Pierre would sometimes drive to visit his grandparents a couple of hours south of Paris, bringing us back *sanglier* (wild boar) that they'd hunted.

The other new Englishmen were Joe Ellyatt and Luke Cozens. Luke had already had an abortive stint in France, spending a season at Grasse in the south. He and I played our junior and academy rugby together at Bath and had been coached by Richard as young players. Luke, commonly known as the Bean due to the shape of his shaven head, was a very skilful fly half with great passing skills and game sense but what set him apart was his kicking. He'd won a competition on the Rec when we were teenagers, the trophy for which was a metal cast of Jonny Wilkinson's boot, and he could hammer over goal kicks from anywhere in the opposition half, sometimes from further beyond. He's now the all-time top points scorer for Stade Rouennais. Luke had bounced around several teams and was about to have a great time rediscovering a bit of his enjoyment for the game at Rouen and, even if his sharp tongue and manner would not always endear him to our teammates, he became a popular and recognisable figure around the city.

Joe was younger than us and had also been through the Bath Academy while studying at Bath University, before moving to Rotherham to play full time in the Championship afterwards where he'd not had much fun. A hardworking and athletic back row with good looks and fox-coloured hair, he proved to be excellent for Rouen by combining his work rate with pace and aggressive play that would often make up for the lack of endeavour around him. His endeavour would be displayed on his face, usually adorned by some sort of decorative wound picked up during *le combat*. Joe was one of our main players during my time in France, both on the field with the consistent level of his play, and off the field where I'd like to think that his appetite for fun is unsurpassable; being able to party for longer than him would be quite frightening.

With a training schedule some way from onerous and a fair bit of free time, it was in our interest to get started with learning the language and Joe, Luke and I were to have lessons once a week with the former Club Secretary, a nice old fellow called Jean-Pierre Botrel who was somewhat of an Anglophile having studied in Leeds and being married to an English lady called Chris.

These lessons were basic in nature with our mixed ability group working through an old school textbook, doing the accompanying listening comprehension and role play exercises. The bits where we would tend to learn the most were when JP would loosen up and hold more everyday conversations with the group, throwing the occasional question around the circle to keep everyone honest. We soon asked if we could have another lesson each week and were delighted that he agreed.

Even if the lessons were not part of the deal, the opportunity to relax in his well attended garden, eat his home grown cuisine from the vegetable patch and admire his paintings, was too good to pass up, even if we would be given the odd bit of heavy lifting to do in exchange.

JP believes in the ideals of rugby; as a young man he was taken in by families affiliated with Headingley Rugby Club, fed, watered and helped out. He told us that paying it forward to younger rugby nomads was something he owed to his own experiences of the sport. That this was of benefit to us, a new generation of cross-Channel chancers, was a large slice of luck, even if I now want to reciprocate in some way myself in the future.

One of the great appeals of living in France for me was learning the language and I'm certainly convinced that it's nigh on impossible to learn a language properly without having a real fluent speaker to talk to. If you're physically in the country then so much the better. We had a good environment in which to learn with actual lessons allied to being in a French speaking working environment where the initial language requirements were quite easy to attain.

Textbook or school French is all well and good but often crumbles on first contact with the enemy. Some suspicious Frenchmen will regard you adversarially and can use your obvious lack of comprehension to avoid helping you out, particularly if you want something that they regard as tiresome or unnecessary. Textbook French doesn't prepare you for slang, loose grammar, abbreviation or crucially, regional accents.

Our scrum half Gabi confused me greatly with his Perpignan accent, rendering me unable to understand the simple word *'moins'* (less), pronouncing it wildly differently. Before going to France I'd not considered that there would be regional French accents, not previously having had to confront the notion. Foolish, seeing as France is a far bigger country than England, but understandable I'd like to believe.

Rugby playing French is somewhat basic and the same words tend to come up over and over again. Drills and exercises are fairly common throughout the rugby world so once you realise what's happening, the words become easy to remember. If you don't understand what's being asked of you, you can always just stand and watch the first group go through the drill, the canaries in the coal mine. The sessions were held in French but sometimes none of the assembled nationalities would understand what was being asked of them, leading Hilly to express his exasperation in the time honoured fashion of rugby coaches. You can speculate as to how that goes.

During training, communication was much easier for us as backs. All the English players save Joe played behind the scrum and tended to be selected as the centre of the backline, from flyhalf to fullback or with Ed on the wing. This meant that calls and in game feedback could be easily delivered along the line between us before being translated to a shrugging Frenchman on the end.

Joe had a much rougher time of it, especially as our forward pack was not well organised (this would be a recurring theme) and he would stand there oblivious as people argued during lineouts, unable to understand much of what was being said let alone contribute. This training ground loneliness probably accelerated his learning as he was forced to adapt to survive, picked it up quickly and became a leader in the team later in our time there.

We were best served by keeping our heads down in training for the most part and letting Hilly dictate a bit due to the potential local sensitivity to our arrival. When new players arrive, they seem exciting and fresh in the eyes of others and are obviously there to play. Inevitably you're there to take someone's place and they might not be amenable to that. The French guys were largely very hospitable but we acted respectfully nonetheless.

This integration was more difficult for Luke; playing fly half thrusts you into a leading role and he likes to get things clear, knowing that it is usually the ten's head on the chopping block if things descend into chaos. He's not known for holding his tongue and lacking language skills so didn't immediately endear himself to some of the more old-school players.

Playing rugby in the UK is quite a homogenous experience. I played for second division English clubs where my teammates were largely English. There would be the odd Irishman, a smattering of real local players and the occasional Pacific Islander but the squads were largely composed of identikit British players.

The Premiership sees a little more diversity but the same applies. There will be a few South Africans, the odd New Zealander and maybe even an Eastern European, but even if they are foreigners, most are English speakers.

The Stade Rouennais changing room by contrast was a veritable UN, peopled with players from all over the world, rugby playing nomads who had found themselves in the backwaters of French rugby at a team that had only recently come into professional existence.

The team was captained by Alex Tudori, a handsome, dark haired former Perpignan second row and Romanian international. He'd been to two World Cups and had played against the All Blacks but was now combining rugby with work at one of the president's businesses, his rugby involvement decreasing as his years advanced. He was backed up by another Romanian, Vili Hordila, a grey-haired and fashionably attired fullback. They would usually claim the back row of the bus for away trips, abusing everyone further forward and talking in Romanian when they didn't wish to be understood.

Our other second rows were Vincent Lointier, a local guy and Michel K, an enormous Polish guy who probably should have taken up another sport that could use his frame to its full advantage. Our front row were club stalwarts for the most part, gnarled French props with bald heads and quick tempers, joined by a very hairy Georgian in Otari Toradze. Bouly the forwards coach would turn out occasionally and the other senior guys Pierre and Thomas were supplemented by Jérémy Clamy-Edroux, a local player who could play both sides of the scrum. His arguments with Hilly over what could be expected of him professionally were hilarious, saying that he'd behave like a pro when he got paid like one rather than the other way around. Anthony Vigouroux, a flamboyantly dressed hooker, partial to whole ensembles in one colour, had passed through Toulouse and Perpignan and was now preparing to enter the police force. He combined his excellent lineout throwing and top level experience with a solid understanding of English, making him important to the team while he was still available.

The back row was a great strength of the team with Joe augmenting a good group. Amar Sy provided speed and springiness in the line-out, Fabien Vincent support play and ball pilfering while there were contrasting options at number 8 with Greg Hanocque playing a more considered style and the late to arrive Feleti Kamoto bringing Tongan power and offloading ability.

There were local French players in the backline, the best player being Romuald Berthe, a hardrunning centre and Polish international. There was speed and nous on the wings, sadly not all at the same time, in French wingers Johanny Labitte, former France judoka Polo and Julien Drut while we also had a Fijian legend in Fero Lasagavibau, a once brilliant back three player winding down to retirement, long after his peak as a player for Fiji and the Auck-land Blues.

Our first preseason friendly was against what Hilly would call 'a bunch of cabbages' where we had already scored 30 or 40 prior to half time. During the first half, we were awarded an eminently kick-able penalty and our captain Alex Tudori elected to take the points. This did seem somewhat strange and Luke motioned for the corner, asking Alex (who did speak some English) if that was a better shout.

He disagreed and motioned for the posts before Luke just kicked the ball out in the corner anyway. We then scored from the resulting driving maul. This was of little consequence to our long haired number eight Greg, a Frenchman who made constant references to his Viking heritage and who had played some decent rugby at Auch previously. He shouted blue murder in the changing room at halftime, stressing the importance of respecting the post of captain and not just doing whatever you want. Ironically Luke was at that very moment doing whatever he wanted by not listening, unable to understand what was going on anyway.

Despite these teething problems, we felt welcomed by the group with a big part of this being the daily ritual of handshaking and air kissing everyone that came to the club. This small gesture of respect initially seems a bit much but you come to relish the daily *bonjour*, developing your own little variations with specific people as you get to know them better. It's a pleasant way to start the day and is taken very seriously. You must look the other person in the eye, unless you're kissing their cheek, and failure to properly shake someone's hand, forgetting to shake their hand, or trying to shake their hand for a second time appears rude and disrespectful.

This ritual isn't confined to rugby clubs; when the French arrive at their place of work something similar occurs and it goes a long way to making everyone in the office feel valued. It's certainly something I think we could bring back to the UK as mornings feel far more awkward without saying hi to everyone.

Greeting is a real leveller and you're expected to greet everyone, whether they're the president or a volunteer serving lunch and one of our presidents rubbed everyone up the wrong way with his lack of respect during the ritual. He'd often turn away at the moment of handshaking, declining to look people in the eye or even face toward them. Eventually, when we had become more comfortable and started to care less about what they thought of us, Joe left him hanging as he turned away, his hand flapping around in space like a fish gasping for air. Great mirth erupted and he was embarrassed but I doubt he altered his behaviour afterwards.

The co-presidents were Marc-Antoine who owned a construction company and Philippe who ran a financial services business. They had taken over the team in the lower divisions when it was in danger of going out of existence and had invested to the point that the club had achieved promotion into Fédérale 2 before we joined them.

They had designs on taking the team into Pro D2 and establishing Normandy as a place where rugby was played. Traditionally rugby is a southern sport and the north lacks the culture and player base of France's warmer climes.

The teams in the south had the budgets and supporters to sustain large well remunerated squads and attracted big sponsors as a result, Toulouse being the obvious case. The tide in France is turning towards a new breed of investor to whom money is no object. Even Mourad Boudjellal, the Toulon president partly responsible for the Galactico culture in French rugby through assembling the incredibly successful side of recent vintage, has begun to balk at the salaries commanded by various players.

The trend is now towards the larger cities where the Parisian teams and Lyon have begun to make their financial might tell while Montpellier have one of the wealthiest investors in Mohed Altrad. These clubs are now paying transfer fees for players, something that wasn't previously unheard of but now, the scale of them is increasing and rugby's first million euro transfer cannot be too far away.

This culture of the president has filtered down the leagues where ambitious businessmen would like a vehicle to market their various business enterprises. There are more places in the top divisions in France than in their English counterparts with 14 teams in the top division and 16 in the second compared to 12 and 12 in England. Pro D2 is extensively televised and even Fédérale 1 has some regular television coverage on Eurosport. Given that there is no shortage of rugby clubs in France, many have taken one over and attempted to get up into the higher reaches of French rugby. Our two presidents were merely the latest.

We did not meet these guys before signing for their team but were swiftly introduced to them on arrival. Marc-Antoine was suave and well dressed, speaking English confidently and telling us what to do immediately. Philippe was more awkward and less charming; his own expensive clothes did not hang naturally on him.

I first had an inkling that there was some discontent between them when I introduced a visiting parent to Philippe as the vice-president. This was how he came across but it was an error on my part. He quickly corrected me, insisting that he was the 'co-president' and that they were joint partners in the venture. They had different allies in the club and were followed about by a cast of characters keen to court their favour.

Marc-Antoine seemed like a lonely sort of guy. Wealthy, handsome and a successful businessman, you nevertheless got the impression that he was quite insecure and always eager to impress you. He had a lovely wardrobe with a range of velvet jackets that people laughed at but secretly coveted.

He could laugh at himself somewhat too. One day he sported a safari style coat and I just said, 'English Patient' to him to which he chuckled. You felt that Philippe, with his ill-fitting expensive outfits would not have found such a comment funny in the slightest.

Marc-Antoine had a glamorous partner with whom he shared a tempestuous relationship; Hilly was often invited to dine with him and would listen to him pour his heart out over various arguments they'd had. Providing relationship counselling to a man who is effectively your boss is quite an odd dynamic to be a part of but you find in France that your remit easily goes beyond what you thought it would when you signed up.

Philippe was a keen golfer and kindly organised memberships for some of the lads at the Vaudreuil club where he was a member. I'm not a golfer but the boys would go down on days off to play a round and even played in a club tournament one year. Our winger took advantage of their extremely generous beginners handicap to win the tournament and take home an array of prizes, politely applauded by the members as he made off with their stash of golfing goods and rendering Philippe jealous.

Our presidents were evidently guys who liked to present themselves as alphas with their designer clothes, expensive cars and a shared love for extended bouts of public speaking, something that we witnessed first hand soon after our arrival.

Our official welcome came at the season launch party, hosted by the Hotel Bourgtheroulde in the centre of town. Although most of the talking would be handled by the presidents and Hilly, we were expected to contribute to the evening by walking out of the hotel, taking a microphone and addressing the crowd of sponsors, players and supporters in the courtyard below before descending to join them for canapés and champagne. As this was our first week at the club, the prospect of speaking French in front of a large group felt daunting so we arranged some stock questions and answers with Hilly to ensure we weren't stood there dying on stage.

One man who did die on stage slightly was a fellow new signing, Argentinian scrum half Carlos Danil. Having already spent time in France, he spoke very good French and was combining his rugby commitments with a job at the wealth management firm belonging to Philippe. He told the assembled crowd that he was ready 'to bleed for the shirt', disturbing the bourgeoisie and striking an odd note. This pride in the jersey stuff didn't ring true due to him having not yet played a game.

Argentina has become a top rugby nation, often peaking at World Cups where the lack of expectations and the focus on the bigger teams has seen them catch out some luminaries of the sport. They seem to regularly knock out Ireland and in the 2007 tournament they dispatched host nation France twice, in the opener and in the 3/4th place playoff.

They've produced some fantastic players and now run a de facto national team in the Super Rugby competition while some of their better players continue to play in Europe where they can command a far higher salary. There are many Argentinian internationals in the French Top 14 including classy winger Juan Imhoff, playmaker Nicolás **Sánchez** and flanker Facundo Isa while one of my rugby heroes **Juan Martín Hernández** spent almost his whole career in France.

Despite the increasing competence of Argentinian rugby, I'd never had a teammate from there until Carlos. Foreign player restrictions in England mean that teams are more likely to take a New Zealander or similar and the fact that there are just fewer Argentinians playing rugby must also account for some of this difference.

Carlos was signed at a similar time to us and lived with Joe. Combining rugby with employment meant that he lived in a different rhythm to us and so he found some of Joe's lifestyle choices slightly difficult to deal with, his heavy brows and dark eyes giving him the air of someone who is permanently tired before any lack of sleep is factored into the equation.

Due to having an actual job, he was justifiably not best pleased when people would come home drunk after Sunday matches and spend time in his living room making noise and playing music while he was trying to get some shuteye. Concurrently to this he would demand silence in the afternoons that he was at home so that he could sleep, making him an awkward customer to deal with socially.

He also had some odd eating habits where he would eat one food-stuff at a time, getting up between each component of the meal to cook the next. He'd eat a plate of peas, then a steak, then some potato and so on. I've never discerned whether this is an Argentinian custom or just one of his.

Carlos had been signed ostensibly to be the starting scrum half and possessed a reasonable pass. His decision making wasn't up to much though and he would often do bizarre things when a simple pass would have been the best thing to do. This didn't endear him to Hilly who, being a former scrum half, was always harsher on scrum halves, and he began to despair of him. During one game, he was hooked after the first twenty minutes due to the paucity of his play.

An early hooking is absolutely catastrophic and the ultimate marker of a coach having no confidence in you. We had rolling subs in that division so he was put back on the field later but didn't do much better. After this he wasn't really taken seriously and he began to play more and more for the B team.

Carlos was an identical twin and his brother Guido came to stay one weekend. Guido played fly half for a team in Fédérale 3 and during his stay he came down to the training ground during the day to do some kicking practice while his brother was at work.

Unfortunately for him he was spotted by Hilly on the field.

'Carlos, why aren't you at work?'

'I am not Carlos, I'm his brother Guido,' Guido replied in his heavily accented English.

This perplexed Richard and he wandered off for a bit to consider this turn of events before coming back.

'Alright Carlos, very good. Now seriously, why aren't you at work?'

'I'm not Carlos, I'm his brother Guido. I'm visiting for the week.'

This really got his goat and he wandered off before coming back one final time and going at him harder.

'Right that's it Carlos, enough of that shit. Why aren't you at work?'

Guido had to go and get his various pieces of identification to prove that he wasn't his identical twin brother so that Hilly was satisfied.

This was about the most notable thing that Carlos did on the field at Rouen and he wasn't actually there.

Later on, he was told that it might be in his interest to find another team and the club were probably keen to save the small amount of money that they were paying him to better cover another position; they wanted to bring a hooker called Robin Becquet back from New Zealand to shore up the front row. The younger scrum half at the club, Gabriel Cremadeills, had had a good start to the year and looked lively off the bench, meaning that there wasn't much point keeping Carlos around to play in the B team.

To be fair to Carlos, why should he move mid-season when he was fairly stable at Rouen? He had a flat and a car provided and was earning some reasonable money. The problem wasn't his to solve.

Unfortunately, when the club has provided you work with one of its own businesses, workers' rights are something of a secondary concern and he was summarily fired from his job. He suddenly found himself out of work, sharing a flat in Rouen with a relative stranger, receiving the use of a car and a few hundred euros a month to play terrible rugby.

Carlos was an odd chap and not a good rugby player but he was essentially a nice guy. He could speak at least three languages and had the wherewithal to hold down a financial services job on another continent. He is smarter and more adventurous than most other guys I've met but he was suddenly in a very precarious position, on the far side of the world from most of his family and without any substantial income.

This is the sort of predicament that is not uncommon in the outer reaches of professional rugby. You're reliant on the club to tether you to wherever you've pitched up and if they change their mind about you, there's not much that you can do about it. Any sort of legal advice is expensive and certainly not going to be provided to you by the club while there is no players' union to speak of.

In the UK, there are people who have similar experiences and even in the Championship, a full time professional league, the players' union won't begin to represent the interests of the athletes there because according to them, 'it would be opening Pandora's box'. The issues are myriad and too serious for them to even begin to address them, meaning that some of the game's most vulnerable players, subject to similar risks and stressors to their top flight brethren but without the financial rewards that those players enjoy, go about their work largely uninsured and without protection.

It's something that deserves to be addressed for the long-term health of the sport and for the sake of those who give their bodies and their formative adult years to it. Unfortunately, someone is always willing to take this chance and can find themselves burned by it. Just like Carlos Danil.

He wasn't to know that at the beginning of the season though and full of hope, excitement and champagne, the evening turned into a big night out with coaches, players and staff moving on to the Irish pub together, the president shouting drinks for everyone. Although we couldn't make much sense of the conversations going on around us, there was a buzz around the team before the season began and I felt more positive about joining the club.

4

ROUEN

ROUEN IS A RATHER LOVELY CITY ON THE BANKS OF THE SEINE, about an hour and a half north west of Paris and 40 minutes or so from the Normandy coast. Famous for being the site of Joan of Arc's execution, Rouen is split across the river with the Right Bank or Rive Droite being the affluent town centre, replete with cathedrals, ornamental clocks and traditional Norman architecture, while the left bank or Rive Gauche is the grimier, immigrant dominated area where the rugby club and our accommodation was based.

It's a large city with about 500,000 inhabitants, the urban sprawl having swallowed up previously separate smaller settlements and it extends right out to the main motorway that takes you to the French capital.

It's not a lively place, although a large university and renowned business school means that there is a sizeable student population and the requisite bars to water them. Rouen's geography makes for a concentrated centre, a large hill borders the north of the city while the river severs it down the middle, dividing it in two.

Cities on rivers tend to be constructed along its lines but Rouen seems to ignore its river. The metro crosses the Seine but there is no option to continue along its banks. Building along it was evidently an afterthought as there are some newer commercial developments on Rive Droite but they are not well integrated into the town itself. This is partly due to the large road that continues along the riverbank and probably due to some poor town planning. The prefecture and law school are based out of the town centre and although not far away, involve crossing one of the major roads into the city which gives it a detached air. You have to drive down to this part of town and it's something of a bolt on.

Rouen was my new home and with our club car, a little white Clio with two seats rather than four to qualify for a certain tax break, and our own feet, we set about exploring the city.

Early in our tenure, the demands of training (and most of the games) were not great so we filled our spare time with extra gym, extra French lessons and extra drinking sessions.

Rugby players can usually make their own fun when they sniff opportunity and while the standard and expectations were low, we headed out as often as we could, partly to escape our rather dreary little flat but also to try to join in with the French way of life. We were new to the city and needed practice speaking as well as being keen to explore.

The French are big socialisers and the terraces outside Rouen's cafes and bars were usually busy until relatively late. In the UK, most people start early and head home whereas those on the continent head straight to bars and restaurants and remain out for a while, tending to nurse their drinks rather than hammering them like us Anglo Saxons. The vibe is more of a civilised *apero* rather than the hurricane of a British happy hour.

Rouen's compact centre means that the various bars and nightspots are not far from each other, conveniently within an easy walking distance. Later when we acquired a motley selection of bikes, our reach was even greater as we could easily hop on and cruise off if the bar we were in wasn't up to snuff.

Biking around meant that we got to know the city centre extremely well. It's focused around the spectacular cathedral, with a cobbled shopping street leading west to the Gros Horloge, a beautiful archway that houses the eponymous big clock, before carrying on through to the Place du Vieux-Marché where the church L'église Sainte-Jeanne-d'Arc commemorates the spot where Joan of Arc was burned at the stake.

This is a bit of a sore point for the people of Rouen as it was the English who put her to death; something that the lads would rib us about. However, I learned in the Joan of Arc museum housed in the archbishop's quarters to the side of the cathedral, that the French were concerned of her growing influence with the populace and so handed her over to us to do the dirty work. Explaining that won't get you very far though so it's best to take responsibility for something that happened almost 600 years ago on the chin. The city has other Jeanne d'Arc memorial sites, including the Tour de la Pucelle where she was incarcerated awaiting trial.

The first place of pilgrimage that we discovered was the Irish pub O'Kallaghan's. It is in a great spot opposite one of Rouen's larger churches and across from the *Mairie* or Town Hall. It seems ridiculous that an Irish pub would be a prime destination but this is common in European cities. Subsequent European jaunts gave me the opportunity to conduct a limited and unscientific study on the subject and I found that Irish pubs are reliable destinations for a younger clientele across the continent.

This one isn't even cheap but attracted a large student and young professional crowd. When we became better known and had made some friends around the city we could reliably bump into them here on Thursday nights. Right next door was a good and lethal cocktail bar, the name of which always escapes me and the two crowds tend to commingle.

We became conversant with the various bars around the city, ranging from Chester's with its mad patron setting the bar on fire if you bought a big round, the Taverne de Thor, an Irish pub rebranded as an unconvincing Viking tavern, the Panda Bar or Bambou, hidden away in a Rouen backstreet selling 3 euro happy hour pints and the Delirium Cafe and Les Berthom with their lethal Belgian beers.

As a sporting city, Rouen's pedigree is very mixed. There was no great history of rugby to speak of, despite nearby Le Havre being the first rugby club to be founded in France, while the football team had gone under with financial problems, the most recent owner of the team being stabbed to death as a consequence of some dodgy business dealings. In a fun bit of serendipity, Rouen is the birthplace of French World Cup winner David Trezeguet, whose Argentinian father played for the football club in the 1970s. Trezeguet scored the winner in the Euro 2000 final, qualifying to play for France by virtue of his father's short period in Rouen.

Apart from this bit of luck, Rouen's sporting excellence has been largely carried by its ice hockey team. The Rouen Dragons are multiple European champions, playing in a small ground attached to the leisure centre on the Île Lacroix, a thin piece of land in the middle of the Seine. We would later get the odd ticket and go to support them, the cramped arena and concrete walls making for a bouncing atmosphere and they would typically win, leaving the local fans satisfied.

We tried various initiatives to join forces with some of the other sports teams but these were usually a bit awkward and lacking in enthusiasm. We bumped into some of the American basketball players in the town centre on a night out soon after our arrival and we got chatting. Excited about our new adventure, we asked them how they found living in Rouen and if they were learning French.

'No way man, I fucking hate Rouen,' one of them drawled, his socks and sandals combination marking him out as a foreign interloper before he even opened his mouth. When we later went to watch some basketball, we saw that this disdain seemed to extend to his teammates and I think he got out of there as quickly as he could.

The foreign basketballers were a good corollary to us; taking the opportunity to play professional sport wherever they could. The European basketball scene is pretty extensive, even if the top level is obviously the NBA, and you can make a living playing sport if you're prepared to move anywhere. The ice hockey guys were on some good money, in the hundreds of thousands per year but us and the basketballers were of a similar ilk, jobbing pros looking for a break somewhere.

Rugby is becoming more of a global game. Previously your options for a professional contract were limited to the UK and France but now there are websites advertising opportunities all over the place, many advertising match fees and part time employment as sweeteners. You can play in the Americas, across Europe, Asia and the Antipodes and I've been proposed contracts in Italy, the US and Sri Lanka with terms ranging from the good to the derisory. The thing it can do for you is get you a local network wherever you go and if you can make a positive impression, either on the field or by being a good bloke, you can open doors that would be otherwise closed.

Many young players don't realise the opportunities that are available in rugby to do something like this. There are countless places to go and play professional or semi-professional rugby around the world and teams will give you a place to live, a car and a means of employment, whether that's coaching, personal training or potentially working with a sponsor.

You can get away from home, earn a bit of money and see somewhere different, maybe even learn a new language. Ed Carne had done this himself. Ed had already arrived in Rouen and was fully installed downstairs from us in the Rue Méridienne when we got there. The other English guys already knew each other to some degree as we all either hailed from Bath or in Joe's case, had been to university there. Ed took a bit longer to get to know.

Ed is an interesting demonstration of what is possible through pursuing rugby as a career path, having taken a big left turn away from English rugby at a young age. He was a guy who didn't have age group caps but he had lived and worked in Italy and France, learning both languages and even picking up a bit of Fijian; a far more rounded set of skills then if he'd remained slogging it out for Redruth as they descended the English rugby ladder.

Ed is from Hereford but spent many of his formative years down in Cornwall, playing rugby for Redruth as well as representative rugby for the county. These pursuits are largely amateur but Redruth were once in National One, were a tough opponent at their place and had some money to pay a few players, including a future teammate of mine at Rouen in the large form of PJ Gidlow. I played against Redruth a few times and they continued to field some decent players with former England 7s ace Rob Thirlby and his brother turning out for them while later they had future British Lion Jack Nowell and Jersey fly half Aaron Penberthy play as youngsters.

Ed played for them, never having an opportunity at playing in a higher division but through an agent, managed to get to an Italian club where he spent a couple of seasons. Off the back of this experience he signed for USON or Nevers Rugby in the somewhat nether regions of France. You're far enough away from Paris to feel isolated, in the centre of the country and without much in the way of nearby entertainment.

Nevertheless, Nevers sounded like a land of milk and honey to us having been bankrolled by an ambitious wealthy businessman, and they were well on the way to achieving what Rouen had in mind. Ed had signed for them in the lower divisions and seen a couple of promotions in his time there before he began to play far less as they recruited more storied individuals. Nevers are now flying high in Pro D2, their facilities and setup ready for their goal of promotion to the Top 14 and they also have another Rouen old boy in their ranks in Zack Henry.

Ed arrived in Rouen with a plan. He had spent a long time playing rugby around Europe and would have a year in Rouen while completing a qualification in Management at Northumbria University through the RPA (Rugby Players Association). He would then go home to seek employment when the season ended.

Several guys leaving Rouen have spent time in Hong Kong and there are rugby contracts to be had all across Europe, in Asia and in the Americas. I know another guy who is a coach at a school in Santiago, Chile. If you're a young school or university graduate you can do a lot worse than get out and explore the world using rugby as your passport.

One of the things is that you need to be a bit of a self-starter and take a chance on something as you probably won't have the opportunity to go and vet it for yourself before you go there permanently. This is what had happened to us with signing at Rouen and how Ed got out to Italy. An agent had phoned him and said:

'Everyone wants that rose on their chest but for most that is a big ask. If you go out to Italy, in three years you could be running out at the Stadio Flaminio'.

Asking around other acquaintances of mine uncovered that this was not an uncommon pitch to green English youngsters. Indeed, I'd received a similar one myself, probably from the same bloke and I declined, at that point set on heading up the divisions. To be fair, I was then on an upward trajectory.

Ed did go to play some international rugby during our time at Rouen, qualifying for Singapore by virtue of having been born there, playing in some matches for them and having a great time. He was a versatile back, able to play from 12 out to fullback, tall, fast and determined and he had a good year for us, opening up a lot during our time there despite being initially a bit peeved at having Joe cluttering up his spare room. It's a classic manoeuvre that what you're sold, your own apartment, is never quite what exists when you arrive and you tend to have to make a bit of a fuss to actually get what you've signed up for. This was certainly the case at Rouen.

5

A FLYING START

THERE IS A REAL JOY IN LOOKING LIKE SHIT AND BEATING AN immaculately turned out opponent. We only played one preseason game due to a cancellation; we hammered an awful team, looking oddly cohesive and enjoying throwing the ball around; but it all felt a bit undercooked and we had no idea what our first league games would bring. We won our first two games against Auxerre and PUC before receiving our first decent opponent in Beaune, a team from deepest wine country, at home.

When they turned up it looked like a real mismatch. They had a rock star bus and all got off dripping in Puma kit, enormous headphones and snapback caps, looking like a real bunch of pumpers. They also had a couple of obvious Kiwis meaning that they had done some of their own recruitment and weren't just a collection of vineyard workers. Their appearance and demeanour actually did spur me on as it appeared that they thought that they were going to wander in and dispatch us easily. Looking at us in our mismatched attire with only the club polo shirts having arrived, standing around with several of the squad smoking and drinking coffee from disposable plastic cups I couldn't blame them to be fair.

In rugby, there is a tendency to judge the other team on first impressions. 'They look massive' is a common refrain or as with Beaune, if their kit is smart they make an impression one way or another. You basically see them as being more professional than you; or more arrogant. It's easy to talk yourself into how a team is and how they will play, based on nothing more than a brief sighting of them walking into the ground and this is only exacerbated by the Chinese whispers effect of the vague snippets of information that your teammates have about the opposition.

We played some phenomenal stuff that day, slinging it around and scoring 40 odd points, delighting our viewing public and allowing the stadium announcer to repeatedly play the snippet of local song that greeted a home try. Hilariously the Puma crew had to head back home with their tails between their legs and their sunglasses in their pockets. Sometimes looking village can be an advantage and it feeds into the plucky underdog narrative; we've got no kit or any mod cons but we're good. Good fun. It offers plausible deniability if you lose too. 'Look at us! We don't even have any kit!'

Our ground did not give a forbidding impression but le Stade Jean Mermoz, colloquially known as le Mermoz, was something of an anachronism with an old-world charm, its stone benches ringed around half of the ground, the recessed pitch having the air of a forgotten amphitheatre. Tall coniferous trees lined one end of the ground on the far side of the small road and the covered stand was bolted on to the dilapidated clubhouse where a small terrace allowed drinkers a good view of the field.

I came to love the ground, even when it was redeveloped during my time there, losing some of its charm as it was moulded by professionalism. On a good weather day, warm or cold, the place seemed inviting and the people there were usually good for a laugh or two, even if many of them were probably at our unwitting expense in the first season.

In terms of pre-match preparations, we were fortunate to have an English coach, turning up for home games about 90 minutes before kickoff for relaxed *bonjours* and maybe a coffee, then meeting in the changing room to discuss strategy, about half an hour dedicated to individual warm ups before a short team warm up of about 25 minutes. This is an atypical experience in France, especially in the lower divisions.

Many teams will meet early at around 9am to have breakfast together before doing a light training session. After this they will hang around and eat lunch together and then wait to be able to prepare for the game. The belief is that by spending time together, you strengthen the team bonds and allow the players the time to mentally prepare for the match.

To me this seems absolutely ludicrous and I would be bored out of my mind by the time kickoff came around. We didn't have to subscribe to this idiocy but my experience of rugby in France would be drastically different if we'd had to put up with this. At our home games, we were responsible for our own morning routine and pregame nutrition, able to roll into the ground not too long before kickoff and keep a bit of a buzz going before the game began.

Away games were a different matter. If we stayed the night somewhere, usually a budget hotel, we would eat breakfast and have the morning largely to ourselves, maybe with a quick strategy meeting and a few lineouts and backs moves in the car park before lunch. If we travelled on the day we would stop somewhere for lunch before arriving at our destination.

Lunch is, without fail, *crudités*, a sort of melange of cold meats and various salads including beetroot and shredded carrot, chicken and pasta, the quality of which varied quite wildly, and a dessert of yoghurt and fruit followed by coffee. This meal would never differ. Ever.

After the first friendly game or *match amical*, we were introduced to the concept of *le troisième mi-temps* (the third half) in earnest. French rugby sees the traditional post-rugby drinking as such an integral part of the sport that it is linguistically part of the match, probably more so than the warm up. The club barman Patou recognised early on that we were up for integrating ourselves into this tradition, helped by not having to shoulder the burden of going to work the next day, and he regularly plied us with drinks without the expectation of payment. He was relieved of his position of barman after a few months when the clubhouse moved into a portakabin at the far end of the pitch, the club unable to reconcile the glaring holes in their accounts with his protestations of innocence.

I was also quickly introduced to the delights of Ricard, foul smelling aniseed pastis, diluted with water to make a deadly concoction masquerading as apple juice. After being made to down two on the bounce by the forwards coach Grégoric Bouly, I gladly vomited off the back of the stand, allowing him his fun and relieving me of further consequences the next day.

All in all, we were proving to be popular acquisitions, both for our play and our willingness to drink, and the club, expecting nothing, had won its first three league games, sitting pretty at the head of the *poule*. In the spirit of *liberté, égalité, fraternité*, it was probably fair that we didn't have to pay for any beer.

6

THE PARIS SUBURBS

IN THE EARLY DAYS, WE WERE FREQUENT VISITORS TO THE Parisian suburbs or *les banlieues* to play against various sides in our pool. To the unenlightened, the Parisian suburbs probably sound like a land of milk and honey, or croissants and cigarettes, where stylish ladies promenade through the boulevards with their small dogs and expensive sunglasses, while old boys play backgammon and drink *demi bieres* in sidewalk cafes.

The Parisian suburbs are actually quite frightening places, stuffed full of unedifying apartment blocks, convoluted road systems and angry young men roaming the streets. Some of these young men make it to the rugby pitch where they make their dislike of you very clear. If they're not there then they are perched at the side of the field, cheering their friends, heckling you and blowing marijuana smoke in your direction.

France has a big problem with *les banlieues*, synonymous with the unwanted immigrant population who have been stuffed into districts and largely forgotten about by those in power. Crime is high and opportunity is minimal. They are largely located in the area outside of the ring road that encompasses the city centre, commonly called

Le Périphérique, enhancing their sense of displacement. They don't belong to the Paris that the rest of the world recognises and aren't wanted there.

My first experiences with *les banlieues* were at university where I did a module comparing literature and film from and about various world cities. Paris was one of them and we watched a great film called La Haine (literally 'Hate').

La Haine is set in the Parisian suburbs in a multiethnic housing project. It follows three young men for one day and documents the banality of crime, racism and violence in their world. The film inevitably ends tragically. It's based on some real incidents and shot on location in a suburb where riots were occurring at the time in 1995. It's a great film.

The scenes of violence depicted in La Haine are seen as part of life in *les banlieues* to this day. While we were in France, there was a widely reported incident where police beat a guy in custody, doing all sorts of appalling things to him which resulted in his death. Racial tension is very high and these areas are regarded as places to be avoided.

For the casual visitor to Paris, the only time you'd see these places is probably if you fly into Charles de Gaulle and take the train to the centre. If you take the slow train then you stop at many of these places, some of which are home to our erstwhile adversaries like Drancy. I once engaged in a ridiculous dance with a pickpocket on one of these station platforms, him constantly trying to move out of my eyeline while I continuously swivelled and pirouetted with a grace and unaffected manner I never knew I had to avoid him pilfering my valuables. Eventually I just went and stood against the wall, his attempts proving too persistent for my patience.

Funnily enough we never experienced anything too extreme during our visits to *les banlieues*, encountering more fighting when we played against southern French teams; apparently their Latin temperament makes them more prone to bloodthirstiness.

Our first visit to the suburbs was to play quite a genteel outfit in Paris University Club or PUC. Their playing surface was appalling, housed in the centre of a velodrome track. They are based within the ring road so acted as something of a warmup for the more niche experience of playing in Le Périphérique.

PUC are a famous old club with a formidable list of rugby alumni. Their most recent high profile product is probably Wesley Fofana who to my mind is one of the finest centres, injury permitting, in world rugby. We faced them in our second game of the season, heading down there having beaten Auxerre in the season opener but we were yet to play a game away from the Mermoz. PUC were considered to be quite good and none of the French guys were necessarily expecting a win, as is the general attitude when playing away.

On a pockmarked playing surface, we managed to shock PUC with some decent rugby and took the lead through some kickable penalties, a couple of decent tries and an absolute monster of a drop goal from our fullback Pierre-Alex Clark. It was later that the wheels began to come off.

Their best player was the brother of current French international François Trinh-Duc and he made a break after a well-timed palm to the chest of yours truly. I pursued him, caught up a bit and dived after him, clipping his foot with a tap tackle and perhaps averting a try. I was met with a blast of the referee's whistle, told I had committed an act of *'grosse brutalité'*[1] and given a yellow card. It turns out that tap tackles are banned below Pro D2 and are seen as a dangerous act.

For a tap tackle to be so harshly regarded in the country of eye gouging and punching seemed quite odd to me but off I trotted to take 10 minutes to myself. PUC were coming back into the game and I hadn't timed this little break very well. When I got back onto the field we'd received another yellow card and were looking a bit suspect.

Then our other centre Romu tip tackled someone and received a straight red card. Despite our general inability to keep cool heads, we managed to cling on to our lead to see out the game and were hailed as heroes by our small band of travelling supporters as we had secured a valuable away win, resulting in us sitting up at the top of the table.

The reason for the jubilation of our supporters at an away day victory, against a good PUC outfit no less, is that French teams traditionally have no expectation of winning away from home. John Daniell explains in his book Confessions of A Rugby Mercenary[2] that 'ideas rooted in the history of France and of rugby involve the concepts of *'terroir'* (literally the land or soil) and *'esprit de clocher'* (spirit of the clock tower). *Terroir* is a prevalent idea in wine cultivation and means that 'a product draws its identity from the soil that it grows in and its character from the culture that surrounds it'. *Esprit de clocher* is the idea that you have a collective duty to the town. To play rugby at home is to defend the very ground you stand on and to represent the spirit of the city. To lose is unthinkable and means that French guys are very pumped up for home games.

Daniell explains that in the Top 14, France's premier rugby competition, these ideas are strongly rooted as some of the teams are still from comparatively smaller towns in the south. They love nothing more than receiving big city counterparts and beating them in a test of virility and honour on the rugby field. Even a decade after publication of his book, these ideas and attitudes still exist, the smaller town team of Castres recently won the Bouclier de Brennus, beating teams who all finished above them in the playoffs to claim the title, but the prevailing trend in France is now that the big city teams are strengthening and that the traditional power lines of French rugby are shifting.

The Parisian teams, from a nadir where they considered merging, are now both replete with new investment and new stadiums, stacking their squads with international players. Racing 92's new ground, the La Defense U Arena, looks like the future of the game, an indoor, fast-paced entertainment product, teams lining up in total darkness before running onto the field in a cavalcade of lights, sound and fury. Lyon are now a force, Toulouse are resurgent and Montpellier are backed by some serious money. More traditional teams like Biarritz have fallen by the wayside and even Toulon are struggling to keep up with the new wave of super investment in French rugby.

How does that pertain to Rouen and their ambitions? Rouen is a big city in a non-traditional rugby area. If their project succeeds in the long term, Rouen will be able to harvest any rugby talent in the north of France and provide a good proving ground for ambitious youngsters hoping to make the Top 14. Other big city teams are trying to do the same thing including our divisional rivals Strasbourg. We met other sides with the same ideas as us during my time in Rouen as well as some teams whose ambitions had exceeded their budgets. Professional sport is a ruthless place where dreams and ideas can often exceed practicalities.

At this point in my French adventure we were not a fully professional team and so had a lot of guys who were more invested in the idea of Rouen than a professional player would be. This meant that the wild swings in emotion were far more prevalent than at my previous clubs where as professionals, each game was treated quite similarly, even if playing at home could maybe be used as some sort of psychological edge.

Us new arrivals became used to seeing some players crumble at away games, eyebrows and ears covered in Vaseline, crying in the changing room, red eyes still evident as they took the field. At home games, they would be the opposite, walking around with chests puffed out, shouting motivational stock phrases to no one and everyone in the home changing room. The front row were often taken into the showers to headbutt each other and squeeze together, a ritual I'm delighted to not have been a part of.

Playing away can be uncomfortable for other reasons as, even at better clubs, steps are taken to make the away team's experience less comfortable. This ranges from painting the away dressing room 'sad' colours to the ball boys not passing them the ball back in a timely manner or not drying it effectively before giving it to a hooker pre lineout. Many away changing rooms include a corner so that the whole team can't sit together in the same space or even, in more nefarious cases, make the showers run with freezing cold water only.

After our maiden away victory against PUC, Joe and I ventured into Paris to celebrate his birthday. It was our first trip since arriving in France but being a Sunday it was not hugely lively; we had a few on the Rue de la Soif before accepting some local advice and heading to the Champs-Élysées.

The Champs-Élysées is the famous Grand Boulevard that runs from the Arc de Triomphe down towards the river. It houses some of the larger stores and luxury brands, being memorable to me for being where the Count of Monte Cristo bought a house and plotted his revenge on those who wronged him in his previous life as Edmond Dantes. That evening it became memorable for some other, less edifying reasons.

We headed to an open bar and ordered some beers. The waiter asked what size so we specified large. Not looking at a menu was in hindsight, a mistake.

He came back with two enormous beers that would be more at home at Oktoberfest. Being already well oiled we were not thrilled by this but set about drinking them anyway. After a short time, he came back over and asked that we pay as they would close the bar before too long.

'Yeah sure. How much?'

'52 euros.'

I was stunned.

'What?'

'I'll show you the menu. It's right here. Look, €52.'

I forlornly handed over a 50 euro note and a coin in exchange for two beers which neither of us really wanted to drink. He then brought some plastic cups over so we could decant them and drink them outside. He'd seen us two fools coming from a mile off.

After being denied entry to a club for not being gay (how they decided that is beyond me), we repaired to somewhere even less salubrious and took shelter from the cold for a bit. We then hit a cafe by the station at about 5am and waited for the first train back to Rouen. Mission accomplished. Kind of.

Our other games in the suburbs came later in the year when we travelled to Domont and Gennevilliers. One thing about France is that some of these pretty deprived areas have excellent facilities and both *stades* were very acceptable, with reasonably large stands, several training fields and decent playing surfaces. Domont had a new athletics track around the playing surface as well as several good warm up pitches with both artificial and grass surfaces. We couldn't point to our surroundings for an excuse; we just had to try and win now.

Win we did not and at Domont, we had mixed the team around to give some of the reserves a go, buoyed as we were by our early season success. We played appallingly and lost to a poor outfit, although there were some mitigating circumstances as, when we stopped for lunch at a roadside restaurant before the game, our coach driver Jean-Paul imbibed a couple of glasses of beer, failed the coach's integrated breathalyser test that was required to start the vehicle and locked himself out for the next 30 minutes, meaning that we were all left standing by the side of the road while he at least had the decency to be a bit embarrassed. I can't imagine many bus drivers for English teams drinking beers at lunchtime.

On the Gennevilliers team was a large back rower who was apparently a drug dealer of some renown in his spare time and it was probably his mates or customers smoking weed at the side of the field. He was a good player and his pack dominated ours in the tight, scrummaging and mauling us all over the place while we replied out wide by scoring a few tries. His own teammates seemed to regard him with some trepidation; when one complained about something, he shut him up with an aggressive looking glare, not even saying anything.

Referees can behave in a slightly partisan manner during away games, perhaps more so when they're dealing with some of the ruffians of the Périphérique and this one seemed to let a fair bit go. I chased a high ball, reaching it just after the opposition fullback had passed and gave him a slight nudge as I stopped, no malice at all.

He punched me straight in the face.

I was about to swing what Luke would call 'a posh punch' when Hilly, stood nearby and in full view of the whole stand, told me to stop. I thought better of it and the referee blew his whistle. Here we go, I thought. Get a red card out for this joker and we'll be off to the races. Not reacting meant that I was in a good spot.

He summoned both of us over, told us to calm down and awarded them a scrum. I was shocked. Luckily, he was a slight little fellow and hadn't done me any harm but the extent of home field advantage became clear to me then. The crowd enjoyed it anyway, chanting '*Chez nous, chez nous, on est chez nous*' at me, meaning 'we're at our place pal' by way of explanation.

Our early away trips had resulted in a mixed bag; one win and two losses. We'd learned about the performance discrepancies, the way refereeing decisions would go against us and experienced the Parisian suburbs. These early away games were the trifling matter of a couple of hours in the bus; later in our French tenure the coach journey to Paris would merely be the start of a *deplacement*[3].

7

LE GROS-THEIL

AFTER A COUPLE OF WEEKS IN THE SADDLE, THE CLUB BARMAN'S appreciation of our foreign idiocy and general propensity for a good time reached new heights and he invited us Englishmen to visit one of his favourite restaurants with him. Patou would speak to us in appalling Anglo-Saxon while no doubt taking the piss out of us in French too fast for us to comprehend at that stage. His fun demeanour, mixed with his idiosyncratic personal appearance; he resembles the main protagonist from the film Despicable Me with a long pointy nose, a Dracula hairline and flushed cheeks from years of Ricard abuse; meant that we were surely in for a good time. We accepted his invitation.

A professional team would not necessarily be pleased that a club employee was taking players drinking in the middle of the week so he was selling this outing as a meal. In France, meals and alcohol tend to go hand in hand and Patou assembled a hard-drinking trio of Frenchmen to accompany us on this jaunt, including the second team coach Bayou, a very overweight and rambunctious character, and the stadium announcer and general club administrator Jean-Louis Bellot, an incredibly unhealthy looking older gentleman and avuncular character who spoke much more English than he initially let on to us. This was looking like being a real session.

Anyway, Patou suggested that he take us foreigners for a traditional Norman meal at his friend's countryside restaurant one afternoon. We suggested a Thursday as these tended to be our days off. It would also give us some breathing space between the inevitable drinking that would ensue and our game that Sunday. He said that that Thursday suited him, that he would organise it with his compatriots and that he would be in touch.

Thursday rolled around and we heard nothing from him, assuming that this was not a serious invitation. After our skills session at the Mermoz on the Friday morning he asked if we still wanted to go. We said that we did and that we had thought we were going the previous day. He waved it off, said that he'd meet us back at the clubhouse at one o'clock that afternoon and that he would drive.

We assembled at the clubhouse ready for our adventure and I went ahead with Bayou as one of the others was late. We arrived at Le Gros Theil after half an hour or so of very stilted conversation in broken Franglais where I discovered a packed traditional French restaurant not entirely unlike an English country pub. I was immediately made to down a couple of house cocktails (*L'Eau de Mer*, literally 'Seawater') and then thrust onto a stage to sing karaoke with a man playing the accordion, who encouraged me to sing 'Stand By Me'[1] with him and then dropped out, leaving the crowd to be assailed by my warblings. Anyone who was in that restaurant could attest that I am not a gifted vocalist and when the others showed up halfway into my ordeal they were understandably delighted.

Jean-Louis tried to stay the drinking knowing that we had team run that evening but he swiftly gave up and joined in, the afternoon turning into a full-on boozeathon, occasionally interrupted by plates of traditional French cuisine. Some of it was lovely but some were challenging. *Langue de Boeuf* or beef tongue was actually very pleasant but *Tete de Veau* or calf's head was awful; stringy and impossible to chew.

We were finished off with dessert, cheese and three shots of *sorbet tonton* (a semi-frozen incredibly strong apple liqueur), the last one of which failed to stay down and found its way into the breadbasket.

We made our escape and were driven to another *stade* in the middle of nowhere while Jean-Louis went for a previously unannounced meeting. The place was deserted and we were left to drunkenly wander around the facility before being driven back to Rouen. Everyone at training had heard that we'd been plied with alcohol and even if they hadn't, Luke's comical failure to catch a very simple pass in the warm up, basically cuddling himself well after the ball had bounced off of him, would have given us away. As the rest of the session went off without any further mishaps, we were spared any repercussions, our long lunch being regarded as an effort at integration rather than subordination.

My experiences of playing professionally in England were that at social occasions and promotional events, declining alcohol was not seen as a strange thing to do. Everyone seemed to understand that your priorities were not drinking with sponsors and the like. In France, especially at Rouen where professionalism was a new concept, declining a drink came across as quite rude and obstructive and you had to pick your battles, being quite strong willed if you wanted to not drink alcohol. The other side of this was that there were cultural niceties and expectations that we had to fulfil and in this first season, when the stakes were lower, we could quite often justify having a few drinks.

Drinking is not uncommon at a higher level of the game and rugby doesn't have the same physical demands as football for instance where they can potentially play three games in eight days. Rugby's contact dimension requires longer between matches and therefore, more leeway in which to consume alcohol. Athletic capacity is a big component of the game but it's not the be all and end all like it is in more focussed endeavours like athletics, rowing or gymnastics, meaning that a couple of beers or glasses of wine here or there will probably not be a great hindrance. If you're going out a couple of times a week and drinking hard, that will eventually get you.

There are some guys at the top of the sport who drink regularly and even in the relentless NBA schedule of an 82 game season, LeBron James finds time to drink red wine in the evenings. If he can do it then I'm sure lower division rugby players, idling around in northern France can (and have).

Sometimes a weekday drink can help an athlete feel a bit more normal, less disconnected from society at large, giving you a small piece of mental relaxation and help you to bond with your teammates. A couple of quiet pints can do wonders for your mental well-being which could be more beneficial than the physical benefits of not drinking them. A total asceticism works for some guys but for others, it can form a mental prison of denial which leads to some sort of explosion, whether that's in a big drinking session or some other sort of destructive behaviour.

Rugby teams have long been known for enjoying a drink or two and team sanctioned drinking can be a good way of bonding the lads, especially when there are a lot of new recruits or times are tough. A famous example in French rugby is when Stade Français were having a tough season despite their star-studded squad. They had some time off during the year and while many coaches would choose to take the team to a training camp or do some extra physical work, Nick Mallett, the South African head coach at the time, took the team off to the Alps for some skiing. This might seem incredibly risky and counterproductive but, after a trip that involved a lot of *apres-ski*, Stade returned to the field full of zest and went on to win the Top 14 title.

Now this could be survivorship bias and there are countless examples of when team drinking goes wrong. Bath Rugby took their players to a sponsor's cider farm and a couple of the more combustible characters later had a well publicised set to that was caught on CCTV in the city centre. This resulted in a lot of bad publicity for the club but occurrences like this are not uncommon at team socials and most of the time, they don't make the press and result in no bad blood between individuals.

Quite a lot of our desire to go drinking was motivated by a need to meet people, both socially and romantically. Our days were often relatively devoid of contact beyond ourselves as the other players were mostly working, leaving our afternoons empty until evening training. Although our French lessons took up a bit of this time, we were often left twiddling our thumbs, usually around the joysticks of the N64 controllers that we used to play Mario Kart over and over again. Going out into town was a way that we'd see some other people.

I didn't have much preconception of what a French woman was before I landed in France. I'd met the odd one before but we were now on their turf and about to encounter some new cultural norms regarding dating. Out of the foreigners, Joe and I were the only singles and we were excited at the prospect of meeting some of the locals. My year in Penzance, largely unable to go out and with the place on lockdown during the harsh Cornish winter, meant that I saw this opportunity as quite a boon.

Our major problem was linguistic. French may be the language of *amour* but we were as yet unable to have an engaging conversation with a person. It's fascinating to watch your own prospects drain away before your eyes as you realise that you have nothing whatso-ever to offer conversationally, watching the object of your affection get increasingly bored at your verbal stumblings and eventually stroll off to find a Patrice or a François instead.

Another complicating factor is that Normandy is a traditional region of France with not many English speakers among the populace. This was fantastic for our language learning, less so for our romantic pursuits. Paris would have been a far easier proposition with its more international profile.

There is a historical perception that French women are an easy bunch. We later learned that American GIs, part of the Normandy landings and the liberation of France in WW2, were given pamphlets for Operation Overlord, containing useful phrases and information that would help them to navigate rural France on their way inland. If they were to get lost or separated, they would have some tools with which to engage the locals.

Now, many were excited at the prospect of bedding down in a farmer's barn for an evening, hoping to be able to coax some young *françaises* to join them for a roll in the hay. Amusingly, these pamphlets were full of information that made it very clear to these young men; French women are not the stereotype that you think.

In fact, the French womenfolk seemed quite difficult for us to convince, evidently used to weaselly behaviour from French men. Or they were merely unimpressed by barbarian foreigners wandering over to them and then drunkenly slurring poorly constructed sentences in their direction.

Nevertheless, we remained optimistic, spurred by some early success and Rouen's packed bars on a Thursday night. There was a rather fetching girl who trained in our gym, her favourite exercise of holding a chin up while wiggling her legs around making her a favourite of the boys during weights sessions. I saw her perusing wares in the *supermarché* and thought I'd chance it. She looked at me blankly, I thought my halting *français* had failed to move her but then she laughed and revealed that she could speak some English. I was in luck! We arranged a coffee date.

She seemed delightful and outlined how she was studying to be a *pâtissière*, leading me to immediately imagine afternoons making croissants together before making other things happen. Sensing this as an avenue to go down, I suggested that one day she show me how to make croissants. She agreed and we arranged an afternoon during the week for her to stop by.

This seemed like a great setup so I cleared the others out of the flat, tidied up as best I could and waited for my first French assignation to take place. She turned up, slightly disappointingly, with the ingredients for biscuits rather than croissants but I must confess that my thoughts were not solely on the baking.

Things were going well, rolling dough, throwing flour around and generally relishing the ridiculousness of the afternoon. After a short time, the biscuits were ready and I was waiting for my moment to strike.

At this point the lads came back in, disturbing the *bonhomie* that had existed in the room. She looked alarmed, then annoyed when they insisted on eating the biscuits, snatching them away before quickly making her excuses and leaving. The boys obviously thought this most amusing, although they were a bit put out that they didn't get to taste her biscuits either.

The next season, I got myself a girlfriend who spoke English and lived elsewhere. This left me able to regard the French dating scene anew with some knowledge born of mostly bitter experience, but also some amusement. Now that I could speak to the ladies, I was often used as a foil for others earlier in their own French journeys who were unable to hold a lengthier conversation. One of the boys brought his date round to my flat, speaking to my girlfriend for half an hour while I conversed in French with his companion. When he felt like sufficient time had passed, he suggested they move next door and she assented, both of them evidently agreeing that the conversational minimum for an evening date had been exceeded.

The French lads found our linguistic struggles highly amusing, telling you how clumsy your efforts were and mocking you for your inability to hold someone's attention. Later, when we began to venture further afield, to other European cities or to England, the shoe was on the other foot as their limited English meant that they were cast as the tongue-tied foreigners while we became the urbane, witty translators, able to hold concurrent conversations and facilitate an international social event.

I came to realise that the French are not great travellers. Many don't leave France due to the sheer range of things to do there; when you can surf, ski, go to the beach and enjoy some incredible European architecture all in the same country, why venture further afield where you can't necessarily speak to anyone? Amongst the players in the team, many had never left France for an extended period of time and tended to spend their holidays *en famille* somewhere within its borders. I think that this attitude plays into their sense of national pride. They don't need to leave so why should they? The place is a joy and they place great store and pride in being French as a result.

8

STRASBOURG

By any measure, we had already been a big success on the field. We'd come in, installed a new style of play using a system vaguely recognisable from the top level of the game and, using our interchangeable backs, were able to sling the ball width to width and get everyone a lot of touches. We were the talk of a very small number of people around the town and I'd begun to enjoy playing at the Mermoz, even if the lack of professionalism and the paucity of our language skills meant that we lived quite an isolated existence.

We were not under the impression that rugby was popular in Rouen before we arrived, even if our player presentation had been well attended, but we quickly realised that not many people were even aware of the team's existence. We were out for lunch one day when our English voices were overheard and we were asked why we were in Rouen. When we explained that we were *rugbymen*, the response came swiftly.

'Pour qui?' / 'For who?'

It remained to be seen how the rest of the season would pan out but our initial plan with Hilly remained in our minds. Play well here and go somewhere that knows what rugby is for next season, preferably in the sunshine. Establishing the team in Rouen, in the face of such ignorance, seemed like a mountainous task.

Soon we were to go away to Strasbourg. If we could steady a few of our away day wobbles then it looked like being a straight shootout between us and Strasbourg for the top of the pool. Fédérale 2 consists of four pools of ten teams, split vaguely geographically, and the top four in each pool go through to the playoffs where 1st plays 16th and so on.

Making the playoffs alone would be a good result for us considering we were technically a newly promoted team but us new guys certainly had our sights set on winning the pool. We were there to lift the level after all.

Strasbourg would be a big test and were on a similar track to us in terms of their ambitions. Strasbourg is a large city in the east of France and would be a good location for a top professional rugby team given that their football team wasn't overly successful. They had a smattering of quality players, including a France 7s representative in their back three and were flying high at the top of the group.

We were going away from home and so had no expectations of a victory from our own players. Games in France up to Fédérale 1 involve the B team playing the same set of fixtures meaning that a bunch of students, old boys and some of the biggest jokers you'll ever meet happily sit on buses for hours, spending a whole weekend to go to some far-flung field and play a very low level of rugby.

If that's not the spirit of the game then I don't know what is. They certainly knew how to play the third half, getting blind drunk and often rolling up blunts to smoke in service stations on our way home and occasionally managing a pregame night out too. Some of them wended their way into the centre of Strasbourg that Saturday night to sample some of the local nightspots.

It did them no harm as they played an absolute blinder of a game. We would tend to watch the first half of the B team game before going off to prepare ourselves but, due to the lack of warm up fields at some stadiums, we would often warm up in the dead ball area during the second half of their games, therefore having courtside seats to the action. No matter how hard you concentrate on your own preparation, it's difficult to completely inoculate yourself from what's going on as you may have to jump out of the way if play makes its way to your end of the field.

You can't help but be inspired by your clubmates if they play well and they turned over Strasbourg at home, understandably celebrating at the final whistle. They'd set a standard and now it was our turn.

Strasbourg came hard at us, flinging the ball around and testing our defence which unusually for us stood firm. We were struggling to get into our game but managed some decent sets of play without really troubling their line before Luke pressured their ten into dropping the ball, scooped it up and offloaded to me and I managed to make the line with a couple of tacklers holding onto me. If we could make it to half time with a small cushion then that would have been ideal.

We couldn't due to a combination of appalling defending and equally poor refereeing. They worked the ball to the edge where their speedy flanker did our lumbering Polish second row Michel on the outside. He dexterously chipped over our cover and made it to the bouncing ball which he only had to gather and put down to level up the game. He managed to knock the ball on so perfectly that we briefly breathed a sigh of relief until he flopped over on it, the referee awarding the try immediately.

This decision was laughable in the aftermath of the game but at the time it wasn't funny as it cost us our lead in the crucial period right before half time. We swore blind at him in English, saying some filthy things. They tend not to understand if you avoid the word 'fuck' but he probably got the gist anyway.

Being a referee at this level of rugby is a tough gig. I'm sure refereeing at the top level is difficult but for different reasons; the theatre and sense of occasion, the stakes and big personalities and the scrutiny of a big crowd and television audience. At the lower level your problems are more a lack of support and a more visceral, partisan environment where personal abuse and disrespect are much more possible. Your linesmen are substitutes from the participating teams, a partisan crowd pressure you into making decisions favourable to the home team and there have been instances of violence against referees in amateur games. You don't get the benefit of a second look at anything and so need to make snap decisions all the time, having to move on quickly whether they are correct or not. I refereed some youth tournaments as part of our promotional duties in England and it gave me an appreciation for how difficult it is.

This ref was probably unsighted as he was running behind the Strasbourg flanker meaning that he could have very easily not seen the knock on. To us it seemed like a disgraceful decision but it was probably a genuine error rather than anything more sinister.

We headed into the changing room and collected ourselves. We were not ahead like we had been but we were in a good position, even if our regular hooker Anthony Vigouroux had gone down injured, leaving our usual B team hooker David 'Petitneuf' Duparc to shoulder the pressure of throwing in to our lineout.

Petitneuf, so named for being absolutely tiny, would turn up to training in his van, replace his work boots with rugby ones and wander around to little effect. That day he was immense, nailing every lineout and anchoring the scrum that won us the game. Pushing them off their own ball on their 22m line, our big Tongan number eight, Feleti Kamoto, picked up and carried wide away from the scrum, taking a tackle and offloading to Joe to score under the posts. After that we never looked like losing, playing a relatively safe game plan to close out the biggest result of the season.

We were pleased at the final whistle but I didn't think that our celebrations were out of the ordinary. Nevertheless, something stuck in Strasbourg's craw and this was the beginning of an ill-tempered rivalry between us. We didn't know it at the time but the similar desired trajectory of the two clubs and the status as group favourites would lead us to further enmity and future confrontations.

Petitneuf became *'le hero de Strasbourg'* for his sterling performance off the bench. This was said partly in jest but he clung on to the nickname for at least the years I spent in France, often drunkenly telling newer signings about how he'd downed Strasbourg all by himself on one autumn afternoon in 2013. Even though it's somewhat ridiculous, rugby lends itself to this sort of mythologising as pieces of play, good and bad, become part of the social tapestry of the team, being retold repeatedly to anyone who will listen. Petitneuf had his brief moment in the sun that day and without him stepping up and playing above himself, we would not have won. We headed home jubilant that night.

9

PRIDE IN THE JERSEY

PRIDE IN THE JERSEY IS OFTEN INVOKED AS A MOTIVATOR; YOU should have pride in who you're representing, literally in the colours on your shirt and the badge on your chest. The *esprit de clocher* of fighting for your town, your community, your tribe.

With professionalism, this is tough to justify. How much pride in the jersey can you have if you've just turned up? This isn't necessarily a choice you've made. It may have been your only option. It's easy to have pride in an international jersey where you represent your country; you've reached the apogee of sporting ambition. It's easy to pull the shirt on of the team you've always supported, where you've come through the youth section, trained with your idols and are now running out at a ground where you've always been a spectator. It's easy to have pride in these things.

Professional pride is something different. You want to do a good job for yourself. To represent yourself in the best possible light. Now this can also include being a good teammate and fulfilling your role in the group but the pride is in your own job, not necessarily the success of the collective.

There are teams that immediately convey a sense of pride in the jersey but they tend to vary by the individual. If you join Manchester United or Liverpool, the shirt hangs heavy on you. If you join grand old rugby clubs then the same might be true. By and large though, pride in the jersey is something that takes time to develop; a relationship that begins contractually can grow to become something more.

The last time pride in the jersey is pure and true for most people is school rugby. I spent 11 years at my school and played rugby all the way through, captaining the First XV and playing with my childhood friends. Of course I had pride in the jersey. You play for fun, social status, competition and you are invested in the success of the school; it's something bigger than yourself.

One of my most cherished rugby memories was a school rugby tour to New Zealand where we spent a month travelling the length of the country, staying with local families and playing matches against a variety of school teams. The first and best team that we played were St Pat's Silverstream.

Early in the morning at an outdoor whole school assembly in Wellington, wrapped up in winter clothes and able to see our breath, we were invited into the middle of the stone courtyard where we were surrounded by the pupils.

One boy moved forward slightly and shouted to his peers. They all dropped into the familiar stance, slapping their thighs and stamping in unison on the floor. The sound reverberated around us as the whole school began to perform their traditional haka.

It was incredible. The sound flowed and bounced off the brick of the courtyard, we stood in a tight group in the centre while a language we couldn't understand swirled through the air, the words indecipherable but the meaning clear. I get chills thinking about it now, fifteen years later.

An ancient challenge rang out, the same words that their predecessors would have shouted, a tradition passed down from year to year, from boy to boy. They were welcoming and challenging us at the same time, letting us know what we would find out on the field the next day. This was pride in the jersey made flesh; those boys unself-consciously participating in an ancient rite linking the warrior traditions of their ancestors with their contemporary sporting identity.

Their team repeated the haka on the field the next day before kick-off, snarling and whooping while we stood with our arms around each other, facing them in one line. It was a meeting of two rugby cultures, kids from opposite sides of the world with completely different experiences and expectations who were all ready to share in the communal experience of playing rugby. I've never been so excited before or since to play.

I played my youth and academy rugby for Bath alongside my school commitments and loved pulling on that jersey too. I had the opportunity to play some second team games for them as an adult, years after I'd left the academy and it was a thrill to put that shirt back on and run out with my younger brother, the only proper game of rugby we ever played together. I hadn't appreciated how much pride I took in wearing that shirt until I'd been away and come back.

Fierté- or 'pride' is often referenced right before the game and it means different things to different people. There's no way we could already have pride in the Rouen shirt; we were a new team that hadn't long existed and we had just arrived. Everyone can smell bull-shit, knowing instantly if something isn't true. Someone demanding this of us would have been ridiculous.

What rugby can do is help you settle in somewhere new, whether you're professional or not. Rugby clubs are always welcoming, playing gives you the opportunity to do something well and be recog-nised for it by strangers, thereby conferring social status. You imme-diately have a shared interest with other guys at the club and you participate in the same practices, experience the same pains and trials and you win or lose as a team. You bond by virtue of shared experience and create a history together.

As we approached Christmas, we began to get to know our team-mates a bit better after playing almost half of the regular season matches. Our language skills were improving and we began to be able to contribute a little in team meetings, even if a lot of what we came out with had to be translated by Hilly for the full benefit of everyone.

One of the big benefits of playing at this level in France is that there are far more free weekends than there are in England. There is no domestic cup competition, immediately getting rid of a raft of matches. We would tend to play three games in a row and then have a weekend off. The other big win was that there was a full break over Christmas with usually just one match in December, followed by a couple of weeks of intensive training before everyone departed to spend the festive period with family and friends.

During one such free weekend I was the only foreigner left in Rouen and our hooker Robin very kindly procured me an invite to a dinner held at another player's *appartement*. He said he'd call me to arrange a lift.

When he did, conversation proved difficult as I tried to explain where our flat was. The problem wasn't just vocabulary but also of geography. I was not very knowledgeable with the street names of the city and couldn't answer him when he tried to suggest some-where to go. In the end, I met him outside the nearby shopping centre. He looked hangdog with red rimmed eyes.

'*Ca, c'etait difficile.*' / 'That, that was difficult.' he said immediately.

It really was and it was my first encounter with a phone conversation in French. You don't realise until you have someone expectantly on the other end of the line but I find that understanding foreign speech relies heavily on being able to see the other person's mouth and at a more rudimentary level, their gestures. Without the cues that I'd never appreciated from the movement of a mouth, comprehension proved nearly beyond me.

Our last game before Christmas was away at Compiègne and we travelled there with the B team as usual. We had no expectations regarding the opposition and played some good stuff, scoring a couple of fine team tries and ending up with an attacking bonus point and a stirring away win.

As we shook hands with the opposition and prepared to leave the field, our watching B team and supporters stood up, linked arms and began to sing.

'*Allez allez allez Rouen, allez le Stade Rouennais!*'

We in turn faced them and sang back to them as the song got louder, faster and more fervent before we all cheered in unison.

For the first time, it felt like we were building something.

10

MY FIRST CHRISTMAS BREAK

PLAYING PROFESSIONAL RUGBY AROUND CHRISTMAS TIME IS A pretty grim endeavour. Christmas is usually very disruptive to both professional teams and to the families of the players and staff who are working while everyone else is celebrating together.

The worst year I've had involved playing a Cornish Pirates-Plymouth Albion derby game on Boxing Day and receiving Bristol in Cornwall on New Year's Day. This entailed getting up from the dinner table at about 5pm on Christmas Day and driving back to Penzance to be on the bus with the rest of the team the following morning. The coach refused to let me travel straight to Plymouth, adding about 4 hours to my journey.

New Year's Eve was uncommonly dry as my housemates went to bed, leaving me to ring in the New Year alone, watching fireworks explode on the television rather than at Mousehole around the corner from Newlyn.

We then celebrated a famous victory as the only people in the pub in Penzance, everyone else nursing their hangovers at home.

That was an exceptionally grim one to be fair!

Being a professional athlete around Christmas time is extremely bizarre as your sense of dislocation from society is heightened by the fact that work shuts down and people get either out or in to celebrate with their nearest and dearest.

In the meantime, you're outside, in the freezing cold, hitting tackle bags and preparing to entertain the masses at packed stadiums full of festive cheer.

You may have to leave your family behind to catch a bus to your away game, spending Christmas Day with your teammates in a hotel somewhere, keeping up with the goings on at home over FaceTime.

I'm from a medical family and so understand that there are other people working during this period too. My parents would negotiate on call shifts year to year, rarely able to completely relax during this time either. New Year in particular sees a rise in activity for the emergency services and one year I became a festive statistic after being jovially pushed at a club Christmas party, slipping on the icy pavement and getting my eyebrow glued together at A&E. Safe to say it was not my finest hour.

Most clubs are understanding during this period and try to organise training around the big days. If you train Christmas Eve you'll try to get everything done as early as possible, potentially starting earlier and thrashing out your sessions before hopping in the car and going back to wherever your family is based. In the professional era, players and staff are rarely from the area near the club so even your English players might have some considerable ground to cover.

Foreign players often band together, unable to go all the way to wherever they hail from, forming new bonds with teammates and their families over a big, shared festive meal.

Teams ring in the period with their own Christmas party, inviting partners if they want to keep a bit of a lid on things. Secret Santa presents tend to be in jokes, referencing shared history or sore points of the recipient, typically causing hilarity in the squad as things are unwrapped with excitement and trepidation.

Our first experience of a French rugby December was brilliant. The previous year had been my Penzance festive non-extravaganza whereas this year we were flying high in the league, signing off with our win at Compiègne and having not much to do apart from a couple of weeks training, attend our Christmas party and go home for two weeks.

A Christmas break is common in sports leagues around Europe whereas at home, sport is an enormous part of the festive calendar. Boxing Day football is a traditional touchpost and the general crush of fixtures is renowned around the world for being tough to negotiate for the clubs and their players. Even if football is not your game there is festive rugby, albeit still probably just once a week, but also traditional events like hunting or sea swims.

We did our two weeks training with minimal fuss, even if it was a sort of mini preseason due to the lack of matches to play, before preparing for our Christmas party. Christmas parties in the UK often get out of hand and rugby clubs are obviously not immune to this; if you want it to be a more civilised affair then you invite partners to keep an eye on things. If you don't, then God help you.

We were very excited for our first French Christmas fête; it was to be held in a sponsor restaurant in the centre of town and was fully comped with three courses and wine. We went to the supermarket to purchase Santa suits, complete with fake beards and hit up the *vin chaud* stands that dotted *centre ville* on our way to the party.

It turns out that French people find fancy dress both incredibly alien and hysterically funny, acting as if they've never seen it before. We were honked and grinned at all the way to the restaurant where we discovered that everyone else had dressed relatively smartly and had brought a significant other. This was no impediment to our fun as we sat down with some of the members of the team more accepting of idiocy and had a famous evening, even treating everyone to a haunting rendition of Silent Night.

Later, the whole party decamped to a bar around the corner where I was given a Christmas gift of a *brouillard normand* (a Normandy Fog).

I didn't know what this was until Bayou and Bouly, two overweight, sweaty, drunken Frenchmen, sprayed Guinness in my face. I was not happy but (much) later saw the funny side.

You could chart the enthusiasm of the club's administrators by the provisions made for the Christmas party. This first year it was a rather delicious meal in a restaurant in town, delighted as they were with our performance, but as success came to be expected, the Christmas party became a slightly sad event that people would regularly try to skip. For now though, we were feted as local heroes, fed and watered and sent back home to our families. We were to reconvene at training camp in Brighton on January 2nd.

11

___

BACK TO IT

It was a fine decision by Hilly to organise training camp for the 2nd January in Brighton. It meant that we could bring all our stuff and hop on the bus back to France with the rest of the team. The benefits of having an English coach.

Brighton was an absolute waste of time as far as training was concerned. The weather was so abominably bad that it was impossible to do anything of any significance on the waterlogged fields of Hove RFC. Some of the players realised this early and were drinking pints with their lunch, despite us having training that afternoon. Doing this in England would get you crucified but they were left unmolested, drinking quietly in peace.

I spent one of those afternoons wrestling with Bouly and another very overweight individual, the second team prop François Vilain. François has a face so heavy that he appears largely expressionless but put him on a dancefloor and he moves like an angel. I saw him twirl our scrum half's wife around the clubhouse until she was sweaty and somewhat excited, while he seemed perfectly at ease with himself.

He had none of this grace that afternoon, trying his best to pin me to the floor as we wrestled over tackle bags. Hilly found the whole thing hilarious and to be fair, it was. François invited me later in my French adventure to coach a local team with him where we achieved a promotion and we became very friendly over the course of my time there.

The main thing I found on returning to England for a spell was how objectionable we seem to foreign eyes. The French guys came to train at Hove RFC and had their valuables stolen from the changing rooms while we were outside, François being relieved of £300 in cash. Someone even had their kit stolen from the tumble dryer. This seemed particularly unnecessary as we did not have what I would consider desirable kit.

We 'trained' for two days and had a team night out on our last evening in Brighton. After having a couple in the team hotel, Luke and I took a group of the French guys to a pleasant looking pub tucked away somewhere in the centre. We walked in past the bouncers and ordered a round for everyone at the bar. There were about ten of us.

The bouncer came over exasperated.

'Who here speaks English?'

We nominated ourselves.

'You're going to have to leave. There are too many of you.'

I ventured that we had walked right past them on our way in, making no effort to disguise that we were a group and that we had just ordered drinks. He'd had several opportunities to tell us that we weren't welcome and he'd waited until the worst possible moment. He said that he was sorry but it was the pub's policy.

The French guys were baffled; we weren't drunk, hadn't done anything untoward and just wanted a quiet pint. They thought it inexplicable that we were being told to leave because there were too many of us. We explained to the doormen that this was some of these guys' first time in England and that this was a very poor way to behave. They seemed suitably embarrassed and we were left alone after that.

Later, during a cultural visit to the Oceana nightclub, our captain Alex, who was funding his nocturnal activities by selling smuggled packets of Camel cigarettes to strangers in the street, had his bottle of vodka stolen off his table when he wasn't there. English people would tell you not to leave things you don't want stolen unattended, but for the French guys this was not something they usually had to deal with. So far we'd been robbed (several times), made to leave various establishments and were just generally not having much fun.

The day after, as we were about to depart Brighton, our flanker Aurelien 'Cho Cho' Choliere turned to me dolefully:

'C'est une ville des voleurs Brighton!' / 'Brighton is a city of thieves!'

Our teammates had not felt welcomed by the city of Brighton and could not wait to get home to Normandy. I couldn't blame them and I was embarrassed by the experience that they'd had there.

I'd lived abroad before and you have a period of adjustment on arrival where things, of course, look foreign to your eyes. You don't know what a 'good' place might look like and small details like the different car number plates or the unusual names festooning the supermarket leave you bewildered and struggling for a reference point.

Before long you accept these things as normal and become accustomed to your new surroundings. Then, after a period of time, what's at home becomes the foreign, the weird, the bewildering.

At this point I was only a few months into my time in France so would not claim at all to have reached this point. Nevertheless, seeing English people from a new perspective was quite disorientating as I began to question why we behaved so differently. One such moment was feeling put out on walking into a shop as no one had greeted me, realising that I was beginning to assimilate some French customs into my expectations.

Brighton was a tipping point as I saw how we appeared to foreigners. Rude, dishonest and unwilling to help out. The other odd experience was on returning from France for the first time before the holidays and finding that first contact with English people in earnest was at Cobham services on the M25.

Services are perhaps the only fully egalitarian venue left; all classes, demographics and ages need to stop there. Here is probably the one place in the country where you see a full cross section of society and the sight of ours, shouting across the concourse, wolfing down fast food and jostling for parking spots was not especially edifying.

We left Brighton and headed for the ferry. In sharp contrast to the way there, where the bus had been subject to a bit of scrutiny, French customs asked who we were and upon hearing *'l'équipe de rugby de Rouen'*, ushered us through without checking a single passport.

On our return to Rouen we were straight back into it with the return fixture against Beaune being our first test of the new year. We made the long journey down to wine country by bus, aware that they would want revenge for the unexpected beating they'd received at our place.

Wine country sounds idyllic and having now driven around Saint-Émilion in the summer, I can see the appeal. In the depths of winter, when the vines are bare and the skies are grey, wine country looks very bleak. If you actually consider what they're doing, the rolling fields are essentially a factory. All talk of *le terroir* doesn't feel so romantic when you think about it like this.

Beaune felt bleak and their pitch wasn't up to much, being a bit waterlogged and slightly on a slope. We lost the game, didn't get to play with a lot of ball and the only real positive was a well taken opportunistic try from Ed Carne, chipping and chasing from about halfway after a turnover. Leti hurt his hand and was taken off, contributing to the slightly sour mood among the group on our way out of the stadium.

As usual there was some drinking on the bus, spearheaded by the B team. Most of us in the first team indulged in a few drinks but nothing too wild, not in the mood to celebrate.

Unfortunately, Leti had been given some prescription pain medication to tie him over until we got back to Rouen and he'd chosen to augment this by drinking most of a bottle of whisky to himself.

He began to get odder and odder, never the most coherent drunk at the best of times and he began to get more and more confused as to who everyone was. He made his way to the front of the bus, saying that he could see 'ghosts', causing widespread hilarity tinged with dread; everyone knew that this could spell curtains for someone if this 120kg man decided that someone was not a friendly ghost.

In hindsight, going to the front of the bus was not the best idea as he took exception to the coach driver, interrogating him as to who he was, believing him to be an apparition of some sort. Jean-Paul answered,

'I'm Jean-Paul. I just drive the bus.'

He was further accused of being a spiteful ghost when Hilly intervened and reminded him that we were his friends. He then changed tack.

'Thank you, thank you. You're like an angel... with no hair!'

He then lay on the floor and went to sleep while word of his vision rushed up the bus. Luckily, he didn't wake up until we reached Rouen.

When we did get there, it was decided that we needed to take him immediately to hospital as he might refuse to go if we stopped at the club to let everyone out. The hospital isn't far but no one was too enamoured with this idea. When we got there the club doctor came out to meet him, hand outstretched ready to shake. Leti, still in his addled state, thought that this was a threatening gesture and went to take a swing at him, just about being restrained by whoever was propping him up. It was another novel French experience and our first brush with violence in our team environment.

From being the star of the show the previous year in Fédérale 3, Leti found himself somewhat on the outer under Hilly. He'd turned up later in the autumn, spending some extra time back home in Tonga with his family and commensurately, was out of shape and unaccustomed to the new style of play that had been installed when he got back to Rouen. Something of a soloist, he was used to picking and choosing when to involve himself in the play and I suspect, that this extended to training sessions prior to our arrival too. This sort of attitude wouldn't prevail under the new regime.

The team evolved away from him, playing a faster, wider and less combative style and the club found that they already had the back row players to pull this off. Joe shifted to number 8, Amar Sy packed down on the blindside flank and Fabien Vincent took the 7 shirt. Fabien was a local boy, recently returned from unsuccessful *espoir* stints at Montpellier and La Rochelle, and he set about integrating himself into our game plan. Able to steal the ball in the ruck, handle and pass with some alacrity and with a natural nose for where the ball was going to go, Fabien proved excellent as a support player and I'd often get the ball away to him after a tackle or find him on my shoulder if I had broken the line, his accented English easy to distinguish.

Other useful local players included an energetic pair of scrum halves in Clément Desportes and Gabriel Cremadeills, even if their energy was not quite matched by the accuracy of their passing, and our wingers Johanny Labitte, not the most athletic but someone who understood both the game and some English, and Paul-Arthur Richardot, a skinny ex judoka with a beautiful girlfriend, his physical gifts and English language skills were the diametric opposite of Johanny's. These two were hilarious, Johanny learning to shout 'yours' in English whenever our forwards left a kickoff to someone else, while Polo, always up for a good time, is still at the club now, his skinny frame belying his strength and determination.

After the first half of the year had allowed Hilly to give most of the club's players a chance in the first team, the back half of the season had seen him largely settle on a lineup. Upon arrival he'd diplomatically given most guys a go whereas now, most people were clear where they stood. The senior guys in the team were the front five forwards, with Alex and Vincent in the second row, the back row were young, fit and keen to play wide, while most of the game was managed by the English in the backline, Pierre and Ed's versatility enabling us to accommodate different combinations. The back three were local players, Johanny and Polo aided by Vili who'd been settled in Rouen for some years, while further experience came from Romu Berthe in the centre.

Romu had been great to us, seeing us as good teammates rather than people here to take his place and he continued to offer a lot to the side, even if his status as the star player had been slightly diminished. He was a Polish national team player, shorter but powerful and a hard runner, putting his scrum cap down and charging at the opposition.

We were discovering a bit of a team ethic and style, scoring a lot of points while also conceding more than we would have liked and we were sitting pretty up at the top of the table along with Strasbourg. The second half of the year would be about refining what we were doing now that the players had sorted themselves into the appropriate teams and trying to achieve a decent seeding for the end of season playoffs.

12

SATURDAY NIGHT FEVER

FRENCH RUGBY HAS BEEN SLIGHTLY AHEAD OF RUGBY IN THE UK when it comes to innovating the live experience. Max Guazzini is probably the man responsible having taken over Stade Francais, turned their kit bright pink (earning them the nickname *les pinkistes*), and moving big games to the Stade de France. Tickets would be cheap to encourage a big crowd, cheerleaders, acrobats, lion tamers and fireworks were there to provide a spectacle and a sense of occasion.

Part of this is down to cultural difference; the French love pageantry and theatre while most attempts at stadium entertainment in the UK feel too corporate and inorganic, leaving everyone feeling uncomfortable. Where the UK gets pregame atmosphere right is in the Celtic crowds, singing songs with real meaning and depth to them. Despite their, let's say dislike, of the English, I still love hearing these songs; they feel real, part of the identity of the club, something that cheerleaders and t shirt cannons will never be.

All this French innovation worked tremendously well, garnering Stade Français a lot of press and French teams have been moving games to bigger grounds for years now. Toulouse go to the football stadium when they welcome big rivals, Toulon move games to Marseille and the Top 14 semi-finals are held in the same city on consecutive days to create a mini festival of rugby. The final was even played at the Nou Camp in Barcelona one year to avoid clashing with Euro 2016 but this proved so popular that I'd be surprised if it didn't happen again at some point.

Our presidents liked the idea of doing something similar to publicise the Stade Rouennais project and discussions to move one of our regular season games to the Stade Robert Diochon, the empty home of the struggling FC Rouen, proved successful. The game was arranged for the first home game after Christmas and excitement began to build.

We were pumped up for our first game at the football stadium. This *stade* lay dormant since the football team went under so there was already a sense of occasion about it reopening for us and we'd been heavily promoting the game which was to be held on the Saturday night.

All our games had been on Sundays, restricting our third half nightlife options considerably, so this opportunity to play in front of a big crowd and go out among the masses after had the squad salivating. Since the training camp in Brighton we'd had a gruelling couple of weeks training, a decent away win at Auxerre tempered by a poor result down at Beaune and were keen to get out and prove that we could produce in front of the Rouen public.

We were well prepared and keen to play, believing that the firmer pitch at the Diochon would suit our running game and that the atmosphere would get to the away team if enough people showed up to watch and we could start fast.

Sure enough there were about 6000 people there, with a brass band, baying schoolchildren and many of our family and friends. Due to some Norman-Viking connection there was a historical reenactment on the field before the game with fighting Vikings, a horse and a lot of flag waving; a sort of less flashy facsimile of the Stade Français experience. Indeed, we were waiting in the tunnel under the stadium before kickoff where we received a guard of honour from the Vikings, who banged their shields rhythmically as we walked through.

It was ridiculous yet got us up for it all the same.

Our home crowd usually varied between about one and two thousand depending on the weather and Sunday afternoon kickoffs meant there was a family day out sort of environment. To play in front of a much bigger public, under lights and in a proper sports stadium was a great opportunity for us.

It was also amusing to have the sport vs war parallel drawn out quite so clearly by staging the reenactment beforehand. Sport is an obvious stand in for actual conflict and although there is still conflict in the world, the idea that as a young western male you may ever have to fight someone is receding further and further from view.

George Orwell said that 'sport is war minus the shooting' - it happens in obscure places in front of partisan crowds who bey for your blood and my time in France certainly took me to some obscure places. The connection between sport and war is made explicit in the language used to psyche up the team in the pre-match huddle. In France, the captain will talk about *la guerre* / 'war' and *le combat* / 'the fight', using militaristic words to outline what's coming.

Back home in the UK we have an elderly neighbour who served in the army. He loves his rugby and talks about how he was never scared on the battlefield but would be 'scared shitless if Jonah Lomu was charging at me on the rugby pitch'. Now, Lomu must have been terrifying, but I've always found the rugby/military comparison a bit distasteful. There are similarities in terms of the camaraderie, the unit mentality, the wearing of uniform and the sublimation of oneself for a common goal but if you serve in the military, you have a much higher chance of going somewhere where the likelihood of killing people and the risk of grievous personal harm is very real. I have friends who have experienced some of these consequences. Rugby, for all the language and trappings, is a game. War is not.

I get that you're all uniformed, told what to do, go out to 'perform' on a battlefield and form closer bonds than normal with people who are effectively your colleagues but the actual threat of death means that to my mind, one form of service is very distinct from the other. Barring something unfathomably tragic, you won't die playing rugby.

I once had to spend an afternoon doing meet and greet in the hospitality suite at Plymouth Albion on a day where we honoured military veterans of the Iraq and Afghanistan Wars.

During the handshaking and socialising, I met a man who no longer had any limbs after losing them to an IED in the Middle East.

I really didn't know what to say to him. He was a quiet and reserved guy and wasn't called upon to make a speech. He was probably not much older than me but his life was irrevocably different because of his experiences. Rugby can cause serious harm to its participants but not like this.

It's the regularity and likelihood of life changing injury that makes military service so terrifying. Normandy is known worldwide for being the site of the D-Day landings and the opportunity to visit the beaches and pay our respects was something that I availed myself of several times while living in the area. To see the scale of the cemeteries in Normandy is to be humbled before swathes of ordinary men whose bravery you'll probably never approach.

On a cold and wet day off in that first year, Joe and I drove to the landing beaches for the first time. We had vaguely researched where we were going, planning to drive along the stretch of Normandy coastline west of Ouistreham and take in each landing zone on the way to the American cemetery at Omaha Beach.

Each zone was designated to a nation - the Canadians took Juno for instance - but the one seared into the popular psyche due to Saving Private Ryan is Omaha Beach, Spielberg apparently effectively recreating the sound and fury of the bloodiest D-Day landing. The beaches themselves are somewhat nondescript, long stretches of empty sand, uninterrupted by many amenities, desolate and grey in the Normandy winter.

Omaha Beach also has the American Cemetery and their War Memorial museum which is phenomenal. The Museum is a striking yet reserved piece of modern architecture, subtly covered in the names of those who died during the landings, full of memorabilia and presentations explaining the planning and sheer scale of the invasion. It's been tailored to an American audience in terms of the voiceover and presentation but, as they are telling you the story of real heroes who put themselves in the way of actual harm for a noble cause rather than NFL players on America's Game, it doesn't feel inappropriate.

The opportunity to visit the D-Day sites, to learn about the minutiae of the preparation and to see the results displayed so obviously before you is something that everyone should experience and we were lucky to be living nearby and able to do so. I returned several times but in my final season, we were taken for a team day out including a screening at the 360° cinema at Arromanche where the rusting hulk of a landing craft remains in the bay.

Although rugby is just a game, it is a visceral one, played with pace, daring and aggression and there's no doubt that the real threat of physical harm does play a part in the spectacle. The body composition of the protagonists has been ever improving since the dawn of professionalism, although a look at some of the guys in Hilly's England team would discourage you from thinking that there's been a change in size. Martin Bayfield and Johnson, Tim Rodber and Dean Richards are all enormous men, Bayfield having played various beasts across the Lord of the Rings and Harry Potter films, while Jeremy Guscott would be a pretty big centre now, let alone in the 1990s.

The power of the protagonists and their conditioning is what has changed completely and, with modern defences strung out across the field, the number of collisions has risen alongside their sustained ferocity. Rugby has a big problem in how to address player safety and at the time of writing, four young players have died in France over the past year due to injuries sustained playing the game. I'd still argue that the war comparison is unhelpful but rugby has a case to answer; how it does this could change the future trajectory of the sport.

Anyway, on that cold January evening, with the Norman sound and fury echoing around the stadium, *esprit de clocher* flowing through our team, I don't think PUC believed that they could win the game. We started fast and went at them with a sustained ferocity that hadn't been present in our previous performance away at Beaune.

Ed Carne scored a great individual effort as we went blind off a scrum. He chipped the ball ahead into space, hacked it on and touched down. We were outplaying them but the score was still relatively close with some good kicking from the Bean keeping us in front.

The second half saw us cut loose a bit and score some very well worked team tries, eventually coming away with a handsome margin of victory and basking in the adulation of our supporters, waving flags and banging drums to show their appreciation.

We then headed up to the corporate boxes for our post-match meal and to fulfil our promotional duties. I was collared by one of the presidents and taken into one of the private boxes to perform for some higher ups. By this time my French had improved a fair bit and although I was nervous, I managed to present a short report on the game as it felt to me on the field and thanked them for their support. They applauded me and as I did a good job, the president took me to the next box to repeat my act for the next bunch. They were a bit more raucous and made me down some horrible drink but were equally receptive to my ramblings.

Our performance was good for the club on several levels; the French Minister for Sport was present as a guest and left impressed by not only the result, but also with the work of the marketing team in attracting a decent crowd to a Normandy rugby match. Other potential sponsors were also in attendance, including the president of

Matmut who had to endure my little performance. Matmut is one of France's larger enterprises and sponsors various sporting endeavours around the country. It has a large presence in Rouen and impressing this man was to prove very beneficial for the club in the years to come. Big occasions need to be leveraged, not only on the night they happen but to ensure that further benefits arrive down the line and this evening at the Diochon certainly made what was essentially an amateur club seem like a serious proposition, to me as well as potential sponsors. The atmosphere and support had been incredible and for the first time, the Stade Rouennais project looked serious.

We were certainly something of a curio around the city, being professional rugby players in a town with no history of the sport and being English. The presidents, who certainly did see us as their property, would use us as performing seals, bringing out their little Englishmen to do tricks for their friends and business associates. We were also some of the only full time players, meaning that we had the lion's share of the promotional work to do and would spend our time giving presentations in schools and signing things in town squares for sparse crowds where people were often surprised to hear that there was any rugby in the area at all, making us seem even more curious.

These commitments were great for our language skills and you just need to put yourself in harm's way when you're learning, getting out and speaking to people. Coaching kids is a great test as they pull no punches, making no allowances for your lower levels of comprehension and peppering you with questions. Later when I had got to grips with the language and could observe new arrivals with some detachment, I could see the difference in learning with the guys who didn't interact at sponsor events and the like and the guys who did.

Once all our duties were finished, we went for a late dinner with our parents, Hilly, Jean-Pierre Botrel and his wife before heading out into town to *arroser la victoire*[1] with the rest of the lads. We went on late into the evening, drunk and happy.

13

RACE TO THE SUMMIT

THE REST OF THE SEASON WAS SPENT IN A STRAIGHT SHOOTOUT with Strasbourg to see who could secure top spot in the pool, guaranteeing themselves an easier playoff draw. The convoluted system meant that you only had to make the semi-finals to get promoted as the division above also contained 40 teams. That meant winning two rounds of playoff matches, both of which were held over two legs.

The difference in points between the teams was negligible and so our second meeting was to be decisive. If we could remain ahead of them on points after this game, our destiny was in our own hands and we had an easy game to finish the season where we were almost guaranteed to win. The firmer pitches and sunny forecast would suit our running game; Strasbourg came to the Mermoz knowing that they needed a win and that they would be facing the top point scorers in the division.

They played incredibly negatively, putting high balls up over and over on a sunny day and barely passing a ball. Sadly it worked as our wingers, never the most secure under this sort of aerial attack, managed to drop almost everything. We were the favourites for this one and you could see how it was affecting us.

Being the favourite or front running can be more difficult. When no one expects anything of you, you can develop the underdog mindset of 'I'll show you'. When you're the frontrunner you can develop a sense of confidence that you'll find the solution or conversely, the pressure of having to succeed can cripple you. We were going for the second option.

Once when playing rugby in Sydney, I turned up for a game not feeling great. Nothing serious, I just felt slightly under the weather. It must have shown because our hooker asked me,

'Were you on the piss last night?'

I did sometimes do that in Sydney as it can be hard to say no to the array of temptations on offer but I certainly hadn't this time. I assured him that I hadn't and that I felt slightly ill.

'You'll probably have a good game then mate. Sometimes when you don't expect anything of yourself you play well.'

I had one of my better games of the season in the end, scoring a couple of tries. Funny how that works.

Anyway, our game against Strasbourg was on a bad track. We had them on the ropes when we had the ball, their defence stretched to breaking point by our wide-wide attack, but our errors had cost us, keeping them slightly ahead. Then we forced a pass, they hacked the ball almost the length of the field and scored, leaving us without even a losing bonus as it stood. Later on, Luke had a penalty which would bring us within a score and within the margin required for a losing bonus point.

With a losing bonus, we would top the pool and go into the knock-outs drawn against one of the lower seeds.

He missed.

That season he was statistically the best kicker in France with a kicking percentage better than Toulon's Jonny Wilkinson, a fact that the local press dug up and crowed about. He'd been on fire that year, given full rein to run the team, pulling out little chips and tricks to go with his often spectacular kicking off the tee. He has always been an excellent kicker, albeit at a lower level of competition than the great Wilkinson, a favourite of English and French alike.

He later missed another slightly easier kick and we lost the game without a bonus. This result was a bit of a disaster, meaning that we were to play Suresnes, a team from a wealthy suburb to the west of Paris, before facing Soyaux-Angoulême if we came through that game. Angoulême were the best team in the division and had been winning all year.

After the game, Luke said that he hadn't realised the implications of missing the kicks. Considering he always knows full well his kicking stats and the ins and outs of the changing scoreboard, I found this hard to believe. It's also not as if he'd have tried harder to get them if he knew what a successful kick would mean. He tries to get all of them. He'd known that they were important and had missed them.

I'm no kicker so I can't completely understand the mindset but this is your lot. If you win the game then you get the praise, if you lose the game then you get the criticism. You have to take the rough with the smooth.

Having said this, no player in the team will blame the kicker. If he's won games for you before then you know and respect this. It's not like you catch every pass or make every tackle, why should he get every kick?

Equally if the team had played better or executed our game more effectively, our postseason path wouldn't rely on those specific penalties. You win and lose collectively. What cost us wasn't even our points total in the end. As we finished on the same total as Strasbourg, the rules dictated that the next point of comparison wasn't points or tries scored but our disciplinary records. Ours was appalling so Strasbourg finished in first.

Discipline is something that's quite hard to explain to a French team and some of them are proud of their hotheaded temperament. Being liable to swing a punch was almost a point of honour amongst some of our players, particularly the older ones, even though it would regularly cost us on the field. We didn't help ourselves in this regard away at Drancy when, having received two yellow cards, we were obliged to take off a back and put on a front row forward in order to scrummage. I was stood in defence, convinced something was awry and started counting the number of players we had on the field.

There were 12 of us.

In the general confusion, Hilly had subbed off a player and neglected to put on a replacement, leaving us another man short defending a scrum in our 22m for no reason at all. When I realised this and started shouting to the bench, my opposite number started chuckling. By this time my French had improved enough to join in,

'*On est vraiment des idiots*' / We really are idiots.

He was not inclined to disagree with me. We went on to win that one but you can see how our casual indifference to the rules in all regards could cause yellow cards to mount up. Combined with the odd act of *grosse brutalité*, it made for a sorry state of affairs and I think we averaged one yellow card per game during the whole regular season. Unbelievable to a professional rugby player.

Wider implications aside, it was galling to lose to Strasbourg and the way they celebrated was appalling. They were fist pumping and whooping shouting '*la revanche*'[1] and dancing together. We had won at their place and hadn't behaved like this.

Most of the team dispersed quite quickly after the game, eager to get home and lick their wounds in private. A handful remained at the clubhouse to have food and a couple of quiet beers. Strasbourg had their food, packed up and went back to their bus.

Suddenly they burst into the clubhouse, dancing in a conga line and singing, led by their coaches. This was quite extraordinary and disgraceful.

As there weren't many of us left there wasn't much could do about it but I have no doubt that had the rest of the team been there,

there would have been a fight. Two of our players went to remonstrate with their coach but he was aggressively rude in his response.
They wanted to fight him but would probably have been set upon by
the whole Strasbourg team.

It's a famous old thing. Win and lose with grace. These guys
certainly hadn't managed it.

We moved on to the playoffs against Suresnes, beating them relatively comfortably away from home in the first leg. This victory was
achieved despite our combustible prop managing to not react when
being punched in the face and receiving a red card for just being
involved. He was furious, storming over to the bench and destroying
their substitutes dugout where some of our players had been sitting.
It was quite a spectacle. The second leg was the following weekend
at our place for which he was now banned.

Being a sportsperson means that your life runs on a different
schedule to most other people. Some of this majority are your
friends. Their lives tend to have a working week between Monday
and Friday with a weekend free to do as they please, occasionally
augmented by a bank holiday or holiday that they can take with a
certain amount of notice.

An athlete's life runs very differently to this. It might seem obvious
but in the case of rugby, the week builds to the focal point of a game,
typically held on a weekend. You are other people's entertainment
and therefore you perform when they are available. This means that
you get some days off in the week when they are working which puts
you somewhat at odds with society at large.

Rugby players can often be seen strolling around city centres on odd
weekday afternoons, sporting flip flops and sipping coffee, whiling
away the time with a series of frivolous pursuits like playing cards or
pulling each others' pants down for a joke. You will only very rarely
see them doing this on a Saturday when everyone else is.

Although the week builds to the focal point of a match, the training
week does not ramp up as the game approaches. This is to avoid

fatigue. To allow recovery after the previous game, you would normally receive the day after the game off or just have a light recovery session. Many teams would also make the next day a lighter training day. If you've played on Saturday then Tuesday and Wednesday will be when you get through the bulk of your training load. Tuesdays always seemed long to me. At least with Wednesdays you can look forward to a day off on Thursday.

Free weekdays seem quite joyous at first. Town is not so busy and you can relish the time when most people are working. Cafes and restaurants are not oversubscribed and you can wander around in a relative state of calm. For a while you enjoy being at a remove from society at large and feel as if you're in on a secret that they don't know. You pay in other ways.

During this first season in France I turned 26 years old. Advancing age meant that non-rugby playing friends of mine began to get married, starting with one of my oldest friends from school. His wedding would normally have been well placed for me rugby wise as the season tends to end in May or even at the end of April depending on the team's success that year. The home game against Suresnes was the following Sunday, the day after his Saturday wedding at which I was a groomsman.

I managed to negotiate the Friday off training to get back to England and help with setup. He's a relatively idiosyncratic chap and had decided to hold a non-denominational blessing in a field not far from where we grew up. This required putting up a futuristic sort of tent and a lot of admin, running around carrying stuff. I'm pleased I was there to help with that.

Unfortunately, the team were less amenable to me missing the crucial second leg of our playoff tie that weekend; it was the biggest game of the season so you can hardly blame them. I booked my flight to get back as late as possible but it meant leaving the wedding at about 4.30 when everything was just getting going. I felt incredibly miserable and this was the first time that I missed a big life event in our friendship group. I gave my reading, shouting into a howling wind, waited until the end of the blessing and then hopped in the car and off to Heathrow.

I felt even more miserable when my flight was delayed, causing me to miss my train connection and had to get a €250 taxi from Paris to Rouen after midnight from a guy who knew he had me over a barrel. No hire cars available. I considered running from him when we got back, mostly because he tried to make me pay the *peage* tolls on the motorway which we'd agreed that he would include in his special price. I didn't though. That would have been mean.

It's perhaps unfair to not mention missing various family birthdays and events over the years, including my parents' 60th birthdays but it's hard to remember each instance in detail as they are so numerous. I was probably in a mediocre hotel in the middle of nowhere, counting down the hours until our game the following day. These things are relatively par for the course and not everyone can make everyone's birthday.

It's not that living out of step with everyone can't be fun or even do you a favour in questioning the routines that society at large lives by for almost no discernible reason; you can even feel somewhat special that your life doesn't follow the same rhythm as other people. It's just that you find yourself permanently out of step with your friends, family and most other people. This really rears its head when you retire from the game and are confronted with how the world works. You can't ring someone and meet them in ten minutes time while many people don't want to do anything on a Wednesday evening as they have a weeknight routine that they stick to. Your teammates live on the same schedule as you, making life easy to coordinate. This is another way in which you are an other. Separate from the world at large. Fun to begin with, grating later on.

Suresnes came up to the Mermoz and all seemed to go according to plan until a flurry of late points made the game incredibly close. Their kicker, a barrel of a fullback not entirely dissimilar in appearance to François Steyn and sharing his penchant for kicking everything, had a kick to at least send the game into extra time. The convoluted regulations meant that no one on the field seemed to have any idea that this was the case but fortunately for us he missed. We were unsure whether, in the event of a tie on aggregate, we would play extra time, it would depend on tries scored across the two games or whether our red card would count against us.

One of our most popular players signed for Suresnes for the next season as they guaranteed him a good job and found him an apartment in the area. He had been living near the Stade de France in the St Denis *banlieue* to the north of the city centre, a rough area near the *banlieues* renowned for being a dumping ground for the immigrant population to be ignored and forgotten about. Despite being bright, motivated, well presented and incredibly friendly, his name Amar Sy immediately marked him out as a black Muslim and he bemoaned how it was impossible for him to find an apartment in a better area. Landlords simply would not let to him.

Amar is the sort of guy you'd want in any organisation and the club were keen to convince him to take up rugby full time. He lived and worked in Paris during that season, his job garnered through a club sponsor, joking that his home was the A13 road due to the constant driving up to Rouen to train and play. He was tall, slim and athletic with a coltish running style, his springy frame enabling him to be a real menace at the front of the lineout where he'd often bat back opposition throws and he was fast enough to chase and win short kickoffs that Luke would put up. His skills were not the best but he worked hard to improve them over the course of the year and by the end, was renowned for his *coup de pied rasant* or grubber kick.

Sometimes rugby can grease the wheels for you and Amar moved over to Suresnes the next season to improve the quality of life for him and his young family. It's odd as a practising Muslim is probably someone that you would want to rent your apartment; they won't drink or party and live a clean existence. On away trips Amar would have halal meals prepared for him in advance of our arrival at whichever hotel we stayed in and would bring his prayer mat to fulfil his commitments to Allah. Speaking with him about his faith was quite fascinating.

I've got a bit of a theory around Islam and professional sport. As suggested, if an athlete takes his religion seriously then he is an ideal employee with many of the temptations of society and sports team drinking culture immediately off limits for him. There are now prominent Muslim athletes like reformed partygoer Sonny Bill Williams who excel at the highest level of competition. Of course, there are others who don't take their religion so seriously; one guy in the B team indulged in every vice that he possibly could, sometimes all at once. The only thing he wouldn't do was eat pork.

We beat Suresnes and then had to face favourites Soyaux-Angoulême who beat us soundly over the two legs. If we'd finished first then we would have had a still difficult but not impossible game against someone else for promotion to the next division, speeding the development of the club immensely. Whether the club were ready for a back to back promotion was up for debate.

Angoulême were obviously a professional team and although they didn't have too much going on out wide, they had a reliable kicker and a very well drilled pack of forwards who dominated our line out and carried athletically around the park. It felt like a bridge too far for us during the game and with their packed stadium, replete with brass bands and banners, they were evidently anticipating winning promotion before the game even began. We had lost to them at home, giving them a fright with our fast style of play, tapping penalties quickly and offloading as often as we could. By the end of the game their bigger forwards were wilting in the heat but we had too great a deficit to make up.

I was interviewed after the home leg and said honestly that I believed in our ability to win a game at their place for which the journalist, our home reporter, basically snorted in my face. You could see how the lack of belief from anyone near the team could bleed over into a performance and our hooker Robin, a midseason arrival from a year spent in New Zealand, had an absolute shocker, falling off tackles and missing most of his lineouts. No one really covered themselves in glory though as Angoulême won a deserved victory and had their party. We had ours on the bus home; a long journey made even longer by Jean-Paul driving an hour and a half in the wrong direction.

Soyaux-Angoulême are now in the upper echelons of Pro D2 and are probably eyeing potential promotion to the Top 14 in future. Tom Varndell recently spent a couple of months there before hightailing it back to England, apparently shocked at their lack of professionalism and archaic approach to training. Luckily for him he didn't sign for Rouen. They are an example of a well backed and organised side who British rugby fans may not necessarily have heard of but who are now a destination for serious rugby players, even if there are still evidently a few kinks to iron out. If nothing else, they provided a good example to Rouen of a model to follow, the main takeaway for me being that we needed a more organised pack of forwards.

Losing to Angoulême didn't put too much of a downer on the year as the club had only been promoted to Fédérale 2 the year before we arrived. We had wildly exceeded their expectations by getting to a promotion decider and expectations were therefore high for the following year. We packed up the car and went home for the summer, new contracts in the bag and reasonably happy with our first year's work.

14

YEAR TWO - OPERATION PROMOTION

OUR SECOND SEASON WAS COMPLETELY DIFFERENT. WHILE US foreigners were secretly holding a candle for achieving promotion the previous year, none of the French guys considered it as a serious possibility. The new season brought different objectives. Promotion wasn't a possibility; it was expected.

To aid the process the club had gone out and recruited ambitiously. Our first season had seen us struggle up front, happy to sling the ball around and run the other teams off their feet by leveraging our fitness but not too willing or able to play a tighter game. We also lacked some finishing power on the wing so a couple of back three players had come in.

The main signings were foreign and so the number of English speakers at the club swelled. Ed Carne and Pierre-Alex Clark had departed to begin new careers in England and were replaced by Leo Montoya, a French-Chilean utility back with Chile 7s representative caps, and Kevin Milhorat, a skinny fullback from Massy who had gained promotion to Pro D2 and barely played him at all. These two would become influential for wildly different reasons.

The foreigners were guys used to a higher level of rugby. Ed Barnes, formerly of my old club Plymouth Albion, Bristol and Narbonne, arrived to take over the captaincy and provide some experience in the inside backs. Ed knew France having spent the previous few seasons there and was married to a charming young French girl, Marion. With his England Saxons (essentially the England 2nd XV) experience and being able to speak French, he was a major coup for the club, even if he was winding down a bit. Richard Bolt, a talented scrum half somewhat under-utilised in English league rugby despite his Premiership title winning experience with Harlequins, arrived to take over the starting 9 role and showcase his brilliant passing game. He and Ed already knew each other from Bristol and were firm friends off the field.

Semisi Taulava and Nick Seymour both arrived from Worcester Warriors, being known to Hilly from his time as their head coach, just as Ed was known to him from his time at Bristol. Semi is an enormous guy, both physically and in force of personality and is tons of fun. He was a replacement for Leti who had proven erratic both on and off the field, even if he had plausible cause for complaint with the club over unfulfilled promises made to him regarding the arrival of his family. Nick was an aggressive, muscular hooker who had arrived to beef up our front row and replace Anthony Vigouroux. He'd moved over with his girlfriend and was to spend three years at the club, even if on arrival he fell afoul of a few of the pitfalls that moving to France can bring.

Other signings included Remi Cardon, a curly haired nutjob intended to replace Amar Sy, Romain Suster, a powerful Czech prop with a lot of Pro D2 experience and Wilfrid Hounkpatin, one of the greatest physical specimens I've ever seen who, despite being a 135kg prop, could post one of the faster 40m sprint times. All three of these guys make for interesting tales and exemplify the divergent paths that professional rugby can take you down.

One of the big factors in squad recruitment was the licensing system. Every professional sports league has some sort of checks and balances to deal with foreign players. Some run a quota system, some reward teams who field home grown players and some have a very strict limit on foreigners. It's an emotive issue and has come to be a big discussion in France regarding the future of the game.

The Top 14 has proven incredibly appealing to the world's best rugby players, giving them the opportunity to increase their earnings, live the French lifestyle and experience another culture. The Top 14 and European Cup competitions also have a prestige and a level that the high paying Japanese competition cannot match. The Top 14 clubs are more than happy to indulge these players and convincing one to sign for your team is a badge of honour amongst the colourful and competitive owners that bankroll the glamour clubs of French rugby. The only nation to remain relatively unaffected by player recruitment is New Zealand who make it very clear that if you leave, All Black caps are impossible. There are still many former All Blacks playing in the Top 14 but they tend to be those who were not quite first choice for their position or who were ageing out of a starting role and beginning to prioritise earnings.

In the top division, the salaries really are night and day compared to elsewhere in the professional game. Dan Carter was earning about €100,000 a month at Racing 92, not including the club car, provided accommodation and the host of other smaller benefits that he'd be collecting. His former All Black understudy Aaron Cruden earns around €800,000 per season at Montpellier while the average salary in the Top 14 is reported to be €235,000.

These salaries far exceed what's possible in New Zealand domestic rugby for most players and so it's completely understandable that 'mid-tier' internationals feel that their interests are better served in France where they can potentially triple their income. This has led to a large number of foreigners heading over to France and taking up places in squads that would potentially be held by French players.

The FFR (French Federation du Rugby) have taken steps to ease this problem by introducing a homegrown player quota, not unlike the EQP (English Qualified Player) regulations in the English

Rugby Premiership. This can lead to a premium being paid for French talent.

In football, the obvious corollary is the English Premier League. They pay the highest salaries and have one of the most competitive championships, meaning that there are shared incentives for players to come and teams to recruit. This is a commonly cited factor in the dwindling number of English players available for selection for the national team and some weekends, a team may field a starting side with no English players in it.

French rugby hasn't quite reached this point but there has certainly been a rise in the number of employed foreigners in the top rugby divisions and a recent lack of success for the French national team. Former national team coach Bernard Laporte was appointed as the head of the FFR upon which he pledged to reduce the numbers of foreign players playing in the Top 14, instigating a series of new regulations around French qualified players.

Homegrown, French academy produced players count as JIFF (Joueurs Issus des Filières de Formation) players and are highly prized for filling the quota imposed on teams by the league. They don't have to be playing at the team that formed them, they just must have been developed by a French rugby academy. The best example I know is Yacouba Camara, a back row forward who has really benefited from the implementation of these rules coming just as his various contract renewals have come up. Blind luck or sensible work from his agent; I couldn't tell you.

Anyway, Camara was developed in Paris at Massy, making a big impact in his first year of Pro D2 competition. He was signed away from them by Toulouse, being a promising youngster who could further develop, JIFF qualified and good enough to contribute immediately without being likely to be called up to the French national team. He's since been signed away by Montpellier, now one of the financial big hitters in France, and is a French national team player. He is more likely to be away for parts of the season but he's still quite young, marketable and counts as homegrown; gold dust for a team stacked with foreigners like Montpellier.

The rules have been circumvented in an obvious way as many French teams heavily recruit junior players from other nations to join their academies rather than waiting until they are established adult players. They spend three years in the *espoirs*[1], becoming French after three seasons and join the first team squad as if they were an actual Frenchman. This feeds into the debate about international eligibility in a wider context; France isn't the only nation to do this by any stretch, but with the financial power of the clubs, opening academies in Fiji is not only very possible, it makes complete sense. You can get island talent over to France cheaply, integrating them into a professional environment sooner and qualifying them as home-grown. They are low cost bets that can pay off handsomely, like Aliv-ereti Raka at Clermont.

Stade Français have been taken over by Hans Peter Wild, the owner of Capri-Sun, subsequently spending much of his juicy cash on French internationals to shore them up against the new regulations. They have even paid a substantial transfer fee to get Yoann Maestri out of his pre-contract agreement with La Rochelle who presumably jumped at the chance to make an enormous profit on a player who hadn't even trained for them yet. French players are commanding a premium, much as young Englishmen do in the Premier League.

Why does this matter lower down the leagues? Laporte decreed that it's in these divisions where youngsters are likely to get a first go at senior rugby and that it behoves them to not have a load of jobbing foreigners clogging up their avenues for progression. By introducing limits lower down, he argues that these players will play and filter up the divisions. Tighter regulation can be introduced in the top league at a later date. This helps to placate those who want to provide opportunities for youngsters without overly upsetting the wealthy owners of the Top 14 who have a lot of costly foreigners on multiyear contracts. If they were suddenly unable to use them in matches then they become expensive dead weight.

When we arrived in France the license system wasn't an issue for us. Later it would become a dominant topic of conversation and speculation.

Players were given different licenses based on where they were from and how long they had spent at a club. As new recruits and foreigners, we were the 'worst' grade of licenses with a limit on the numbers of us you could have in a match day squad at any one time. As there were only a few of us and two of the English guys qualified for the French player licenses, this was not a problem in our first season.

Later, as our foreign legion swelled with recruits, we began to rub up against the restrictions.

For any player, the golden ticket was a *license blanche* - a white license. This meant that you were a homegrown player of which the club had to field 6 in every lineup. To qualify as a white license, you had to have been developed as a player there or have spent four consecutive seasons there, becoming eligible for your fifth year.

This sounds like an admirable policy and in some ways it is, encouraging homegrown players or recruits who stick around for a long time. For a team in a hurry to get up through the divisions like Rouen, it was quite a hindrance. The guys with white licenses weren't necessarily the best players, they often weren't, but they needed to be included in the squad. Sometimes, due to injury or unavailability, a player from the *espoirs* would be called upon to sit on the bench, only to make up the numbers with regards to licenses. Anyone with a white license was very aware of their relative power and so needed keeping happy in between times.

Our second row Vincent Lointier was one of the few who resisted the call of professionalism. Coming to the end of his rugby shelf life, he preferred to continue working as a chef where he cooked in a school, winning a national award for the quality of his cuisine. He was suspicious of the foreigners on arrival but warmed to us as the seasons went by, cracking jokes and leveraging the power of his license to remain in the team.

In a small squad, there is no selection conundrum. These *licensiers* are always going to be included. Problems arise when they don't start or when they have other commitments they'd prefer to do instead. Vincent was granted several bits of time off or the ability to skip sessions he didn't fancy. Weights was conducted in his own time and I suspect mostly at his leisure judging by the lack of change in his physical appearance. No one resented this of him; it was a fact of life that anyone else would have taken advantage of in a similar fashion.

Vincent started the final in my last season, playing for the Jean Prat trophy. Everyone knew this was not on merit but merely because he knew that with his licence, the club needed him to play. The other two second rows, both English, went away and missed training sessions the weekend before the final, knowing that it wouldn't make a blind bit of difference to whether they'd play or not. When this knowledge is pervasive in the squad it doesn't necessarily breed resentment towards an individual player taking advantage, the reaction being mostly envy at his privileged position, but it does make you question how other selection decisions are made.

In my final season the new foreigner limit was brought in and was to apply to the next year. This meant that you could only include 6 foreigners in the match squad at any one time. If the white license system had held, the three of us who arrived together in my first year would have qualified as homegrown players and therefore not counted as foreigners. Being better players than most of the home-grown alternatives, we would have been in a very strong bargaining position when it came to contracts, looking at being ideal squad members and facilitating the recruitment of more, better foreign players. Sadly for our bank balances, the licence system in that form was scrapped and two of us left anyway. Luke said that this was a fine metaphor for our rugby careers overall; nearly but not quite.

Sometimes contractual situations can turn on changing regulations or other factors out of your control and the general disorganisation of the FFR means that these factors aren't always clear right up until they happen. 'When in France' as Semisi would say. The influx of foreign players to Rouen was the first sign of professionalism really altering the fabric of the club, engendering a greater us and them environment between the English speakers and the French; juggling the demands of the licence system, as well as the emotional responses sure to result from changes in team selection would be a big part of Hilly's duties.

15

LA RÉSIDENCE

THE SUCCESS OF THE TEAM IN MY FIRST YEAR LED TO A GREATER investment in the team from principal sponsors, enabling the recruitment drive that had occurred during the off season. One of the big developments was that rather than housing players in different apartments owned by private landlords across the city, Matmut had given the club the use of some of their employee apartments, situated in the suburb of Petit-Quevilly and part of a residence right down the road from the Mermoz. This was great for the social life of the team and for the ease of getting to training. Luke and I moved into a top floor apartment which was a huge upgrade on our previous one. Light and modern as opposed to gloomy and tired, the new place was a big fillip for us.

The state of the residence on arrival wasn't to everyone's liking and although we were also moving to a new house, we already had most of the things required to furnish a place, albeit in a relatively spartan fashion. Players were turning up from more organised teams expecting an apartment that was ready to go. This was not how things were done at Stade Rouennais.

Barnesy rolled in to Rouen late at night with a wife and crying baby, hoping to be able to dump his stuff and go to sleep until the next morning. What he found was an unfurnished apartment with no hot water or electricity and no one to call until the morning. He'd played several seasons in France but his experience of Rouen was quite different to what he'd previously encountered.

Having spent his French years in some of the more scenic destinations in France, near the beach in Narbonne and in the beautiful environs of Avignon, he did not find the dilapidated urban environment of Petit-Quevilly too appealing and neither did his young French wife who hailed from the hilltop, picture postcard town of Carcassonne. It's hard to overstate how lovely these towns are and although the centre of Rouen is classic French town material, it's fair to say that Petit-Quevilly is somewhat grittier.

Being poorly prepared for a player's arrival was not uncommon and treated as somewhat of a joke. To some extent you're an adult and ought to be prepared for some turbulence when moving house but you are being given a place to live as part of your contract and may have moved countries. It's not unreasonable to expect some help. Or a liveable apartment. When we moved, we were made to share an oven with our teammate over the corridor, our requests for our own cooking apparatus being laughed off for some weeks. It doesn't exactly engender goodwill between the club and its employees, creating an adversarial atmosphere at work.

Ed is a classic case of bad luck and timing. I'd played against him previously during his Bristol days and he was a fellow graduate of the Graham Dawe school of very tough love down at Plymouth Albion. A big guy for a playmaker, able to take the ball to the line and offload as well as play a more considered game, he was also a prototypical hard tackling ten with one particularly stiff shoulder that was worth avoiding. Ed was in the Premiership and at Bristol at a good time when they were competing in Europe.

This doesn't mean that he ever really saw the big bucks as a result. As he'd been with Bristol when they were promoted he was probably there a little below market rate and had it all to prove. He played well enough to be selected for England Saxons even though he told us that he felt he hadn't been playing too well when the call came in. The selectors told him he was effectively the third choice 10 in the country as far as they were concerned which came as a surprise to him because he felt he could have been playing better.

He then tore his Achilles tendon and didn't see another Premiership field as Bristol were relegated down to the Championship, where he recovered in time to play a small part in that season. After a lot of palaver there involving the mass culling of player salaries when they failed to achieve an immediate promotion, he decamped to France and to the sort of chaos that I've been describing.

Ed struggled to immediately adapt to our style of play and took the ball into contact a little more than necessary; our pattern and the lower level of competition meant that you could often make a lot of ground by just moving the ball wide early and then using our structure to manipulate the defence. If you watch the Crusaders play Super Rugby you can see the apogee of the sort of rugby that we had been aspiring to; occasionally they score by almost out-systeming the opposition. Ed thought he was to play 10 but he ended up playing mostly at 12, even moving to fullback for a bit which he did not enjoy, the inclement weather that year making his life of catching kicks very miserable.

We basically aimed to use a dual playmaker system where he and the Bean could interchange at 10 and 12 in phase play, with one at first receiver and the other behind a pod of forwards as an option to move the ball. Me and the back three players would be more strike runners although the idea was that anyone could slip into the pocket if needs be to maintain the movement of the ball. That the two of them were both good kickers as well as forming a left foot/right foot combo was just another reason why this should have worked out very nicely.

It seems impossible that two perfectly capable players don't mesh but it happens quite regularly in sport. It wasn't like there was a lack of will from them but sometimes you almost want to be too accommodating. The Bean would sometimes follow play around the corner as he would do normally and then duck out at the last minute, deferring to Ed, trying to give him time at first receiver. The problem was by moving round as he was accustomed to doing, everyone else would set their depth and timing off him. Ducking out at the last minute would throw off everyone outside and we would be bollocked when it occurred, even though it was a wider rhythm issue.

If you were a suspicious person you might think the Bean was sabotaging Ed's chances of being the playmaker by making him look like an idiot but he's not that sort of character. He always wants to do things well. Nevertheless, the chemistry issues precipitated a move to fullback for Ed to put a bit of distance between them. It didn't really suit us or Ed though.

I think they could have been a bit more up front with each other on arrival in terms of what they needed from the other but there is an element of social awkwardness when dealing with someone you don't know. Some of it is also down to the coach to address and Hilly seemed to completely prioritise Luke's views over Ed's which was odd seeing that he'd installed Ed as captain. I got a bit of flak for what I was up to outside them but when I pointed out how out of sync they were as a pair the actual problem wasn't solved; Ed was just moved outside. He was more flexible positionally and Luke was scoring a lot of points at fly half.

You could see Ed's quality in his passing skills and the ability to stand in the tackle and offload. When he did play at 10 he had that ability to go straight at the line and take on his opposite number or attack the gap that can exist between the 10 and the flanker. In the modern game where defences rush, having a 10 who can go right at the line is often the shortest way to gaining ground, being that a rushing centre can catch you metres behind where you started.

It wasn't all bad and I pointed out that we couldn't have been doing too bad a job as our two wingers scored 16 tries or so each. If your wingers are scoring then they must be getting the ball in favourable situations somehow so it wasn't all doom and gloom.

Rugby players can be a pessimistic bunch, with gallows humour often used to deal with the day-to-day. At Cornish Pirates, one of our props would frequently bargain with me to see how much money I'd pay to leave a wet and miserable training session that very instant and this was no different in France, where such talk was commented on by a visiting coach who would mutter 'it'll rain tomorrow' whenever he heard something slightly negative.

With the propensity of team management to review everything, spending hours poring over video footage, it can be easy to overlook what's working and talk about errors all the time. This prevailing attitude can infect a group, leave you all feeling like nothing is adequate and start to inhibit play on the field. Coaching and leading is a fine balance between not getting too carried away with the good or the bad and occasionally celebrating the big successes.

We were sat in the shopping centre branch of Paul cafe after weights later during the season and a lady approached us having heard us speaking English. She'd lived in Rouen for about 15 years and was curious as to what a big bunch of us were doing there. We were becoming even more of a curiosity as we swelled both in numbers and in size with the addition of Semi. There aren't too many beefy Pacific Islanders walking around regional French cities so they tend to draw attention.

She asked us how we liked it and Ed, at this point over the whole enterprise and prepping for retiring back to England, said that frankly, it was shit. She looked quite shocked. He ranted about where we lived, how it was grubby, dirty and didn't seem safe.

We tried to rescue the situation by asking if there was anything that she recommend we do around Rouen. She told us that 'I just walk around the city centre,' which we found incredibly underwhelming.

By the time I left Rouen we would regularly spend our free afternoons drinking coffee in the square and then strolling aimlessly around the beautiful city centre, looking up and pointing out details on the various buildings, the way the upper floors of the timber framed houses extended out above you due to only being taxed on the area of the ground floor, the bullet holes in the Palais de Justice from the Second World War, the secret courtyards you'd catch a glimpse of when a gate was left open, little oases of calm in the cramped backstreets around the Cathedral. It turns out that her advice to enjoy the place was good and that we were idiots for thinking that it was too simple.

Sometimes we think that doing something requires an activity. You have to be playing a game or competing or going to an event. I'm certainly an out and abouter, always keen to do something, but sometimes it's ok to do nothing and just walk around. The French certainly excel at taking things slower and enjoying their surroundings; if you go down to the quayside in Rouen on a Sunday you'll find swathes of people strolling aimlessly along the banks of the Seine.

I think this is partly a wider societal trend in that life has become a whole game of one upmanship where people on social media look as if they're permanently on a thrill ride but I think it's also partly just part of being a person. You become dissatisfied with your normal existence before beginning to enjoy it for what it is as you prepare to say goodbye to it. The French linger over moments in company and appreciate the small things, taking satisfaction in what seem like life's interim moments. I've learned a lot from their attitude and now, I make an effort to appreciate my surroundings and slow down.

16
———

YOU CAN'T WIN EM ALL

Not every game is a winner. Matches can be not much fun. Some of them can be downright tedious or annoying.

Part of being a professional is that you have to do a professional job. You have a plan, iterated and practised during the week and you must 'execute' it.

Some teams play in a higher minded manner; they throw the ball around and 'play what's in front' of them. This is really the end goal of a rugby team, able to adapt to any situation that arises on the field and find the appropriate solution. Rugby really is a sort of violent chess where there will be a seam to exploit or a space to attack; you just have to have the right implement and be able to spot the opportunity. The best teams have a range of solutions to counter any defensive tactic they might see, whether that's using forward power, incisive back play or a smart kicking game.

Most teams are just not that good, certainly in the French lower divisions. Even at the top level of rugby, most teams mitigate what they would like to do against a superior opponent to give themselves a fighting chance. The most obvious example is when people play the All Blacks.

The All Blacks are quite literally the best team on the planet. In any sport. Their win percentage is in the 90s and they have won the past two World Cups[1]. They have even refreshed the team very substantially, moving on a host of storied players without compromising their continued dominance.

In some ways, they beat teams before the game even starts due to the aura they carry. In other ways, teams rein in their tactics slightly, knowing that they are unable to go 'toe to toe' with them and need to box clever.

Rugby is often painted as a gladiatorial game and the language I've been using would back that up. Boxing analogies abound as teams 'trade blows' and it is an apt comparison as increasing numbers of players leave the field each game to have their heads examined for signs of concussion or sanity.

This is a long-winded way of saying that most teams recognise when they're facing a superior opponent and develop some sort of plan. They then go about trying to carry it out, even if it runs counter to what they would normally do. This can be seen as a fear based strategy or just as sensible. As ever, it depends on how you look at it. James Haskell reflecting on his time with the Otago Highlanders said that beyond what foot the other team's kicker used and a basic appreciation of their pattern of play, the team did no analysis whatsoever, preferring to concentrate on their own game. This certainly runs counter to my experience of playing professional rugby but in a way, the worse the team the greater the need for a clear plan.

We tended to be the favourite in most matches in France. The first season we had no expectations on us until later but from my second season onwards, we were largely regarded as a team to beat. Our perceived status as a team of Englishmen added fuel to the fire and we were seen as a big scalp. This meant that the other teams would usually play very negatively against us to mitigate against turnovers, from which we would often score, keeping the game tight.

Our early season results certainly encouraged this approach against us as we hammered some poor chaps in a preseason game before going to Domont, where we'd contrived to lose the previous year, on the opening day of the season and putting sixty or seventy points on them away from home. Once teams realised that we were going to be a tough afternoon out, they completely altered their own plans to avoid the humiliation that would have probably occurred in a shootout.

The reason that this was also sensible was that our pack of forwards tended to struggle in the maul. This meant that most teams would maul against us from anywhere on the field to try to win a penalty. If they did they would kick to touch and repeat the process for as long as possible. They wouldn't often put the ball wider than inside centre, meaning that as the outside centre, I would quite regularly make 2-5 tackles in a game. Scandalously low numbers.

Tours took this approach extremely seriously and we played out an incredibly dour 10-6 win away at their place. The game barely got out of jogging pace and was what I'd call an old fashioned maulathon.

We even tried to maul them as our approach was predicated on scoring tries. We turned down a slew of kickable penalties in favour of kicking to the corner for an attempt at a pushover. A maul from the 5m line should be a pretty reliable scoring strategy but we managed to fail with all our attempts and went into the sheds at half-time with the game very tightly balanced.

We were yelled at in the backs for our 'embarrassing' performance while the forwards were lionised for their efforts. This beggared belief as they had been staggeringly incompetent in their attempts at scoring and we had passed up a lot of points from the tee.

Kicking to the corner rather than taking points is regarded very suspiciously in France and it made our older forwards feel very uncomfortable, especially away from home. They felt, even if they didn't say at the time, that you're lucky to get a penalty away from home and should accrue points at the earliest opportunity. We were obeying the coach's edict to go for the tries but it made our own forwards feel uncomfortable and riled up the opposition.

We always wanted to play fast and offensively and were often met with anger by the other team. *'Ils ne respectent rien!'*[2] was a common cry coming from our adversaries when we tried to run out of our own half and it could spur them to greater levels of resistance. Sometimes you do need to use the death by a thousand cuts approach to get ahead; once they feel that they need to chase you then the cracks will appear for your offensive game to exploit.

We creaked to victory against Tours and looked forward to the prospect of a week off. In one of the finest demonstrations of insouciance that I've ever seen, Polo, replete in his finest casual clothes including some very flash leather boots, picked his skis up from underneath the bus and strolled off to catch a train to the Alps, eager to hit the slopes. No one batted an eyelid. This was France after all.

This second season wasn't often that much fun on the field due to our status as favourites and the fact that there wouldn't be many meaningful games before the end of the season. Even then, we were only required to reach the quarter finals to get promoted. This coupled with the fact that most other teams just tried to spoil games against us did make for some dour afternoons out and we got bollocked again for our performance during a laboured victory away at Plaisir.

It's frustrating when you know that your team has the capacity to play well and to enjoy the games but it's just not coming together. I was struggling to enjoy my rugby and I ended up suffering a minor tear of my medial knee ligament in the run-up to Christmas that although boring, allowed me to take my mind off playing for a bit.

The new signings were beginning to settle in and to realise that they couldn't turn up and expect anything to be like it was at a bigger club. Semi and Nick, initially quite shocked at the lack of professionalism were beginning to come around and Semi in particular, began to partake more and more of the local culture.

Semisi was a larger than life character. He is enormous, standing at about 6ft5 and weighing something like 130kg, although this could vary quite wildly. He was a formidable ball carrier and tackler, absolutely destroying some poor opponents in our preseason games, although he was not the most mobile.

Semi's shock at how lax some of our systems and sessions were, was recognisable to us. You knew what he was going through but just had to let him figure it out for himself without being too patronising, lightly warning him about getting too worked up about everything.

Luckily his placid manner led him to really lean in to the slower pace of French life and the next year, he could advise newer guys in the same way. Everyone has their initial freak out on arriving in France it seems.

Semi was used oddly by us. Upon turning up, he looked ready to carry and hammer people in the line but in France, there is a bit of a tradition of having the number 8 regularly patrol the backfield to return kicks. Ball playing 8s like Christian Labit and Shaun Sowerby would do it but so would bruisers like Isitolo Maka so it seems to be a positional thing rather than individually motivated.

I thought it odd to take Semi out of the front line where he could whack people, especially as he was not too mobile or proficient under a high ball and got caught out a couple of times. It also meant one of our back three players would be higher up in our defensive line, taking pace and theoretical kicking ability away from our backfield. It was an odd decision.

Semi was practically unstoppable near either line, able to pick and go and carry men with him as well as the ability to seriously disrupt the other team's maul. Given that our maul was largely appalling during my time in France, he was an enormous boon to us as we could now make the most of the 5m lineout opportunities that typically presented themselves from kicks to touch.

Sadly, someone cannonball tackled him in an early season game at the Mermoz and he limped off with a fractured leg. The guy had even had an earlier go and not received a red card but he got his marching orders this time and had to go and hide in the bus to avoid some rough justice from Semi afterwards. Without him our maul suffered somewhat, as did Semi's physical conditioning.

It wasn't that he didn't work hard. He did and he did care. All the while with his broken leg he would bang battle ropes up and down at one end of the field, working on his physical conditioning while he was unable to run. The problem seemed to be that he stuck to this regime, even as he got fitter and preferred it to running as he was far more proficient at it.

I don't know what it feels like to cart around that sort of bodyweight and I can completely understand that with some of the big guys, it's better that they do more biking or rowing to preserve their joints. The thing is that eventually, they have to do some running. He managed to largely avoid it and his game, as well as some of our collective capacity, suffered as a result.

He developed a real love of red wine, a readily available pleasure in France, and this probably didn't help his conditioning during his time off the field either. He was a great host and would often get his wife Amy to cook great dishes of food to supplement the numerous barbecues that we had at his house in the *résidence*. He had two young kids and so had claimed a proper house with a back garden and attached garage.

The garage proved to be a real boon as he put together a wooden bar and turned the place into the Bar Tranquil; a venue for the team to go and unwind and forget their troubles, or merely to avoid prying eyes after home games when Hilly would suggest that everyone leave and not drink beers all night. Full of sofas and rugs, the Bar Tranquil was a fine establishment where the beer flowed freely and we could chat away until the early hours.

Semi didn't charge for entry to the Bar Tranquil but he doubtless managed to keep a few extra beers that were left over from all the sessions held there. There were other entrepreneurial efforts made by the boys to monetise their club sponsored apartments. One of the best things about moving to France was the more comprehensive package you receive as a player; even during the first season when our salary was very low, the little Clio we were given to run around in and the flat between me and the Bean meant that we got by reasonably well. We had Ed Carne downstairs and Joe lived with Carlos the crazy Argentinian not too far away, giving us a little community near the St Sever commercial centre and the club gym.

Being given a flat eliminates your biggest expense and our car was also a boon in this respect. The cost of living there otherwise was so low, 80 euros a week between the two of us gave us plenty of good food to eat, that we were saving money each month. As our salaries increased over time and we moved to a bigger apartment, we began to live very comfortably.

Contracts in England tend not to include accommodation, although I did live in a club provided flat during my first season in Plymouth. I had a lovely view over the train tracks from my bedroom window and we were very cramped, all our meals being eaten in front of the TV as there was nowhere to put a kitchen table. The house was located within a short walk from the city centre and by the end of the year I'd dump my stuff and leave pretty much as soon as I was back from training. It was claustrophobic living with five of us in such a small space.

Our first French flat was not in a salubrious area, located on a corner that bordered a busy crossroads, down the street from the Clinique Mathilde, one of the bigger hospitals in the area. This coupled with the tabac downstairs meant a lot of traffic and we were lucky to have a small garage for our car, otherwise it would almost certainly have been sideswiped or messed about with by passers-by.

The garage was a source of amusement, having a somewhat temperamental lock. We'd normally just pull the door to or leave it open. One day, we came back and found a collection of cardboard and other effects in the back of the garage. We weren't certain but given that there were a load of bins in the street, we guessed that this was probably the temporary situation of a tramp.

Loath to cast someone out into the street when they were already sheltering in a garage, we left the stuff alone. The poor person was just trying to sleep somewhere slightly warmer and we never saw them once.

One day the landlord, a jovial old boy, came by to ask us how we were, me doing my best to keep up with his conversation while Luke nodded at him. He then asked us if we could lock the garage from now on as there was a *'clochard'* who had taken up residence. From then on, we always remembered the word for tramp. Small incidents or associations make words stick in your mind and I don't think I'll ever forget our *clochard*. I was a bit sad that he was casting this unknown back out into the elements and we didn't make much effort to lock the garage anyway. They were doing no harm.

At the end of our first season, I went to look around a three bed right over the street. It was the same price as our place but would house three of us, saving them cash. It was also brand new and much nicer, with balconies all the way around on the top floor and underground parking.

You could raise an eyebrow at the fact that they hadn't found something like it earlier but we were now growing used to this sort of general incompetence and apathy towards doing a better job.

We ended up not getting it thanks to Matmut's sponsorship of player accommodation taking us to *la résidence* and as we were happy with our new place, all was good.

Nick Seymour was not best pleased to discover that his place was totally unfurnished when he arrived from the UK with his girlfriend, nor did it have the second bedroom that he'd agreed. He kicked up a fuss and was moved into a two bed on the ground floor in the building opposite.

His girlfriend left after few months and moved back to the UK, leaving him on his own in the flat. For a while his mate Cam came to stay, rehabbing a knee ligament injury while jonesing for a contract for the following season. Cam is now back in New Zealand but his brother is currently playing for the All Blacks in the centres.

Cam was not unusual in taking a face to face approach at trying to get a contract. Rugby clubs all over the world will take a triallist. Even big clubs, in the Premiership or elsewhere, will have someone to train every now and again, unpaid, in the hope that they are a diamond in the rough.

When I played at Plymouth our coach Graham Dawe, a Bath legend who knew of my background and affection for my hometown team, asked me why I didn't just go there and trial. I asked if this was possible.

'No team has ever turned down a player,' he responded.

In some ways, you can see how this would be true. The risk is very small to the club; let a guy come and train and let him leave at the end of the day if he's not up to it. If he's brilliant then you can probably get him at a low price, given that he's prepared to do a trial with you.

In this respect, rugby players are similar to auditioning thespians and being available to trial or audition is an immediate indicator of a position of weakness. You're trying to get a gig. If you were really good then there would be no need, they would be pitching you. As Zlatan Ibrahimovic famously said on being offered a trial at Arsenal:

'Zlatan doesn't do auditions.'

Matt Hopper was another centre at Plymouth who had turned up midseason and become the club's player of the year by virtue of his outstanding performances. The year I played with him, he spent the year injured or on the periphery of the team, unable to get back to his previous level. He took an offer from Cornish Pirates and after a stellar season found himself fielding offers from Premiership sides.

'It's weird just sitting there and having them try and sell you' he said afterwards. 'Normally it's us saying 'Please give me a contract".

A triallist could be a well-known player who's on his way back from injury but this is more unlikely. At our lower level, it's someone coming on a wing and a prayer, hoping for an opportunity.

With its informal way of doing things, France is ripe for this sort of behaviour and triallists were a common occurrence at Stade Rouennais. Guys from the UK would come and maybe train. There would be someone's friend or relative, or just another French guy looking to prep his next move around the lower divisions.

We had a few memorable ones. One was Will Takai, involved in a legal dispute, without a club, vomiting on the training field during touch games. Another was Balthazar, a sprightly little chap with a predilection for inappropriately timed tricks and chips.

When you're a naive young guy, it's possible to think that being good at rugby means you can do these things. That what will get you a contract is the ability to pull off something outrageous. There was a memorable interview about becoming a professional player that described how, after signing a professional contract with Saracens, the guy began to constantly try ridiculous things in training thinking that this was both his prerogative as a professional but also what was expected of 'good players'.

Good players tend to be those that can do all the basics, make no mistakes and slot in well to a team with an established way of playing. Every now and again there is a freak athlete or real maverick for whom it may be worth breaking the structure slightly. For most of us, that sort of leeway is not available.

Even supposed 'maverick' players like Danny Cipriani know exactly what the team structure is and run around manipulating both the defence and their own teammates by calling a series of established plays, deviating from the script only when they see fit. Where Cipriani is actually a 'maverick' is in his propensity to challenge coaches and create the structure himself. To succeed with a player like him, you have to trust him, hand the keys to the attack over to him and live or die by the sword. To get the best out of the Bean you had to do something similar. Imposing a system Cipriani disagrees with on him is a recipe for disaster but he is a facilitator of a system. If you were a ball carrying back row forward who broke structure playing with Cipriani and pissed it up, he would certainly let you know about it.

Triallists do need to look good and if you can do something eye catching then great. The problem is that if you humiliate a regular then you might find some rough justice administered with no friends around to back you up.

Back to our prospective friend Balthazar. His attempts at tricks just came across as ill advised, a bit crazy and not a good fit. His was the wrong sort of standing out. He was a small guy and had some speed but he didn't necessarily seem in control of what he was doing and pitched himself all wrong.

Another guy turned up from Massy, the Parisian team who at that point were yo-yoing between Pro D2 and Fédérale 1. They had some foreigners and some recent success in terms of players moving to the top division. Sekou Macalou is now tearing up for Stade Français but back then he was just making the progression from the grimmer environs of Pro D2, standing out with his speed and athleticism for a man of his considerable size.

This guy, whose name escapes me, was a 10/12 utility sort of player, able to kick and be a playmaker. He was looking for a contract for the following year. Sometimes these trials come about when you're on a day off from your parent club and are conducted discreetly to avoid pissing anyone off. Your current team could regard your visit as an act of treachery even if they had no intention of keeping you beyond the end of your deal.

This poor guy came along on a light training day and threw a few balls around. He then finished up doing some kicking practice with the Bean. The Bean, not a man in need of an advantage when it comes to kicking, quickly trotted down to the other end of the field, guaranteeing himself a stiff following breeze. He then succeeded in pinging some monstrous spirals down towards the clubhouse end of the field, leaving this poor guy to run and fetch them before finding himself unable to send them back anywhere close to where they'd come from.

Basically he was being made to look like an idiot.

We pointed out after that the Bean could have offered him the wind at some point but he shrugged and said it wasn't his problem. He was right. It wasn't. The guy didn't get a deal with us in the end.

Another guy turned up from one of our rivals in the division and was a big, slightly overweight back row forward. He looked like someone who would serve you your kebab before menacingly telling you to get out of his restaurant and was a formidable ball carrier, if perhaps not one to last a full game.

This guy scuppered his chances during conversation in the day rather than anything he did on the training pitch, saying to our conditioner Olivier that he wasn't one to bother in the gym or in training but that he would 'die for the club' on the field. Bearing in mind that Olivier was not only the conditioner but essentially the man in charge of contract negotiations with the French players, this was not a smart move. Saying 'I'll be up to fucks but I'll make it up to you on the weekend' is again, something that the very very talented can get away with and usually, only after they've proven that they've got anything to offer. This guy seemed quite deluded as to how strong his bargaining position was. He didn't get a deal either.

Delusion about your place in the game is quite commonplace and you see it with both young guys, convinced that they're doing some-thing no one has seen before (they're not) and old guys who reckon they have a reputation that precedes them everywhere. Largely no one knows who you are and are quite content to carry on in their own little sphere, interrupted only by the odd triallist who comes and goes. Rugby is an itinerant game where nothing lasts forever. For some people, it can last just one day.

After Cam left, Nick hatched a little scheme. He would move into Joe's apartment where he lived alone and they would put his place on Airbnb, saving the money for a summer road trip in Joe's recently acquired camper van.

Now I doubt top level players are pulling stunts like this but you never know; small amounts of money can add up. Rugby players are known for being happy to up and go on a bit of a wing and a prayer, not too bothered about sleeping arrangements or exactly what's going on. Players sometimes come from the other side of the world for the chance of a professional career so they don't sweat the details early on. It's this sort of hope that enables clubs to treat them mean and keep them keen.

I spent a couple of weeks down at Toulon the year after I'd left Rouen, helping a friend settle in. We did the usual things and got hold of a phone, the internet and other basics for him to be able to get by. He lived in a nice house but it was older and less rockstar than I was expecting. His agreement was that as he was only there for 6 months, he would have half of the accommodation allowance that he would otherwise potentially be entitled to, up to the value of about €2000 per month.

That figure could be a salary at Stade Rouennais, never mind the accommodation allowance. There were other players at Toulon with double that allowance, renting outrageous villas on the French Riviera with pools, huge terraces and the rest. Apparently, some players even overspent their allowance.

We asked them why they hadn't bought houses and used their allowances to rent each other's properties, effectively getting the club to pay off their mortgages and they all looked a bit disappointed that they'd not considered this. You can understand when they say though that they come from the other side of the world and that life has progressed in two year increments. You don't know if you'll have to up sticks and go at the end of your contract when you sign it, making it hard to commit to buying a house and putting down roots.

It's hard to feel sorry for them though. They're putting away a lot of money if they have any sense at all.

Back in Rouen, Nick moved into Joe's place and was sleeping on the floor in his bedroom. Two grown men sharing a bedroom is quite odd but it was something we were used to from our away trips. This was definitely unusually intimate though, especially when the supplements they were taking began to give them nighttime 'eruptions'.

To be fair, Will Takai, who arrived much later, would often have friends and relatives to stay with him and his young family, who would sleep on the floor of his place. It's by no means unusual. Some of my friends came and crashed on our fold out bed or I'd make up the sofa for them.

I was not renting out club provided accommodation for profit though and if management heard that this was happening, you'd think that they would be quite annoyed. They never did though and the lads tootled off on their summer rampage at the end of the year, paid for by a load of Airbnb guests that they'd serviced throughout the second half of the year.

This was not the only wheeze that the lads tried in the hunt for extra cash or 'spondoodles' as Hilly called them. Some of the French guys reported a break-in to their apartment, claiming against their insurance for a variety of electronics. There was a suggestion that they had staged this themselves which seemed hard to believe until you saw the lack of real damage to the place.

Some of the lads tried to flip English cars, prized in France for their ability to avoid parking tickets, although this ran aground when the 'fixer' they were in touch with made off with their car for a few days before panicking and leaving it unlocked in the city centre. Someone tried home meal delivery, others took wine back to the UK to sell and two of the boys started selling pool floats; an ill-fated venture that eventually lead to them developing their post rugby career paths so not time wasted in the end, even if they never quite figured out how to get physical products through customs.

The flats in the residence were oddly distributed, some girls in their early 20s would have semi-regular drinks parties and you could see the bar that one of their friends had constructed inside. Downstairs from us was an odd flat, perpetually reeking of cigarette smoke with a regular stream of labourers going in and out. Sometimes the door would be open when you passed and you could see that the place was stuffed with sofa beds, bodies laying all over the place. Evidently some building company used the cheap flat to house their workers, resident in Rouen during the weeks only and napping between shifts. You realised that there was an undercurrent of cheap, doubtless extra-legal work going on around the place, something that I'd never seen quite so obviously.

Employment in sport is often extra-legal though, with underhand payments, players registered as students to avoid paying taxes, spouses earning disproportionately large salaries for low level employment or other jobs for brothers or dads. Top level guys are often compensated in other ways with property investments or limited companies set up for them to avoid disclosing greater figures on the salary cap. The guys downstairs in the construction game weren't too dissimilar to us; bussed in and thrown together for a job, away from families and friends, there to work and not leave much of a trace, earning off the books. I suspect the accounts at our team would not have passed muster either if scrutinised by someone so inclined.

We also had a Muslim family next door to us who we never spoke to, engaging only in the usual bonjour and door holding pleasantries. It took us a while to realise that the discrepancy in how our greetings were received was because the guy living there had two wives. Having seen them obscured by their traditional dress, we had originally assumed that they were the same person. It was another small bit of cultural acclimation for West Country white kids.

Living in *la résidence*, among families, oddballs, friendly pensioners, a host of rugby players, our kitman Patrice and his wife Danielle made for a convivial atmosphere, all the more convivial when Semi opened up the Bar Tranquil. We had a little community there, however incongruous we were together, settled in Normandy where we never quite knew what was going on.

17

THE BIG BIGS

THE MAIN REASON THAT MY SECOND SEASON AT ROUEN WAS memorable isn't so much because of the quality of the rugby we played but for the characters that we assembled. The first season had involved some oddballs but we were still settling in then and were less able to communicate with our teammates. During the second season, Joe and I really hit our stride with our language skills while Luke, who had ceased his own French education midway through the previous year, went back to class to dominate the new guys. This was mean of him but he likes to be the best. Rather than take lessons with JP, the new guys were sent to language school in Rive Gauche where they had to mix in with other displaced foreigners based around Rouen.

There were several big characters who joined this season, two of the more notable being Remi Cardon and Leo Montoya. Remi came highly recommended from Aurillac, a good team in Pro D2, while Leo arrived from Cognac having bounced around various teams in the division above us. In theory these were two good, ambitious signings by the club.

It turned out slightly differently as Remi, a man who expected to play and was slightly delusional regarding his own capacity as a player, was miffed when he realised that he was effectively the fourth back row forward. He would often moan if not selected, winding up some of the other players, although he was impossible to dislike, being a genuine and warm bloke who was just somewhat confused about how to go about things.

Remi is one of those guys who makes outlandish claims about what he's capable of, not finding it odd when evidence fails to back him up and just carrying on in his own way regardless. After strength testing day, always a bit of a dick swinging contest for some, he was doubtless a bit flustered by his inability to lift similar weights to those in his position. He was surprised to find that not only were the existing guys fairly strong from being in the gym all of the time the previous season, the new arrivals were very strong having arrived from Premiership teams or by just being enormous physical specimens.

His first approach was to tell some of the other French guys to train with him, guaranteeing that in a short space of time they would make some outrageous gains.

When these gains failed to materialise within the three weeks that he'd postulated, Remi decided that it was the products that he was not consuming that were the issue, not just that the other players were further down the strength and conditioning track than him. This sent him down the supplements rabbit hole in his quest to get what he called 'big big'.

For these he went to the biggest consumers of supplements in the squad, one of whom played in his position and was physically outperforming him. This is a smart move, go to the experts, but after taking what they recommended and still not making progress as quickly as he would like, rather than address his own shortcomings and accept that weightlifting was not the be all and end all, Remi decided that there must be *dopage* (performance enhancing drugs) afoot.

'Big big' then became 'big big dopage'. He never actually went and purchased any but he often referred to everyone else's drug use, miming using a needle to those he would accuse, all of it a product of his fevered mind.

This fevered mind was down to his personality but also due to his consumption of junk food, incessant rugby coverage and predilection for pornography. He would go to great lengths to tell you about his masturbating, pronounced 'big big wonk', and would regularly ask you if you 'do big big fuck last night'. He also had a rather lovely girlfriend who would visit every now and again, always begging the question of what was wrong with her to accept all of this as fine.

He had an irritating habit of always speaking to you in English, even though his English was poor. With other people this would seem like they were trying to improve their own language skills but Remi is one of those guys, like a Parisian waiter, who you get the impression considers themselves more able to speak to you than you are to speak to them, if that makes any sense. His English often didn't. He would persist with it anyway, making any conversation with him take about twice as long as it needed to be but what he took away from you in terms of time and the will to live in conversation, he gave back to the squad by virtue of being himself.

Guys like Remi are so key to a team environment, giving people something to laugh about. He is inherently a great guy and everyone became friendly with him. Sure, he was very open with his personal habits but he was also open with his hospitality, offering regularly to have people 'come in my home' and watch rugby. His idiosyncratic interpretation of the English language was one of the main drivers behind the creation of our own team vernacular, a twist on the common use of Franglais.

Franglais, as I'm sure you can deduce, is the bastardised cross of English and French, substituting a word in from your own tongue when you don't know the alternative. It became fun to substitute French words into our English conversations, dropping a *voiture* here and a *clochard* there. Early common ground was found in the char-

acter of Brian, the subject of English textbooks for French schoolchildren, and if you're in a pinch, saying 'Brian is in the kitchen'
should raise a smile from a French person.

Remi drastically accelerated the melange-ing of our linguistic tenden-
cies as 'big big' became his rallying cry and something that he would
insert into every conversation, French or English. As he became
more and more of a cult hero in the squad, more people began to use
it. It began with getting 'big big' then became about sourcing 'big big
pro-ty-eens' or protein supplements as the rest of us know them but
it came to mean almost anything.

Something, indeed anything, could be 'a big big'.

Remi's performances on the field were certainly not big bigs and he
didn't have much luck during his time with us. On the field he wasn't
up to much, often giving away penalties for hands in the ruck or not
letting go when directed to by a referee. He was actually pretty
decent over the ball but would often get penalised, blaming the
referee for their interpretation rather than listening to them in the
first place when they would tell him 'hands off', leaving him feeling
persecuted.

He was also a little dozy on the side of the scrum, which isn't great if
you're a back defending the blind side; I fell afoul of this several
times when, as one of the faster backs, I'd be sent to cover the possibility of an 8-9-15 move. If the flanker neglects their duty in this situation you're really left in the *merde* and so you'd try to encourage him
to pay attention.

He was just not much of a learner and did not like receiving advice
or criticism from anyone. It was a bit of a shame as he could have
played some good rugby for someone and one of the finest moments
in our third season was when he scored a decent try at an away game
and the whole squad descended upon him, banging him on the head
and chanting 'big big' over and over again.

Leo Montoya was another fascinating character. He turned up at the
club, a slim and skilful utility back with a suspicious number of clubs

on his CV. A well travelled rugby player is not unusual and there were a number of more nomadic players in the squad. Lower division rugby is like this as most clubs offer one year deals, or even 11 month deals to avoid compliance with EU employment law, so life can be a case of upping sticks every year. Luke had played for a variety of teams in his time, partly explaining his reluctance to buy any sort of furnishings for our flat; 'We'll be off in the summer so there's no point.'

Leo had all the gear, sporting training kit from a wide variety of French clubs including Stade Français and Racing Metro where he'd played for the *espoirs*. He also had a roll call of big name French players in his phone, exchanging Snapchats and messages with Mathieu Bastareaud and Eddie Ben Arous who he referred to as his 'Padawan'[1]. His claim of friends in high places was not a spurious one and he would often have a new pair of boots, hand-me-downs from luminaries of Parisian rugby.

Most of the time a player turns up at a new club he's aware that he needs to impress in some way. This is slightly less so in France where they are more focussed on an actual game and aren't too concerned with setting personal bests in the gym or during fitness tests but most people still make some semblance of effort. Leo arrived and quickly succumbed to an Achilles complaint that wasn't serious enough to prevent him from partaking in some sessions but was serious enough to prevent participation in others. He would happily stand on the side spinning the ball on his finger or juggling with his feet, showcasing an impressive dexterity.

We've all seen someone like this and usually they are quite annoying. When you're all there working hard and there's someone who isn't, it quickly breeds resentment. Leo however was nice and friendly, speaking reasonable English and making a great effort to get to know everyone. Antipathy towards him seemed mean and uncharitable. Maybe he did have a real problem?

I asked him one day how his Achilles was. He hadn't done much over the previous couple of days and so I thought I'd test the water.

'Don't worry,' he winked. 'I'll be ready'.

This seemed pretty clear. He felt that he had no need to bother and that he would be selected regardless when the actual season began. I found this annoying but amused myself with the thought that he might have more of a struggle to get into the team than he was assuming.

He scored in our first game, a rout of Domont away at their place, coming off the bench and finishing off a move nicely. Perhaps he had it all right and he was going to be a big player for us.

It was around this time when his social media output ramped up as the season had begun, his involvement now seemed more likely and he had some fresh content to put out there. The boys had been previously unaware that this was something he set a lot of store by but someone saw one of his posts and realised that he was called 'Leo Papsy'.

When pressed he was unforthcoming. It seemed that Papsy was a nickname he had given himself, a piece of personal branding.

His posts ranged from videos of little tricks he'd pull off at training to longer stream of consciousness rants containing life advice and tips for success. He used to caption these insights '#papsytalk'. He would occasionally run a #papsyquiz, usually with himself as the subject matter, giving out prizes to the winner. I won some #papsymerch from him, the prize of two t shirts are probably somewhere in my box of old kit.

Papsy was an unfortunate attempt at a personal brand, a man blinded by the direction of the culture and the examples of far more successful athletes like Paul Pogba with his #pogback campaigns. I've seen other examples in lower division rugby and they are nothing short of cringeworthy. One guy, playing at Rotherham, would sing short excerpts from various popular songs to his dog and brag about his trainers. This sort of behaviour stands at an antithetical remove from the values of rugby which has always historically prioritised the team over the individual.

The fact is though that Leo could have been joking. Some of his output was deliberately hilarious and he kept it up in the face of a fair bit of opprobrium from the boys. He had a giant teddy bear called Lebrun that he would take on road trips or video pleasuring himself, surreal clips that were quite humorous. He didn't seem to take himself too seriously, adding to the mystery around how important he saw this. Was it a performance art piece where the joke was on us? I don't think so but the fact that it could have been gives him some credit.

One player came over from the UK to visit and negotiate a contract for the following year. The backs were outside doing extra kicking in pairs with a line of players strung out across the Mermoz, blinking into the sunshine, ready to receive and kick back towards the clubhouse end. The prospective signing wandered out onto the field with Hilly to watch a bit of the practice.

Leo saw this and proceeded to take all his clothes off, sporting only his boots and socks, before carrying on kicking as if everything was normal, dick swinging in the spring sunshine. No one could believe it but Leo carried on with his usual degree of insouciance, catching kicks and sending them back to where they'd come from.

Small moments of idiocy like this keep morale high amongst the boys. Training can become repetitive and kicking practice is not usually one of the more thrilling exercises. Moments of levity like this can bring a bit of joy into the day and our visitor can't have been too put off by it as he signed the deal on offer.

Unfortunately, Leo's performance on the field was somewhat hilarious too as his lack of a training ethic combined with a predilection for sugary foodstuffs began to catch up with him. He put on a fair amount of weight due to what he called #ladiet, lost any speed that he may have had, while also trying to pull off #papsytricks during games that never went well. Once he ran across the field, threw an outrageous dummy switch before launching the ball directly into touch well over the winger's head, leading Hilly to yell at him and mutter to the substitutes that he would never play for the club again.

If you begin to make a joke out of yourself, in the digital realm or the real world, it's easy to play up to it and before long you have become an actual joke. The only way of avoiding this is by combining your high jinks with on field performance which Leo did not do. If you play well, you can by and large be as weird as you like. #Papsy became a permanent punchline which was a little sad as he undoubtedly had some talent. Once you've lost the confidence of the coach and become a laughing stock, it's very easy to not feature and become someone who is there but not really contributing. He would instead frustrate others in training by dropping the ball and messing up, even if he was still quite funny to have around.

Having said this Leo managed to hang around for another year beyond that one so he must have convinced Hilly that he would get it together. By the next year his stock had fallen so low that he was allowed to leave for a few weeks to play in the South American Championship for Chile in a vain attempt at World Cup qualification. Papsy and Rouen never quite hit it off.

Now any follower of professional sport can see how a player is no longer just a player. They work in an entertainment business and are expected by supporters to be entertaining, have an odd haircut, sell their mate's streetwear label on their Instagram or spout off on Twitter.

Even people who opt out of this, trying to just be a player, are seized upon by parody accounts like Boring James Milner, encouraging the real version to engage in a meta dialogue with his own public image. We live in the age of the personal brand.

Personal brands are now ubiquitous and many young people aspire to be an influencer. This can be in almost any field, made possible by the rise of social media and the desire of brands to sell in the most effective way possible. People with a direct line to 'consumers' appeal to brands, who are happy to pay for access through sponsored posts, product placement and branded content.

Social media is awash with athletes thanking various brands for gifted kit or other perks; these are supposed to be labelled as adverts or sponsored posts. Rugby is not as flush with free stuff as you might think with even decent Premiership players having to buy their own boots on occasion. A lot depends on your agent and what he can source you but even then, he may just buy whatever boots you're after and sneak the cost onto his invoice to make you feel special. Some of the guys in the squad would buy their boots and then put up a social media post insinuating that they were gifted to them, tagging the brand in question. I don't think Adidas would fall for this brazen attempt at sourcing further stash but it only needs to go right for you once.

Athletes have been brands for some time but now they have the means to communicate directly with their fans. The authenticity in these arrangements is up for debate but with some players, you can tell that the material is genuine and there is some sort of actual self-expression.

I'm now 32 and can remember the inception of the various social media networks. My flatmate and I opened Twitter accounts while sat on the sofa in Plymouth and in some ways, we were at the ideal point to 'build an audience' and brand ourselves.

The problem was that self-promotion in such a nakedly obvious manner was different then and viewed far more negatively. The word 'selfie' wasn't added to the Oxford English Dictionary until 2013. Even if self-promotion wasn't the goal, to express yourself quite so honestly and openly would not have been common and could even have landed you in hot water with an employer.

This is certainly true of rugby with its old school honour culture and suspicious coaches wary of anything that reveals an insight into what goes on at a club. The importance of the team is para-mount and star culture has never gone down too well in rugby, with most players happy to be self-effacing and eschew any sort of limelight.

The other thing with engaging with these platforms or expressing strong views is that it puts you there to be taken down. If you don't back up what you're saying, or if you're just not very good, then the perceived value of what you have to say and how good a bloke you are can decrease quite sharply.

In terms of my own personal branding I regret not having written more during my time as a player, even if it was to no one. We experienced the years of initial growth on these now ubiquitous platforms and could have built an audience as our careers went on, even at a lower level of competition. More elite players experience greater stresses from competing at a high level but their lives also become somewhat more monotonous as they play in the same places year after year, rarely have time off and need to maximise any recovery time available to carry on competing. On the fringes of the game lie some different stories to be told but our own reticence, combined with the insular, guarded nature of the sport meant we neglected the opportunity to tell them.

18

DOPAGE

REMI'S CRIES OF 'BIG BIG *DOPAGE*' WHEN CONFRONTED WITH stronger teammates was an ongoing joke within the squad but is potentially a big problem for the sport as a whole.

Dopage is a big topic in France where teams have always prioritised size more than we do in the UK. Considering that Premiership rugby players are already very big people, it's quite shocking to see the size of some of the guys playing in France. Rumours abound about *dopage* and I think that part of this fascination is due to its influence in other sports, like the Tour de France, coupled with the French food culture where the natural ingredient is prized over the modern, artificial alternative.

The French by all accounts were slow to adopt even creatine into their weight training regimes, suspicious of something synthetic, whereas in England we were encouraged to take supplements as schoolboys. These were nothing more than whey protein mixes but recently, several schoolboys in both the UK and South Africa have been caught taking harder steroids and banned. As rugby becomes more of a viable career path, doping seems like an attractive shortcut to some.

I've always found the idea of doping abhorrent, for both sporting and health reasons. To me, the risks of being caught are not as big as the risks that you take with your long-term health and I find the trade off a stupid one to make. Nevertheless, you hear whispers of some top-flight careers having been aided and abetted by taking performance enhancing drugs but this could be absolute rubbish. In all my time playing rugby I've never seen someone on my team using anything of that nature, even if one or two have displayed a suspicious amount of knowledge on the subject.

The guys I've seen able to lift the biggest weights and dominate the power tests are guys that have huge natural athletic capacity. Funnily enough, there will always be someone stronger than you; that's why teams like Clermont open academies in Fiji where the natural athletes are far more numerous than elsewhere.

One report did come out in France where anonymous testing revealed several drug takers in the Top 14 but that this was more of a recreational drug issue. A top-flight physio was quoted as saying that many of the players were dabbling with them after games on the weekend and that by the time they were tested in the week, the drugs had been metabolised by their bodies making them clean for the purposes of a test. Most drugs pass through your system very quickly and are gone within 48 hours or so. A hair test is harder to beat as metabolites can remain in your body hair for a couple of months. However, no one is tested like this in rugby and when the subject comes up, people speculate that it's the reason for Britney Spears shaving her head back in the 2000s.

Rugby players have gotten bigger. There have always been big men playing rugby but there was usually a spectrum of physiques. Now, muscle is packed onto everyone, regardless of height and the risks of playing are increasing commensurately. The thing with rugby players is that all together on television, they don't necessarily look that outsize. This is because they are all stood next to each other and you're comparing them to other rugby players. Some of our guys at Rouen were absolute monsters, dwarfing your average man in the street. As a rugby player, you become inured to this through familiarity while my visiting friends would be amazed at the size of my teammates.

Drugs are certainly a bigger problem for society than they are in rugby. Drug use amongst the norms or the rank and file are far more prevalent. In rugby, you are required to live a relatively clean life-style and are susceptible to being drug tested after matches as well as the odd random test during the week. I've seen more drug use amongst my school and university friends and other acquaintances than I've ever seen from professional rugby players for whom I'd say that alcohol use and abuse is far more prevalent.

Yet.

I had left the Bath Rugby Academy by the time their drug scandal hit the newspapers. There had been a culture of recreational drug taking that had blossomed within the squad and was probably more widespread than the guys who were sanctioned. One guy had acted as the whistleblower and then the club put themselves in jeopardy by acting in an extra-judicial manner, trying to drug test their players themselves. One guy admitted to taking recreational drugs and accepted the termination of his contract. The others fought their case against the club but all ended up leaving.

The RFU changed their drugs policy after Matt Stevens tested posi-tive on a match day. As rugby was signed up to the WADA and IOC Doping procedures, Stevens was given an immediate two-year ban from any involvement with rugby. He was not even permitted to walk in the door of a rugby club, or give talks to youngsters about the dangers of recreational drug use.

As a result of this positive test, the RFU changed their policy. Ironi-cally, as Stevens was experiencing personal lows and a self-confessed dependence on cocaine, he was in the form of his life as a ball carry-ing, offloading prop forward who could play both sides of the scrum. Professionally he was gold dust. He was also a magnetic personality and a big friendly guy. Exactly the sort of player and person the RFU doesn't want to catch taking drugs.

The change in the RFU drug policy was, I believe, designed to not catch these players. There are still very harsh and justifiable penalties for taking performance enhancing drugs but a positive test for a recreational drug now more closely reflects the NFL. A first out of competition positive will get you a slap on the wrist and reported to your team physio. A ban would only come into effect after a third positive test.

There is a lot of anecdotal evidence about rugby players taking recreational drugs. Midi Olympique reported that many Top 14 teams had a problem, with Montpellier namechecked. James O'Connor and Ali Williams were arrested in Paris trying to buy drugs and were sanctioned although not suspended as a result. Some of our players have been out and witnessed Top 14 players indulging while completely informal chats with social acquaintances have reported England internationals partying hard in Marbella. Eliota Fuimaono-Sapolu has tweeted about how 'your favourite All Blacks' are out taking drugs; Israel Dagg and Cory Jane were caught wandering around in a dishevelled state during the 2011 World Cup and it seems they had taken some prescription drugs. This is common practice amongst Australian Rugby League players and the Australian swim team had to investigate their athletes' use of the sleeping tablet Stilnox. Prescription drug abuse is rife in the culturally dominant USA and is often glamorised by hip hop artists, leading to the dissemination of the idea that it's cool.

A lot of this is obviously hearsay. Fuimaono-Sapolu is someone who sounds off about a lot of things. That doesn't mean that he's lying or wrong. He often has a point. It's just that a lot of what he says is unpalatable so people try to ignore him.

All I can report is what I've seen. I've never seen a teammate using any sort of performance enhancing drug. I believe that two guys were using some performance enhancers or dodgy supplements during my time in France but I never saw them do it, nor did they ever fail a drugs test.

Now, French drugs testing policy and process is a little different to the UK. They do not take drug use lightly and probably think they are doing a good job but their lack of discipline around it is hilarious.

The first time drugs testers came to training there had just been a week off in the calendar and the players had scattered to socialise. One of the trips was a multicultural tour through Belgium to Amsterdam which was particularly loose, involving a lot of drinking and recreational drug use. I have never taken recreational drugs, beyond taking one pull on a homemade bong near the skate ramps in a West Country park as a fifteen-year-old before coughing my lungs up; and had not been on this trip, giving me a smug sense of superiority and the ability to watch the unfolding events with some mirth.

The testers had turned up for our evening session unannounced and were waiting on the touchline, sending panic rippling through the revellers in our team huddle. Olivier went to deal with them and returned saying that they were off to the changing rooms to set up their gear and would call the required players in when they were ready.

Now this in itself is ridiculous. In the UK the testers arrive, name who they are going to test and then do not let them out of their sight until the test is complete. Any last minute measures such as affixing a rubber phallus filled with clean urine or claiming absence are then impossible. Not the case in France.

The session had recently got underway so the team were in full training kit complete with studded boots. It was then put to the group if there was anyone who would benefit from leaving the session immediately to avoid being tested, now was the time. As this particular rampage had involved about 8 players, the session would suddenly be suspiciously light on participants. They made their excuses, trotted up the bank on the other side of the training field, hopped the gate that led to the adjacent road and jogged back to *la résidence*, studs click-clacking on the tarmac.

When the testers specified who they were after and some of the players were unavailable they became suspicious. One came back out to the field to investigate, found a session that was suddenly somewhat less heavily populated than before and began to remonstrate with Olivier, saying that there were players missing. He was challenged to name or identify them but couldn't, having never taken a register or named players in advance of going inside. He resorted to saying, '*Où est le grand noir?*' or 'Where's the big black one?' This then became farcical as the existence of this particular big black player was debated with other players of various shades being proffered up instead. There were other players he could test if he so desired. He didn't like this and threatened to return and test the whole squad, convinced that our equally disorganised support staff were running a coordinated, US Postal style doping program when in fact some idiots had just been away taking illicit substances while believing that there wouldn't be any consequences.

They were right as they never faced any consequences, even if they did spend a couple of hours in a darkened apartment with the shutters down, victims of a rather good joke from Luke that the testers were coming to *la résidence* to look for them. The coaches let it slide and they were never caught.

I didn't experience this problem but I can understand the annoyance of some of the reserve players who saw their competition in the team avoid any consequences for taking drugs. If you're competing for a place and see that sort of behaviour go unpunished, it causes a deepseated sense of unfairness and harms team spirit in a way that might not be immediately apparent. It also raises questions of the coaches and the club environment that permits that sort of conduct.

The testers did come more frequently and would occasionally insist on performing both blood and urine tests which were onerous, taking a lot longer than usual. On one occasion, three of us were too well hydrated, not able to leave the Mermoz until about 11pm when we managed a sample that they deemed acceptable. When they came to take blood during a later visit, our big tough Northern second row Dave Markham passed out at the sight of a needle, much to the delight of everyone else waiting.

These tests are discomforting; having a stranger carefully watch your penis while you urinate causes varying degrees of anxiety amongst the squad. You pull your pants down and hold a plastic cup in one hand, over the toilet but turned on an angle to allow them to see exactly what's happening from their position stood a metre or so behind you. One member of the *anti-dopage* team eschewed this less awkward approach, instead resting his chin on my shoulder and peering down while I tried not to laugh.

The other discomforting aspect is that no matter how clean you are, you always feel a twinge of fear when taking a drugs test with a host of what if scenarios running through your head. Contaminated meat, dodgy supplements or mistaken medication are all plausible but unlikely reasons you could fail but it only needs to happen once for you to face some serious consequences if your cheating is deemed to be in pursuit of performance enhancement.

Personally, I am dead against performance enhancing drugs and am opposed to the use of recreational drugs, although I believe they should be treated differently with the latter seen as a personal problem that requires help, not suspension. Such a problem should result in help, counselling and education as well as probably a financial penalty to deter reoffending and show the other players that poor conduct is taken seriously.

In France, it was never taken seriously and one of my friends there never took a drugs test, slinging his bag over his shoulder and strolling home whenever any testers came to the ground. It was frankly amazing that he could get away with this and that it was never addressed by anyone at the club. He is a bit of an anomaly in that he can hammer the beers and smoke away but will be right up there in terms of his physical conditioning and performance on the field. The fact is, at most teams, if you have a problem but play well, they will leave you alone.

Recreational drugs were not a regular thing in the team; guys who used them would tuck into them on weeks off or during the off-season. A much bigger problem in sport is probably the abuse and misuse of prescription drugs. Many sports people regularly experience pain, ranging from minor to debilitating, and are provided with a stream of prescription drugs that are probably inappropriate or too freely available and in the interest of personal responsibility, too often demanded by the player.

Caffeine pills are not a prescription drug but are often taken pregame to sharpen up before kickoff. These are easily purchased and handed around but often lead to people developing a sort of dependency on them and can interfere with sleep. However, compared to anti-inflammatory and pain medications, they really are not a problem.

Anti-inflammatories are often given to players to help with recovery and injury. Again, these are readily available over the counter but players often have access to stronger ones through the club medical staff. The culture of supplementation encourages taking these sorts of measures as players naturally want to be back on the field as quickly as possible and will explore most avenues to get there. It's when these pills are no longer appropriate but are still used that they become a problem.

Anti-inflammatories have been associated with a range of other health conditions and can lead to digestive problems that will go on years after a player's career is finished. Pain medication is another easy one to become habitual, especially when stronger drugs are used.

Some of the guys at Rouen got prescribed tramadol to mitigate their pain as they were playing with injuries that potentially required some sort of surgical intervention. There were a couple of guys with neck and shoulder problems that caused them a lot of discomfort.

I think tramadol has about 1/10th the strength of heroin and is well known to be habit forming. They were given more than they would be given in the UK and were re-prescribed a couple of times before the doctor stopped. Oddly in France you don't necessarily hand over an actual prescription document, often it's a typed and signed letter which the pharmacist often just gives back to you. The fact that it's often emailed to you in what is basically a Word document means that you can go back to the pharmacy and get prescribed again, altering the details quite simply on your computer.

This was done multiple times without any repercussions; you'd think that it would be recorded that a certain doctor had repeatedly prescribed the same pills for months on end but I can only assume that their recordkeeping system was so antiquated that this never happened. The only time that one of the guys got close to getting rumbled was when he tried one of the more salubrious pharmacies in the city centre, scarpering before the pharmacist could get any details out of him about who he was. He should have perhaps considered that he could be in danger of forming a habit when he couldn't wait another day for his usual pharmacy to reopen.

The guys would do this relatively regularly and then use the tramadols on a quiet evening, taking a few and just chilling out in a medicated haze. To my mind this was not good and I brought it up with them. You could tell that they weren't too bothered by my intervention nor were they going to change their behaviour.

It's hard to address behaviour like this in an appropriate way. I was concerned for their wellbeing and didn't have a personal agenda for intervening beyond being their friend.

At an old club one of my teammates, just out of school and doing well in his first year as a professional, was not earning much money and was just a bit naughty. He would go to the supermarket, ring through tubs of Maximuscle protein powder as bananas at the self-checkout, thereby paying a couple of pounds for something that they were marking up to around fifty quid and sell them to the boys at £20 per tub. This gave him a bit of extra cash and saved the boys a lot of money in supplements.

This time I did have an agenda. Having known him since he was very young, I felt some responsibility towards him. He is also quite distinctive looking and would often wear his team kit, meaning that if he was caught then there could be repercussions for the whole squad. I felt like I had to have a word with him. He listened but you could see he was just being polite. He had no intention of curtailing his behaviour. After a couple of weeks and as I watched him carry on his thieving ways, I gave him money for a tub myself.

That made me complicit in his behaviour and wasn't fair. You can't hold someone to a better standard of behaviour and then enable them shortly after and I was aware of this at the time. It was just that I didn't feel like I could do much more. The fact that I didn't try perhaps doesn't reflect well on me but no one else did either.

A much more serious instance is when someone's private behaviour comes out as news in the squad. I've heard of instances where someone has apparently given their wife a slap or in France, one of the French guys threw his girlfriend onto a car bonnet. Their private behaviour is none of your business but in such an intimate environment, it's hard to not hear about things of this nature as the girlfriends speak as well.

Where is the line between who you are and what you do? If you are what you do then these people are abusers. And by being silent you are complicit in their behaviour. Equally what happens when someone makes a mistake? When does something wrong become someone's normal? Equally some cultures you encounter through rugby don't have the same norms and expectations as yours which can lead to some pretty fundamental disagreements over what is and is not acceptable.

This extends to the coaches or management in the team environment. If they preach respect, hard work and all the rest but let certain behaviours slide or hold people accountable to different standards of behaviour, people quickly call bullshit. You need to set parameters, enforce them and if you deviate from them, be prepared to admit fault. If not, the culture that you're trying to create can be compromised very swiftly.

19

BACK TO THE DIOCHON

THE SEASON WAS GOING WELL AND WE WERE SITTING PRETTY AT the top of our pool at Christmas after winning every game. We had faced the usual mixed quality of opposition with a few teams providing a stern test, a couple who could cause us problems if we had a bad day out and a couple who were barely worth playing against. Before Christmas we'd beaten our main rivals for the group, dispatching Niort in the first home of the season, narrowly beating St Jean D'Angély with their dangerous veterans and getting a great win away at Nantes after a disastrous first half performance.

These games had been costly though as Semi had his leg broken against Niort, compromising our tight play significantly and I picked up a small muscular problem, missing the Nantes game before tweaking my knee ligament against St Jean. Despite all our victories, we had not played to our potential and our defence was liable to ship points, even in games against teams who were not of our level.

Despite these concerns, we'd shown that we had a bit of character, managing to beat the better teams and turn around some poor performances, giving the team an upbeat mood going into the new year and the first big test away at Niort.

Playing loads of rugby can leave you inured to the basic joy of playing. When you're obliged to train every day, your enthusiasm for the actual game of rugby can dwindle somewhat. This is where being professional comes in; you have an obligation to turn up and do your work and with the way the games had been panning out during the first half of the season, it had felt more like work than play. This second season was testing my professionalism by leaving me alone for stretches of rehab with the motley crew of therapists that the club had links to around the city.

Injured athletes will try almost anything to get better. Time away from the field is boring, injuries are painful and you can find yourself feeling socially isolated and useless when you're unable to contribute.

Injuries can be welcome if they're not too severe and you're in need of a break. They can even be a sign that that is what's necessary. Sometimes though, they're the result of bad luck, poor technique or the confluence of the two and you'll do anything to get back up and running.

The first port of call are the club's own medical staff. You'll spend most of your time with the physio and could maybe have to see the doctor if you've got something more severe or need medication.

Where you go next can come down to many factors.

Perhaps your director of rugby credits someone with saving his career and therefore has great faith in them. Perhaps the president's girlfriend runs her own alternative medicine clinic. Or it might be that someone has a flashy new cryotherapy chamber and their brother plays in the B team. That's all a therapist needs to get an in with a sports team.

Joe had a bad elbow in our first year in Rouen and the president's girlfriend was an alternative therapist. As the business end of the season was approaching and Joe was a key player, the president insisted that he go for some treatment with her. Turning down this offer would have been a bad look so Joe dutifully went along.

I'd had acupuncture from her earlier in the year for an ankle problem and hadn't experienced any side effects. I quite like acupuncture as it goes and have some vague faith in its restorative powers. It didn't go so well for Joe as the needles caused him some extreme discomfort, exacerbating his injury and leaving him to tough it out for longer than he would have had to if it had merely been left alone.

Medicine as a discipline has always attracted an element of quackery, pseudoscience or snake oil and a pretty amateur rugby club owned by charismatic oddballs attracted a diverse cast of characters throughout the organisation. Alternative therapists were certainly part of the deal.

One guy called Michel was some sort of massage practitioner, although this does him a slight disservice as he also deserves credit for Luke's successful goal kicks, claiming that he was willing them between the posts with his mind. His version of massage involved some sort of relaxation therapy, leaving you laying on the ground before he would strip off his shirt, thankfully leaving on his high waisted white linen trousers, and rolling over you with a beaded mat in between your bodies, applying pressure to you with his bodyweight.

I once walked into the upper floor of the clubhouse to find this going on, Nick stranded underneath this guy looking at me desperately for help.

'Ben, don't leave me' he implored, his eyes conveying the depth of his discomfort as a middle-aged Frenchman continued to roll over him. Michel did not like me being there at all, evidently preferring that his treatment was conducted privately.

'No no - I don't want to disturb you old chap - see you in a bit!'

I scurried off, leaving him to swear after me down the stairs as I escaped, chuckling to myself that he'd got himself in this predicament.

Elite athletes have their bizarre therapies reported in the press from horse placenta treatment to more scientific blood spinning sort of stuff. They can even get in trouble as Samir Nasri did when putting his IV drip treatment on Instagram, violating football's policy regarding intravenous treatment and getting himself banned from the game.

We had a guy who'd come from one of the world's elite sporting environments. Alejandro had been a therapist at Barcelona FC where he specialised in movement but had moved to Rouen to facilitate his wife's career and to open his own shop. We used to pester him about Messi and Fabregas, telling him to call them and prove he knew them, all of which he accepted with good grace in the face of our idiocy.

I'd rolled my ankle and went to see him wearing loose clothing appropriate for a physio session, basically how I'd dress around the house or to lie on the sofa. He proceeded to 'warm up' my injury by making me do squats on a vibrating power plate for 45 seconds of every minute for 12 minutes. I was absolutely dripping with sweat, hadn't brought a change of clothes and eventually could have fallen asleep when he got around to poking and prodding my injury. He then made me cross my legs and stretch my hamstring while standing on the power plate, pushing me deeper into the stretch even as my hamstring was screaming at me to stop. I'd never experienced anything like it.

I went back to see him again so must have thought there was something in it. When your choices are between a mad Spaniard or a half-naked masseur, he was definitely the lesser of two evils.

When someone medical loses the confidence of the coach then a player can be sent all round the houses for second and third opinions. It can cause some social discomfort and offence if an opinion is disregarded and the player can be caught in the middle of a preexisting disagreement between a coach and a doctor or therapist. Our doctor in Rouen kept making outrageous pronouncements, telling one guy his small haematoma could be cancer, meaning that his later opinions, even if correct, were up for debate.

A coach can also just not like the diagnosis if it means the player won't be available for a while and will seek another opinion that puts the onus on the player to get back quicker than expected. This happened in my final season when PJ and I both got injured in the same game, leaving the team short on specialist centres. We were sent to clinics all over Rouen, looking for a diagnosis that would satisfy the coach and failing that, an injection to help our injuries recover quicker. The sports clinic agreed with our doctor in any case and the coach was left disappointed.

Sometimes you are loath to believe someone and seek your own explanations. I felt something 'go' when kicking and the next day felt as if my lower back was fused in one place. A back problem leaves you feeling especially diminished so I sought out our other doctor. He took a very quick look at me and told me I'd pulled my hip flexor and that my back had tilted to compensate. I thought he was talking rubbish and that he was too sure of himself. He'd only looked at me for about a minute.

It turned out that he was correct and that his explanation had been entirely reasonable. It was my opinion of his method that had coloured my interpretation of events and cost me a couple of days of appropriate rehab.

Another endeavour that cost me a day or so was when our physio, someone whose opinion I usually trusted, was convinced that Bolty and I each had one leg shorter than the other and sent us to Rouen's rock star chiropodist. We underwent a battery of measurements and physical tests, including running shirtless and barefoot on an adapted treadmill before I was informed by his assistant that I had no such problem. She went on to inquire as to where we spent our free evenings as well as giving us a list of bars where we might find her. The physio had wasted our time in one respect but it wasn't all bad.

Belief in your support staff is so crucial. Even if you think you're being reasonable you're probably not; if it's someone you like and trust, you'll go along with what they say. If you have doubts, you'll go looking for other solutions. The effects of placebos are well documented and I suspect that many of these alternative therapies are just that. However, if someone believes in them and recovers then are they so bad? It's hard to say.

Being injured is a fine way of rediscovering the basic joy of being out on the pitch. The small tear in my medial knee ligament had precipitated about 6 weeks away from the field and I was itching to get back and prove myself. Our collective form in the backs hadn't been fantastic and in the game where I'd sustained the injury, I hadn't been having a great time of it.

For our first game back after Christmas, I was on the bench away at Niort, our major rivals in the pool. My injury had struck fortuitously before the festive break so I hadn't missed many games. I was feeling fresh and powerful, not match fit but neither was anyone else after their festive fun.

We were struggling to get ahead of Niort, hampered by a difficult pitch and a hostile environment, the crowd baying at our errors. I came on early in the second half and felt like I'd made a difference, taking the ball to the line and putting our blindside winger away for a break in one of our set plays. I'd taken a late hit from their centre but I was never bothered by this too much, it meant he was out of commission defensively and leaving a hole on the inside to exploit.

At the end of the game we were behind, pressing for a score and couldn't break their line. I noticed they had no one in behind and as the game was down to the wire, all their energy was concentrated on rushing wildly out of the line to stop us from advancing.

The Bean noticed as well, our years of playing together as youngsters manifesting in that moment. Without a call or even an indication he ran sideways as if switching with our inside centre while I ran a wide 'pop' line outside my man. He chipped the ball over instead and it bounced over the line. I slid and touched it down, bringing the ball down with me and finishing it smoothly before jumping up and losing it with the rest of the team, sealing an important away victory and opening up space at the top of the pool.

For a second I was concerned that I'd touched the ball down too cleanly and that the referee, using his home team sensibilities would disallow the try but he blew and we'd won the game.

The perils of being a referee were in full evidence afterward as when he tried to enter the pavilion to claim his post-match feed, he was hounded out of there by the irate Niort president screaming blue murder at him. You could see why it would have been easier for him to not award the try but fair play to him, he did the right thing by making me the hero.

Hilly didn't see me as a hero, pointing out that I'd been 'sat down' by their centre after passing the ball earlier in the match. I felt this was churlish having just come up with the decisive try and pointed this out to him. 'Well that was Luke chipping it over wasn't it' he retorted. Yes and no. I don't think he'd have chipped it to another player nor would they have necessarily anticipated it or finished it if he had. It was poorly judged at a time when I'd been injured and was obviously just going about recovering some form and confidence.

Being a coach or a manager is a constant experiment in finding out the appropriate words for each player. Some react well to criticism, some enjoy being bantered with while some are sensitive and need a bit more of a soft touch. These profiles are also fluid, shifting depending on circumstance or how the season has gone for them up to that point. In this regard, considering that I'd just won us the game against a team who had been in the division above the previous season, would it have been so hard to just say 'well done'?

Anyway, this was a good win away from home and we followed it up with a miserable game in the wet against Plaisir the next week at home. Plaisir means 'pleasure' in French, one of the presidents even made an easy joke out of it, but we had not had much fun playing against them in either encounter. Nevertheless, we had another game at the Diochon to look forward to the next week when we would receive the obdurate Nantes, doubtless keen to avenge the comeback victory we managed at theirs earlier in the year.

Another stadium game had the squad excited again and this time, several of us foreigners had convinced our mates from home to come and stay for the weekend. Mine, despite being smart chaps, didn't realise that going to France required a passport meaning that they had to dash back to London to get them before reconvening with the one non-idiot at Dover to get the ferry over. This freedom to just pop over and visit is something that may, for all that anyone knows, become much more restricted. My thoughts on this are pretty unequivocal.

Showing people around where you live is something of a joy and you of course want to paint the place in the best possible light. My relatively barren apartment stood in contrast to the delights of the Rouen city centre and as it was my second season, I'd begun to find the more hidden and esoteric spots that had been unknown to me the previous year. The vast improvement in my French made dealing with the local cafe owners much simpler and I booked a lunch in a delightful cafe, secreted away in the back of a homewares and design store in the older part of town.

You could never get a walk in at this place, it was always reserved with limited seating, and it was very design heavy, filled with curios and British references which didn't tally with the patron's seemingly hostile attitude towards foreigners, his greeting not the friendliest over his round spectacles.

He warmed to us somewhat and the food was excellent. As it was a special occasion we ordered a little *pichet*[1] of *vin rouge* to accompany the lunch and I didn't see much harm in having a small glass. My mates didn't mention it at the time but were a little surprised that I'd done it. My views on preparation and alcohol had certainly relaxed 'When In France' and I felt loose and confident about the game, despite there being an almighty tempest forecast on a cold January night.

Our usual game was to throw the ball around and the inclement weather meant that we might have to adapt this slightly. Semisi was still out injured, leaving our maul a little underpowered and so I was of the belief that this would be a night for the Bean to dictate with his kicking. Barnesy was playing fullback, meaning that we had another top kicker and could cover the field. Kevin Milhorat, quicksilver and light on his feet, had yet to develop his own kicking game and had shown absolutely no sign of kicking the ball in his appearances at fullback. He was sensibly stationed on the wing for this one.

Nantes were not cowed by the occasion like PUC had been the previous season; they were bigger, tougher and more aggressive, playing a bit of a rush defence and trying to pressure our passers. The game was tight and we were playing into the wind, meaning we'd probably have to try and hold on to the ball rather than kick it away as Nantes would be able to return it with interest relatively easily.

This invited pressure on to us and Nantes managed to score a good try, carrying aggressively and making ground in the inside channels. This gave our forwards too much work to do around the corner and we were left short handed out wide, blitzing in as a last resort. They used the overlap and had the extra man strolling in on the outside.

This was a setback but we played some decent stuff, getting the crowd roaring with a big breakout from our 22. Kev ended up being tackled at about their 22 and I played 9 to move the ball quickly before making the effort to get out of the back of our pod of forwards on the next phase. Sometimes you have an intuitive sense of where the space is and as they were scrambling back after a break up one wing, they would be both stressed at having to cover the whole field and likely to 'honeypot' towards the ruck, a natural inclination to defend the area where the ball is.

These inclinations are why there is often a cross kick on in these situations. A back three player is probably involved in the tackle as a big vertical break has been made so the other will probably have the dual concerns of being in the defensive line to combat an overlap and the worry that they are vulnerable to a kick in behind. The cross kick can be the quickest way of getting the ball to the far side of the field where the space is but that night, into the wind and rain, it would have been both a tough kick and a tough catch.

We moved the ball quickly and I threw the long ball out to our attackers out wide. Unfortunately, our reserve number 8 was the receiver rather than someone more adept with their hands and the chance was lost. Nevertheless, we had put the pressure back on them and we scored some points from penalties, leaving the game pretty much level at halftime.

Now we had the wind and it was time for the Bean to go to work. He spanked over an enormous penalty from behind halfway and we decided to pepper them with mid-range high kicks, deliberately targeting the openside winger. The openside winger is often in a half and half position, ready to advance in the event of a pass but also ready to drop back and help his fullback with any kicks. It's a horrible place to have a kick put on you as you have no run-up to the ball, meaning that getting off the ground to compete is far more diffi-cult. You are also not far away from any chasers and thus are far more liable to get tackled man and ball than you are at fullback. It can be a lonely place to be.

Nantes were really struggling to deal with these kicks, their errors giving us easy yards down the field. Our game plan was always to keep the ball in hand but when Luke and I consulted each other during a break in play, we agreed to keep doing it. If the other team can't handle something, you might as well keep doing it until they find a solution. You need to have the discipline to keep poking at their weak points, even if it seems dull, too easy or not to the crowd's liking. This involves some maturity in your decision making as it's easy to do something else just for variety's sake. If their back three players had dealt with the first couple of kicks then we would prob-ably have shifted strategy but they hadn't. If you are one of those guys back there, you really need to deal with the first couple of testers that are sure to come your way. If you manage to give off an air of security early on, you can save yourself a whole game of potential humiliation.

In the end this is how we scored the game sealing try. Luke hoisted a kick towards their openside winger and it was at the perfect length for me to chase and compete. Their other backs didn't impede me, giving me a clear run to where the ball was coming down and the ability to keep my eye on it all the way.

I outjumped the winger, catching the ball into my chest and as I came down and was seized, got my arms free to feed Kev who had an unopposed run to the line. The stadium broke out in celebration and the air went out of Nantes. We knew we were home and dry.

20

OFF TO THE PLAYOFFS

WE WERE NOW UNBEATEN THROUGHOUT THE WHOLE SEASON AND had the potential to win every game. It wasn't something that was spoken about as the objective was solely to get promoted. We really did take it week to week and we knew that St Jean D'Angély away from home would be a tough test.

It proved to be too tough as we failed to get any league points on a miserable afternoon. St Jean scored an individual try through their veteran Fijian winger Bolakoro, who rounded our defence and chipped ahead. Kev really made a hash of it as it bounced around in the mud, allowing Bolakoro one of the simpler tries he'll ever score. Aside from this we never got our attack going and were outmuscled slightly up front.

St Jean didn't field Lesley Vainikolo this time; at our place he'd formed a nasty physical centre pairing with Bolakoro. Although he was certainly on his way out of the game, Vainikolo was still an unpleasant proposition, crashing the ball up and using his power to swat away would-be tacklers, even if his speed had really dissipated. Bolakoro on the other hand, still retained plenty of speed, running around me relatively easily one time when he was put away on the overlap. I had been confident of catching him but he eased away, his natural athleticism too much for me.

I had played some A League games with Vainikolo back in the sands of time and he'd always been friendly and gregarious, having nothing to prove to anyone nor feeling the need to play in any away fixtures that he thought too onerous. Fair enough. For those who don't remember him, Vainikolo was one of the most formidable wingers in rugby league, being about 6"2, stocky and fast. He formed a dangerous pairing with Shontayne Hape for Bradford Bulls and both ended up playing for England in rugby union, even if they were never as impressive as they had been in league.

The reason such a storied player was plying his trade in the lower divisions of French rugby was probably for two reasons. Fun and cash. Vainikolo had been signed by La Rochelle, probably on an excellent deal for an older guy, and the likelihood was that St Jean were taking advantage of France's incredibly generous benefits system, known as *le chômage*.

Chômage is spoken of in hushed tones by English rugby players, never sure if it's a myth or not. On finishing a work contract of at least a year, you go to the job centre and sign up for chômage. After the formality of an interview you are entitled to receive up to 80% of your previous salary from the government while you look for a new gig, up to the value of something like €8000 euros per month. I must confess that I'm not entirely conversant with how the UK benefits system functions but I certainly don't think that it's similar.

Now, the top salaries in our team at that point were something like €3000 per month, not including the house, car and other benefits that you could potentially negotiate. Given that the tax you would pay on this salary was negligible, you find that you can save a lot more money than the equivalent contract in the UK and you will easily out earn the average Championship player where salaries are largely paltry and the benefits not as extensive.

This system means that teams in the lower divisions of French rugby often have former top division players, sometimes even internationals, turning out for them on an amateur basis, usually with their chômage topped up with 'expenses'. Being able to draw a salary of up to about €10,000 per month with a house and a car for training twice a week and playing a game is not a bad deal at all. These guys can usually also use their spare time to set up a business or network their way into something that will occupy them when they hang their boots up for good. I believe Vainikolo was coaching on the side as well; a well-trodden path for retiring players to take.

Chômage seems on the face of things, slightly immoral and doesn't sound appealing. In the UK unemployment benefit or 'the dole' is not something that is regarded as sought after or desirable, even amongst struggling rugby players.

Chômage is not regarded in the same way in France. France is a republic and sees itself as a place that takes care of everyone, even if this isn't necessarily true. They don't have a monarchy and regard concentrated power with suspicion.

These are generalisations but my point is that in France, they see chômage as more of a right than a punishment. It's something that you can take for the month you're between work or almost to give yourself a year off. Two bargirls from town that we knew socially took chômage and went off to travel for a short while. It's not an uncommon thing to do.

The other reason that chômage sticks is that clubs propose this to you as a solution. Players are recruited using chômage. This seems incredibly immoral to people in the UK, and the idea that a high earning professional can carry on earning at that level seems unfair to me but it's part of how business is done over there. We had an (ageing) Fijian international second row sign for us in my final season, claiming the lion's share of his Pro D2 contract from chômage while receiving a top up from us and a free apartment to live in. This is not uncommon at all.

I was on holiday at the end of the season informing my non-rugby playing friends about chômage and my plans to get a hold of it. They asked if I was ok with that. I hadn't seriously considered that I wasn't before as it was regarded as more than acceptable in the rugby fraternity. I did claim it for some time but realised that I was limiting myself for what was a comparatively small sum of money as much of our contract had been paid as expenses, therefore making it unclaimable as chômage.

You also hear the odd story of chômage gone wrong. Our Fijian second row had a bung knee and went in for an operation. After that he was rushed back onto the field but his knee wouldn't let him contribute much. The club believed that he had pulled one over them when he'd signed in the first place and that his injury was preexisting. This is not necessarily unlikely but they hadn't done their due diligence in the first place in that case. Not really his problem.

His problem was that they had not filed his paperwork immediately so he was several months behind receiving his payments. He had been living on the smaller amount that the club were paying him. This made him understandably quite angry but it's odd to see how someone can get worked up about money that they don't really justify being paid.

In the end, the coaches told him not to report to training or to the gym with the other players so he spent the rest of the year training on his own, getting physio and drinking. I saw him in the carpark at the residence and asked what he'd been up to.

'Game of Thrones.'

He was on a bingeathon in his apartment, hammering his way through various box sets and sneaking off for the odd beer with the lads. I loved this guy and it amused me how he was winning, in a slightly miserable fashion, his battle with the club.

Chômage can get you in other ways too. Foreign players often claim when their contract comes to an end and this would be all above board if they continue to live in France. If you leave, then you play a dicey game with the Pole Emploi[1] as if they get wind that you're elsewhere, you can be on the hook for all the money you've received and some sort of other sanction. You have committed benefit fraud after all.

One of our teammates knew a guy who claimed and signed for a team in Italy. He was then giving an interview after a match that was televised and just as luck would have it, his case officer in France saw it. He really suffered as a result.

These sorts of shenanigans are part of navigating life as a lower tier rugby player where a few thousand either way is going to make a big difference to you. What is ridiculous is that it's the guys on the bigger salaries who can benefit the most from the system, able to remain in France when their careers end with no pressure on what to do next.

It's also a reason that there are many of these guys in the lower divisions, happy to not hang their boots up where a UK professional player probably would. There are also some interesting ways of using the system to your advantage on your way out of the sport. In my second season, we signed a big Czech prop from Pro D2 named Roman Suster. Roman seemed dour on first meeting him but he was actually delightful and extremely intelligent, speaking four or five languages and studying for a masters degree. He essentially used his year at Rouen as a deload year from professional rugby, spending all of his gym time on the spinning bike and doing neck rehab to lose bulk that he would not need in retirement and alleviate the pain that comes from being a professional scrummager.

This was to the dismay of the coaching team who saw a guy that they thought would be the cornerstone of a big pack lose something like 12kg over the course of the season. He was largely used in the B team as a sort of punishment but this didn't seem to concern him and he had employment lined up back in Prague when the season finished. The other players weren't bothered by his approach; so many players get misused or harshly done by, we'd seen that with Carlos the previous season, that someone who games the system to their own benefit like this is something of an inspiration, even if they aren't much use on the field as a result.

ON THE WAY UP, PASSING THOSE ON THE WAY DOWN

On the way up, passing those on the way down

Rugby is a competitive sport, usually conducted in a respectful manner. This respect largely carries over to the professional game where although the results are more important, the fact that your livelihoods are at stake every time you take the field engenders a certain camaraderie or brotherhood, even between rivals. There are exceptions; there wasn't much respect between us and Strasbourg for example and respect was something often referenced in our own team environment in France that came to mean less and less as time went on. How the respect inherent in the sport manifests during a mismatch is an interesting point of discussion.

If you're playing for a team and are being hammered, you can usually respect that the other team are just better and that possibly, you guys are having a bad day at the office. I'm fortunate that I've not been involved in too many games like this but even if you just get a solid beating, you can sometimes dissociate yourself from the result. I played an A League game for Newcastle Falcons away at Leicester Tigers while I was studying where our merry band of students and academy players took a bit of a beating from a group of current and future internationals. They're so much better that it doesn't really reflect on you personally.

In an amateur game, a real mismatch tends to result in preventative measures being taken. Sometimes the game is ended early to spare the losers' blushes. Sometimes the winning team will take players off and not replace them, trying to even up the match by competing with fewer players. We played a youth game for Bath where we were approaching 80 unanswered points so we took players off and swapped our positions around, the losing team taking it all in good grace and happy to play for longer. The referee will also often humour the losing team, awarding them soft penalties and turning a match into a bit of a conditioned game.

In the professional game this is not an option and can lead to some odd scenes on the field. The famous 8-2 beating of an under-strength Arsenal away at Manchester United springs to mind where the players on the field almost felt sorry for how far their perennial title contenders had fallen. We had an early finish to a Plymouth game where we were 25 points ahead in a freezing cold, snowy cup game in Scotland that no one was too interested in; the captains drew the ref's attention to the possibility of an early finish as the result can stand after 60 minutes of play. There weren't even any handshakes as everyone sprinted to the changing rooms.

We travelled a few hours to play the small team Vierzon in the last game of our regular season campaign. They had shipped 80 points to us at the Mermoz in torrential rain and we were going there in good pre-playoff condition to play in sunny, dry conditions.

It got unpleasant as we scored 70 points or so by half time. They were really, truly terrible.

One of their players asked us to ease off but we didn't know what to do. You can hardly walk around the field and they were comically bad. Nevertheless, as the tries continued to rack up, it wasn't possible to feel too good about it.

They scored from an interception that we all cheered. It was that much of a mismatch. We scored some great team tries, able to use the match as a training exercise and the most memorable piece of play was a ridiculous forward pass from Wilfrid, using a completely straight arm. It was dubbed *'le WilfGrenade'* and lived on in infamy for the next couple of years.

Vierzon had been hammered by everyone in the pool and we were the strongest team; the final score was 7-136 making this their worst ever defeat. They were to go down a division and possibly cease to exist due to a lack of funds and interest, their players crying after the final whistle. There's no way you couldn't feel for them when we shook hands on our way off the field.

That's one of the odd sides of professionalism and the nature of that division. We were a project, on our way up to bigger and better things, not only ending amateurism at our own club but wiping another amateur team out of existence, trampling them on our way up the leagues. Professionalism has no mercy and we were told at half time to put our feet on their throat, be ruthless and do our job. Harsh words for a sometimes harsh game, respectful or not.

We were then straight into the playoffs with an away tie at Gennevilliers, foes from our group the previous year. As is the way with these things, the sunny weather of the previous few weeks evaporated and we had to play in more tropical conditions. Gennevilliers were not as good as us but did possess a decent maul, the area where we were weak.

Fortunately, Semisi was now back and ready to anchor our pack. He was the best at mauling and could finish a try when we were close to the opposition line, his experience allied with his sheer size making him almost impossible to stop. Unfortunately for us, some French administration prevented him even getting on to the pitch.

During the warm up, officials are receiving finalised team sheets with the details of all the players on it. This is to check that everyone is a registered rugby player, anything that occurs is covered by insurance and that neither team is exercising a competitive advantage by fielding extra foreigners or ineligible players. Usually this is a formality.

This time it was discovered that something about Semi's licence made him ineligible to play. Not only was he ineligible for that game but had been ineligible all season. His long-term injury had prevented his licence from being scrutinised many times but he had played two games at the start of the year where the inconsistencies had gone unnoticed. Our officials tried to make out that this wasn't a big deal but Gennevilliers were adamant; this guy can't play.

Think how ridiculous this is from our perspective. We were turning the club into a fully professional team; that year most of the guys were full-time rugby players; and this was our first playoff match away from home. We were playing to advance the club and accelerate its future. This was up to that point, the most important match in the club's history and our staff had failed to properly register one of our most important and expensive players. Staggering incompetence.

France has an odd relationship with admin. In some respects, the French attitude of *laissez faire* is completely accurate. Getting someone to come and do something; fix the plumbing in your apartment or service your car; requires constant cajoling, buttering up or sometimes a bit of posturing. If you know someone who knows someone else then so much the better and this was largely why our forwards coach Bouly remained in his post; his enormous network of contacts around the city meant that he could expedite things that you would struggle to get done yourself. His willingness to do this for you varied day by day as he inevitably became the conduit through which anything had to go to get done. He both enjoyed and resented this.

In other respects, they are incredibly strict and need their paperwork doing exactly as specified, even when it seems convoluted and unnecessary. On arrival, we had to sign up to the national health insurance and get our *carte vitale*, a miraculous piece of plastic that enabled you to receive a lot of free and discounted healthcare, including dental work, subsidised designer glasses and physiotherapy. Despite going to the office with our friend Bouly and filling out all the possible paperwork under the supervision of someone who knew what needed doing, we were told to ignore the torrent of paperwork that was to flow through our door. The system would roll on regardless and we had to ignore it, allowing things to churn through to their conclusion. We received our cards a few months afterwards.

With this attitude towards documentation prevalent in rugby as well, we were never going to get Semi registered for kickoff in thirty minutes' time. Gennevilliers were delighted and saw even more opportunity to go at our maul while you could see our forwards visibly shrink, knowing that they were in for a tougher day at the office without their physical and spiritual bulwark. Semi looked a bit embarrassed despite all the fuss being absolutely not his fault and he took up a place among the substitutes to watch events unfold.

A pretty scrappy and uneventful game ended 21-21. Their maul overpowered us somewhat but they did nothing apart from keep the ball tight, afraid of engaging us in a more open battle. We wanted to use the ball but were not well positioned to give it away too often as Gennevilliers would cling on to it, running down the clock as much as possible and hoping to nick the game. In the end, a draw was a good result for us as we would play at home the next week, the game moved to the Diochon.

The Sunday afternoon was bright, sunny and the ground firm. Semi was now actually allowed to play for the club and we had a full-strength team to choose from. Gennevilliers, fierce in front of their own supporters, were meek in front of ours and we put on a bit of a display for our crowd, winning 44-7 and scoring some good team tries.

When you play well individually you leave the field personally satisfied but there's a true delight in playing well as a team, finding synchronicity with your fellow players, being able to predict outcomes and following up on the actions of others to take things to the best possible conclusion. We'd shown some flashes of playing how we wanted to play against Vierzon but they were so poor it wouldn't be fair to hold those instances up as successes for us.

Teams probably don't practise support play enough; it's one of the most important parts of the game. I've spent interminable hours on ruck technique, which is important as speed of ball is often decisive, but decision making from the ball carrier and support runners can turn unpromising circumstances into a try or make the most of a half opportunity. When you change your run to accommodate a team-mate or predict a break before it happens, appearing on a shoulder to receive a critical pass, you feel as if you've been let in on a secret.

Pieces of team play, unscripted yet patterned, are known as automatisms, a term used frequently by Arsene Wenger when describing his football ideal. Players moving and interchanging rapidly, automatically, without conscious thought, using the programming given to them by the coach but unconsciously, allowing the flow of the game to dictate their actions and finding that their responses and decisions arise naturally, without opposition and with ease.

The prime example for me would be the famous Invincibles side who went a season unbeaten. I'm a fan so I hope that this record will never be approached. The great Manchester United sides also played with this combination of ferocity and ease, players streaming up the field like birds in formation. I saw an exhibit at the Millennium Dome that drew a line behind each running United player, showing how each reacted to the movements of his teammates, drawing a tapestry on the grass. You could see how following and marking each attacker would be nigh on impossible; the only way would be to constantly swap defensive assignments on the fly, something probably beyond most teams.

In rugby, my old favourites Stade Toulousain deliberately practised to achieve the degree of unconscious competence. Offloading the ball requires the combination of physical control, technical ability, anticipation and trust that automatisms engender and that Toulouse team would always look to do it, not compromising for anything. An automatism is a movement that occurs automatically in recognition of a cue or stimulus; when Sonny Bill Williams takes the ball to the line, people flood through in support, anticipating an offload coming out at an ungodly angle or unexpected time from his enormous hands.

These movements can be practised, recognising when a teammate is going to be likely to have the possibility of an offload and going for it, but they also need to develop over time as you learn the quirks, foibles and preferences of your fellow players. Playing time together creates chemistry and leads to the development of unconscious solutions to the problems defences pose.

Sometimes the automatism isn't even a response to play near the ball. If a break is made up one wing, the likelihood is that there will be space on the far wing and a smart winger or speedy forward not involved in the break should make a beeline for the touchline. If a team recovers their own box kick, it's common for there to be space immediately in behind and a scrum half could immediately do the same thing to exploit space. The recognition of a situation developing leads to knowing what to do, without thinking about it.

This game was probably the best we played all season. Playing our natural game meant we kept attacking them and as we began to open up a margin on the scoreboard, the Gennevilliers had to gamble more to prevent the game from getting away from them. This created further opportunities for us as they were more likely to make mistakes and leave holes to be exploited. Desperation set in and their fullback tried to chip out of his 22, doubtless feeling the need to force the game. I saw this coming and had ducked out of the chasing line, caught the ball on the full, evaded him and a couple of his mates before Joe, a bit of a 'Jonny on the spot' himself, appeared on my inside shoulder to take the last pass and surge in under the posts. It's one of the most indelible images of our time in France as a group as everyone is running towards the posts, some are celebrating, the Diochon crowd in the background, me lying on the floor having been tackled by the last defender, everyone in synchronicity.

I had a good game, scoring a try and setting up another couple. Despite the large margin of victory and the fact that we were through to the promotion deciding round, Hilly wasn't too complimentary again, leaving a sour taste in my mouth as he seemed unwilling to appreciate a job well done. No one was getting carried away but he was being unnecessarily sour in my opinion.

Due to the vagaries of the playoff system we were to face Niort in a two leg promotion decider. Niort had come down from Fédérale 1 the previous year while we were looking to elevate the club to new heights. The two legs are played as if they are separate matches, meaning that any bonus points, offensive or defensive, count in the reckoning. If you went away from home but came away with a losing bonus then you had an advantage going into the next game.

Not only did we win the first game away at Niort but we denied them a losing bonus, leaving the return leg at the Mermoz as an opportunity to both seal and celebrate the season's objectives being achieved.

21

BEING A MAN

WE'VE PROBABLY ALL CALLED SOMEONE GAY. NOT BECAUSE THEY are but to insult them. A proxy for pathetic or rubbish or under-whelming.

Calling someone gay is now something to be ashamed of. Great strides have been made in awareness terms. Most places apart from professional sport.

Being able to be vulnerable is a sign of strength. But to come out to your teammates or even to arrive, fully formed as a gay person is to put yourself right out there. Not everyone is prepared for this and not everyone wants to expose themselves in such a manner.

I will go further and say that almost no one does this. Across the major sports there are almost no 'out' sportsmen. Rugby has had some high-profile retirees come out and prominent referee Nigel Owens is gay but I never had an openly gay teammate until I went to France.

It's hard to talk about this in a respectful manner and I wouldn't want to openly talk about exactly who he is, even if I really believe that he wouldn't mind.

At our first ever training session near the football stadium, where I was underwhelmed by the quality of what was happening, there was an impressive display of athleticism and commitment from one of our bigger forwards who ran down a winger on the diagonal and tackled him into touch.

This guy was very friendly and welcoming, even if we couldn't really communicate at that time due to our lack of a common language. He was committed when he was playing rugby but was slightly less committed off the field, with a propensity to arrive late for sessions on his bike, smoking before joining the session. He's the sort of guy who would cycle in wearing his training kit with smart black shoes, having come straight from a shift as a waiter somewhere in town.

I can't remember exactly when I found out that he was gay but I think I asked him if he had a girlfriend; most of the other French guys did. He told me that no he didn't and that he was gay. I wondered if he was having me on, it is the sort of extended joke that could be played on a newcomer, but he was looking at me sincerely so I took his word for it. He asked me if it would be a problem and I assured him that it absolutely would not. I was pleased that he'd felt able to tell me this so directly but that's more of a reflection on his character than mine.

He broached the subject with me later in the year and I took the opportunity to ask him some questions, telling him that I'd never had an openly gay teammate before and asking if he had a problem with some of the language that was used in the group.

French insults can take a similar tack to English ones as the equivalent of 'faggot' is used quite readily. He said that it wasn't a problem for him, that he knew gay slurs are thrown around somewhat indiscriminately in sporting environments and that he didn't let it bother him. He said that they were generic insults for each other and not words used to denigrate him. You can have your own opinion on this but this is what he said.

David Pocock actually called out an opposition player for using homophobic language on the field and was lauded for it. There is a perception of Pocock that he is a bit holier than thou and painful with his opinions but I applaud him sticking to his principles. Being authentic is difficult for people and he certainly puts himself in situations that don't necessarily benefit his rugby when it could be easier to 'shut up and dribble'[1] or jackal in his case. If he wasn't good on the field, his opinions and his injury record combined would probably make him easy to ignore from an employment perspective but he is one of the best. Being able to hold an opinion publicly in sport is the luxury of the powerful.

I've certainly used gay language as insults before despite retaining an objection to the word faggot. There's no point in pretending I haven't used it and it's relatively common parlance in some rugby clubs that I've experienced but I don't like the word itself. I made more of an effort to avoid using language of that sort after I spoke to this guy for sure.

We were new to the squad so his sexuality was only news to us. The French guys used to joke about it a bit but he was popular socially and had played rugby with some of the others since their teenage years.

It's a great way to consider what being a man is in a rugby context. Coaches often say to 'man up' or 'be a man'. Is being a man smashing the opposition? Is it being a good teammate? Is it playing with an injury? This guy did all those things. He was no less of a man than the rest of us; just a bit less committed to being an athlete and that was nothing to do with his sexuality.

What is being a man? I like this anecdote from Michael Kimmel, an author and founder of the Center for the Study of Men and Masculinities:

> Once, when he asked cadets at West Point what it means to be a "good man," their responses included things like honor, duty, sacrifice, responsibility, standing up for the little guy—i.e., being a good person. When he asked them to "man the f up"—to be a real man—their responses shifted: being strong and stoic, never

showing your feelings, playing through pain, getting rich and getting laid.[2]

Being a good man equates to being a good person where 'manning the fuck up' is about putting on a front. The two are different and to do one is more difficult than the other. The team environment is a tough place to admit vulnerability, although there is a burgeoning awareness of the importance of mental health in professional sport.

Rugby at its core stands for the principles of being a good man; these are all parts of being a good teammate. The characteristics of being a 'real man' are also rewarded by rugby culture. The two aren't antithetical necessarily but the pursuit of getting rich and getting laid, selfish impulses, can lead to the contravention of the ethics of the team environment.

Showing your feelings is something that can make your teammates uncomfortable so being a good teammate can perpetuate a sort of omertà; it's not on to admit that something is affecting you or that you have a problem.

In my last season, I was probably slightly depressed and what I let on to the others that I wasn't having a good time, they weren't exactly forthcoming with help. I didn't express myself well enough and they felt uncomfortable with what I did share. They just thought I was seizing the day by drinking more regularly, which to some extent I was.

Reflecting on the squad I'm quite proud of the general reaction to having a gay teammate. A team by and large is a very accepting environment and we were a diverse bunch in many ways. Why would this be different?

We would shower together as normal which reminded me of a guy from school talking about how he wouldn't be able to change near a gay guy; I thought how ridiculous and arrogant this is. Is this guy going to jump you in the shower or come on to you? Of course he isn't. He doesn't find you appealing in all likelihood. The changing room is a bit of a sacred space for a team and that this didn't have any bearing on that was a good thing in my book.

Difference is to be celebrated or even better, just accepted. If there was truly no issue around being different then it wouldn't be celebrated. It just would be. On the other hand, perhaps it's fun to celebrate what makes us distinct from each other. It's complex.

Our mate was simply just one of the team. The other thing with difference in a rugby environment is that it is there to be laughed at. Being privately educated, I've developed strategies to deal with my poshness and how I can come across to other people. If I couldn't laugh at myself while doing this then I would have been hounded out of rugby changing rooms a long time ago. Being laughed at is usually a sign of acceptance; if someone likes you then they joke with you. The better they know you the harsher the jokes can be. If they didn't like you or found you suspicious, they wouldn't joke with you at all.

It doesn't necessarily need saying but rugby clubs are not very politically correct places and the humour can be borderline or pretty dark. The way you're spoken to, even by your boss in the form of the coach, can be on the edge of abusive. At an old club, a coach told one player 'I would call you a cunt, but at least a cunt is useful for something.' It got a laugh but if you hear this sort of thing every day, it can get you down over time. I don't know too many other lines of work where being spoken to like this regularly is deemed acceptable.

Over time, this guy became more comfortable around the team and could joke with us about his sexuality. If it wasn't accepted then it wouldn't have elicited laughter and he would never have brought it up. It became another opportunity to laugh, especially on away trips.

Dating apps have elicited a big change for professional sports teams when they go on away trips. With the rise of Tinder and its alternatives, players can prepare for their arrival in a new city by changing their location and swiping away, organising their rest and relaxation before arrival. In doing so they avoid the need to go to local bars or clubs to find partners for the evening, ensuring that not only are they satisfied on that front but that they can get a normal night's sleep and not drink any alcohol as their predecessors might have done. For these reasons, conditioners love Tinder.

The gay hookup app Grindr has the same functionality but is known for being a very reliable way to set up assignations. Away trips would see this guy sleep most of the way down and after dumping his stuff in his hotel room, he'd either call a taxi or get picked up by a friend and deposited back later. He was quite prolific in this regard. For our end of season awards do one year, our 'players player' award was split into home and away and he won the away version quite decisively.

The one bit of ugliness that occurred because of his sexuality wasn't precipitated by his preferences but they became a stick to beat him with. Before our promotion decider against Niort at the end of our second season, the starting team was revealed to us before team run.

Due to the idiosyncratic league structure, this game was the last home game of the season and any team going through would be promoted. The remaining teams would then play off to reach a final and the possibility of being the overall champion of the division but these later games would be played at neutral venues.

One of our older players was retiring from Rouen at the end of the year and would play lower level club rugby instead, lessening his commitment to the game and giving him more time to spend with his family and friends. He was a combustible sort in the tradition of Gallic forwards and was known for not being able to control his temper.

This game would be his last in front of our home supporters and he fancied the idea of being subbed off to a round of applause. When the team was named and he saw his name on the bench, his mood darkened immediately.

'Anyone got a problem with this?' said Hilly out of habit rather than expectation.

'Yes'.

The whole room went silent.

'I can't understand why you've done this to me. It's my last game here at the Mermoz. I don't have a problem with you (his replacement) at all. It's about respect for me and I just can't understand this.'

'Let's talk about this afterwards.'

'No. We're going to talk about this now.'

This was good from him. If you're getting dropped then a coach will usually grab you beforehand somewhere quiet and tell you on your own. They might ring you up before training and tell you. They usually do it in a private way that is more sensitive or more weaselly depending on how you feel about it. They rarely get confronted in front of the group like this and you could see Hilly panic a little, knowing how angry this player could get.

The squad sat there while there was a brief back and forth but training was called quite quickly. It was just too awkward.

We trained and this guy went out to try and smash his replacement, our gay friend. This is not abnormal as a behaviour but is quite unacceptable in a non-contact team run and there was a minor scuffle as a result. At the end of the session which passed without incident, we dispersed to do extras, have a stretch or just sit around and have a chat.

Our starter walked to the clubhouse to get his shoes and was followed by the man he'd replaced. He held the door open for him and received a headbutt to the face for his trouble. A real fight broke out and people piled in, the instigator was pulled away, yelling homophobic slurs at the object of his rage.

I really think that being gay had nothing to do with his anger but that it was the first thing he could seize on to attack. It was absolutely unacceptable.

We called a meeting the day after to discuss whether this guy should play. He had been a long-term servant of the club and the forwards coach defended him, saying that he was from an older generation and had some ancient attitudes towards selection and homosexuality, as well as a propensity for violence that we all knew about. He said that as a long-term servant of the club, he deserved a last appearance.

Playing in the forwards involves a bit of a job share, the starter often being replaced on about 50 minutes, giving a replacement 30 minutes to close out the game. It was a slightly insensitive selection decision as it denied this guy his big exit but equally, it was the biggest game of the season and if you really believed that this was the best choice then you had the right to make it. Disagreeing with the selection by no means excuses his behaviour, I merely outline why it was maybe avoidably contentious.

Our friend spoke out, saying that he had no problem with this other guy and that he could play if needs be. I do think he meant this but I could foresee some awkwardness, as could everyone else.

I spoke up saying that if one person thinks he shouldn't play, or that they couldn't concentrate if he turned up, then he shouldn't play. This was slightly weaselly as I wasn't making any decision but I wanted to make it clear that if there was anyone who felt this way, they should speak up.

Immediately Joe said that he thought this guy shouldn't play. We all decided that if one person thought this, there were probably others that did also and then agreed he wouldn't play. The guy never came to the rugby club again.

This is slightly sad as he'd given years to the team but in my opinion it was completely justified. A training ground fight during practice isn't uncommon but one that continues after the session is and is far more serious. It is a real assault and, if you insist on throwing homophobic slurs around while you're doing it, it becomes a hate crime.

We knew this behaviour was outside the norm while we were there but it was only upon leaving and thinking about my time in France that I began to realise how serious some of these instances were and how inured to them you become as a rugby player. My friends asked me about any fights between players, having witnessed a night out which boiled over on their group visit, and were horrified when I told them this. It's just that in your odd little world, things happen and you move on from them quite quickly.

22

PROMOTION ACHIEVED

ALTHOUGH NIORT PRESSURED US AT HOME, INVOKING MEMORIES of the tighter than expected game against Suresnes the season prior, we ended up winning 40-19, the supporters and staff all running onto the field to celebrate with us at the final whistle. On a beautiful day in Normandy, we felt like we'd achieved something special and enjoyed the evening drinking beers on the grass until the early hours.

The next possibility was that we could go on to claim the Fédérale 2 title by winning the knock out matches. We were technically now into the quarter finals where the ties were now a straight knock out match at a neutral venue rather than the two legs we'd played previously. One of the big differences in schedules between France and the UK is that, with the Christmas break and a healthy amount of rest weekend during the season, the knockout games come thick and fast with a potential 7 games to be played in a row for any team that reaches the final. This also means that the season can carry on well into June, a time when a lot of English teams will be coming back to preseason training.

Considering we'd achieved what was set out for us at the beginning of the year, there wasn't much appetite for the rest of the knockout stages, even if our next opponent was to be Strasbourg. We were happy to knock them off but most people didn't like the idea of their holiday being compromised, particularly as Hilly would doubtless have everyone back in to training for the next year as quickly as possible to prepare for the better level of competition that we would face.

This is when things took a bizarre turn. Due to the contracts that we'd signed, we were technically only committed to work for the club until the end of May. Our game against Strasbourg was to be held on the 31st May 2015. If we were to win the game, there would be another 3 matches for which none of us were contractually obliged to play. Another administrative oversight of quite spectacular proportions.

We could have all demanded a lump sum of money to play during the month of June or negotiated a bonus for winning these games. Rumours began to fly that the club wouldn't pay us for that month, meaning that no one was much inclined to play. The glory of winning the French Fédérale 2 wasn't why any of us started playing rugby, we'd achieved our season's objectives and were looking forward to our holidays. Slogging around France to play in neutral venues in the increasing heat without being compensated was just not going to happen.

We were called into the changing room before training one afternoon during the next week to listen to a speech from our presidents. They assured us that they wanted us to win the game and that they would stump up the cash for the next month of rugby if this was to happen.

They claimed to want the eternal glory of the championship and that we would be rewarded with a glorious *fête* if we were to achieve it. Despite these exhortations, no one was convinced and the slightly changed-around team that was named for the game really made it seem like winning was not their priority. It wasn't a ridiculous selection but there were certainly some odd inclusions.

We made our way to the Champagne region of France to face our old enemies. They had done some recruiting of their own and had some big physical centres as well as a number 8 that we were allegedly interested in for the next year. This wound up our flanker Fabien Vincent no end as this guy could potentially take his place in the team.

Why these games were played in neutral venues was beyond me. Two teams that could have drawn a decent crowd were sent to play miles from their home grounds in front of maybe one hundred people or so. It was a sad occasion and a sorry result for us, their two tries coming from a poor kick chase and a shocking missed tackle from Remi on their inside centre. We were not too disheartened as it seemed no one at the club had really wanted a victory and our holidays were upon us sooner than expected.

Ed Barnes was slightly tearful at the end of the game; he was moving back to England with his young family and had just played his last game of professional rugby. He'd never been to university and had only ever known our idiosyncratic way of life since his schooldays, experiencing everything from top flight English rugby to the fourth division of the French game. He'd captained Rouen to a historic promotion in his final act as a professional and could look back on a varied career with pride.

It's odd to see your teammate and friend come to realise this right in front of you; inevitably you think about how you'll feel when your time comes. Ed was going to play and coach some rugby back home in Devon but at a local level. After a couple of false starts he now creates video content for rugby apparel portal Lovell Rugby, combining his passion for videography with his love of the sport. Ed's certainly one of the good guys and although I enjoyed my year getting to know him, he deserved his rest.

As for the rest of us, we were coming back, ready to test ourselves in the next division and further advance the Rouen project. During the season, Hilly had organised a clandestine meeting with the foreign players in an out of the way hotel in Rive Droite where we were unlikely to be stumbled upon by anyone connected to the club. Here he outlined the new plan.

Where he'd initially sold Luke, Joe and myself on the idea of playing at Rouen before moving southwards towards the sunshine and the more established teams, he'd come around to the idea of remaining in Rouen and shaping a club from the ground up. The meeting was to let us know explicitly that this was now the plan and to see if we were on board with it. He was excited by the prospect and confident that he could manage the expectations of the presidents while making more of a difference than he could at one of France's more storied teams where the accumulated history and personnel would be more difficult to harness.

What he needed from us was to be leaders in the team environment and to be evangelists for the project, something we'd had to do up to this point anyway. I was to be the vice captain the next year, providing a diplomatic link between the French and foreign factions in the team but we would all need to pitch in on this front, representing Stade Rouennais at sponsor events, to potential signings and in press engagements. These requests were nothing out of the ordinary but by including us, it felt exciting, that we were building something meaningful together. What had been an amateurish affair was becoming something more ambitious and we left for our holidays united in our shared goal; to bring professional rugby to Normandy in earnest.

23

YEAR THREE - FÉDÉRALE 1 AND BECOMING FRENCH

WE REPORTED BACK FOR DUTY WITH EXCITEMENT. AFTER THE drudgery of much of the promotion year, we were back to being underdogs and had new places to visit. Promotion meant that the format of the season was the same as in Fédérale 2 but due to the historical dominance of the south of France when it comes to rugby, we would be undertaking some longer away trips as a matter of course with three games in the Bordeaux area.

As ever we'd recruited and hadn't lost many contributing players beyond Ed Barnes. There would be more bodies at training and more competition for places in the starting lineup.

Notable new signings included Marno Meyer, a big South African winger recommended by Barnesy on his way out of the club, Harry Spencer, a very large English second row who had spent most of his playing career in France, PJ Gidlow, a crash ball Samoan/Kiwi centre known from his days at Redruth and in the RFU Championship, tight head prop Jeremy Boyadjis, an enormous prop from Auch with a beard like a Viking raider, Thomas Fontalirant, a debonair fly half from Périgueux, his mate Florent Guion and

Bastien Le Picaut, two mobile and genial loose head props, who were used to job sharing.

The club had put their money where their mouth was and recruited well. We now looked and acted more like a full-time squad of professional rugby players, some of the older guys in both body and attitude having been moved along. Another knock-on effect of promotion was that the B team would follow our schedule, immediately raising the standard of our reserve players due to the better level of competition that they would face.

Relations with the B team had soured the previous year as some of the players grew to resent not being selected for the A team, drinking heavily and smoking a lot of weed on the way back from matches. This would change as many of the disaffected players had moved on, some to local clubs around Rouen while others had dispersed around the country. The new look B team were younger and more focussed on improvement, being occasionally aided by a first team squad member in need of game time.

The B team is something that doesn't really exist at a similar level in the professional teams in the UK. Of course, the reserves and the academy players will form an opposition for the purposes of training, sometimes learning the plays of that week's opposition in order to practice effectively, but they won't often have an actual game to play. In France, the B team play the same schedule as the first team. There are also the *espoirs*, who are taken very seriously with a three-tier competition involving Top 14 teams but also traditional clubs with strong juniors like Biarritz or Narbonne.

When reserves train against the first team they will usually do a more professional job of opposing, offering choices to take and not putting up too much resistance. Training against the B team can be a different matter.

A collection of jokers, youngsters and the generally not that good can suddenly grow ten feet tall and swarm all over you, flying up in defence and generally dominating play. You'll never face an opponent so motivated, training ground heroes the lot of them. When this sentiment of being unappreciated is allied to actual bad feeling, as it had been the previous year, training can become quite fraught and liable to boil over.

This season, with some of the more resentful B teamers having moved on, they would become more of an *espoir* team peopled mostly by our young players and augmented by the odd first team squad member. It made for a more relaxing training session, even if they did usually show a much greater aptitude for the game on Tuesday nights than they did on the weekend.

Some of this animosity could have been seen as directed at the foreigners but we had not been very numerous the season before; it was more of a reaction to suddenly not being required in the first team. Now, with the arrival of the new guys who were obviously intended to start, there would be a large number of foreigners in the squad with an ideal starting team probably consisting of 9 foreigners and 6 Frenchmen.

Socially this would have an impact as the split became more pronounced. Oddly, there were never any social issues between foreigners and French; arguments tended to occur between different factions in the French group unbeknownst to us, causing surprise when we would arrange social events and find that only very specific combinations of the French guys would turn up.

Despite our increasing foreign legion, our team performances became more French as we spent the whole first half of the season losing all our away games and winning all the home games. Part of this was down to the fixture list, with us facing Lille and Vannes, two teams with Pro D2 experience and aspirations respectively, while some of it was also down to the general step up in level.

The first time we could get on to a field and see what we had was against Ampthill, a visiting team from National 1 in England. They were similar to us with some reasonably paid former top flight professionals, an ambitious owner and with designs to go beyond the division they were in.[1] It was encouraging then that we dominated them, winning comfortably and scoring some decent tries. We handled the ball well, offloading in the sunshine and backed each other up to run up a bit of a score before half time. It was an enjoyable game made more enjoyable by the disappointment of their affable coach Paul Turner afterwards, making excuses by telling us about all the guys who weren't available. They had guys who went on to play for Bedford, as well as former Cardiff number 8 Ma'ama Molitika, so I didn't feel too sorry for them. Confident about what we had to offer, we travelled up to Lille for the first game of the season.

Here we received a reality check. Apart from Marno looking very dangerous, we didn't really threaten them and our scrum took a pasting from their large, experienced and well organised pack. We were shoved off the ball time and time again, receiving a couple of yellow cards and a good sound beating on the scoreboard. Lille had ambitions of going back to Pro D2, played in the old football stadium which although almost completely empty, had wifi, and made us look not up to the task. Niort had taunted us during our meeting last year, '*Fédérale 1 c'est différent*', and on this evidence, they had been telling the truth.

The consolation was that Lille were probably the best team in our group and it may not have been a bad thing to have a bit of a reality check right at the beginning of the season. We also had new players to integrate into our unfamiliar way of playing so could not be expected to be the finished article just yet.

We won our first home game pretty comfortably against St Nazaire which they did not like, resorting to a series of cheap shots while moaning constantly at each other. It's amusing to watch a team socially disintegrate as they get annoyed and they had signed a couple of South Africans, neither of whom spoke much French and were evidently disgusted at the performances of their teammates.

Irritatingly, their fly half caught me with an outrageous forearm to the face while I was stood in a tackle that went completely unsanctioned. This is the sort of play which is being scrubbed out of the game by some very prejudicial high tackle rules that have caused consternation among some sections of the fan base. As far as I'm concerned, anything that saves someone from being hit in the face is a good rule.

Rugby is certainly a concussive sport and I've had my fair share of knocks to the head. My neck clicks slightly alarmingly every day and I can remember the first time something untoward happened to it, feeling hot, electrical tingling shooting down the side. I've been fortunate to never have been knocked clean out but have seen stars on several occasions, been booted in the head and have been sick after a match due to a head injury. These are mild symptoms compared to many of my rugby playing brethren and I have two former teammates who were forced to retire due to behavioural change brought on by repeated knocks to the head.

Part of the ethos of the sport is to play through pain and most players will be experiencing some type of pain when they get out of bed each day, let alone when they take the field. There is far more awareness around the dangers of playing injured, especially with head injuries, but not only is there a constant pressure to make yourself available from other people, it's easy to put this pressure on yourself through letting your commitment to the group trump your commitment to your own continued wellbeing.

Sometimes guys are suspicious of someone sitting out of training and call into question the veracity of their injury problem. This can begin innocently as a bit of banter but can quickly become a genuine disbelief, often coloured by the general perception of that guy; is he someone who tries hard in general or is he a bit of a shirker? Even personal feelings can cloud these judgements where if someone isn't well known or is disliked in general, their problems become not real, a manifestation of their deficient character.

Concussion is the injury most likely to be overlooked and as symptoms are internal and not uniform at all, it is impossible to know exactly how affected a player is. Some guys can seem fine, while others can suffer long term consequences. There is a return to play protocol but it can be unreliable and easily gamed. The last one I did involved a series of card based memory and reaction tests on a computer and I couldn't even achieve an acceptable baseline score uninjured, quite a blow to the ego of someone who considers themselves mentally agile. Another guy I know who went on to play for the Lions did deliberately badly in his baseline test in order to make it easier to pass in future. When he suffered a head injury, he came in to take the test and surpassed his baseline by an enormous margin, rendering any diagnosis of his brain other than that he had a cavalier disregard for it rather moot.

Our next away game was at Langon where we lost by one point. We had not played well with our defensive and offensive structures disorganised and amateurish, even in comparison to our opposition. For some reason, Semisi was still being deployed as a sweeper in the backfield and contrived to drop several high balls, gifting them easy yards up the field.

We then demolished Libourne at home, using a variety of set plays and finally implementing a bit of structure before getting our first away win at Limoges, our forwards getting their act together and winning the game for us, despite the best efforts of their fallen Top 14 star on the wing, a small slender Tongan winger, electric and untackleable when in the mood but whose predilection for drinking had driven Racing Metro to release him.

Limoges were a team who'd had grand designs but had fallen by the wayside and their stadium was a phenomenon, the definition of a white elephant. We parked outside, the ticket bureaus closed and the larger gates chained up, the enormous white stadium behind surrounded by linked fencing and adorned with placards describing the project, projected to have finished two years before our arrival.

The ground had never been completed; we got changed in the away dressing room before having to exit the stadium, walk around the outside of the tribune and enter at the open end, jogging into the pitch from the corner of the field. Instead of another tribune at that end of the field there was a large portakabin that served as the home team dressing room and they entered shortly afterward. What could have been a reasonable crowd was dwarfed by the size of the stadium, initially intended to showcase Pro D2 rugby on national television as well as rock concerts and *les spectacles* of which our French friends are so fond. Instead it housed a middling Fédérale 1 team, hosting almost no one, a monument to failed ambition with a wistful air about the place.

At least they boasted a good playing surface and we could play a decent game of rugby. Pitches are something that professional players obsess over. At the top level, most pitches are an absolute joy to play on, perfectly flat, firm yet soft and covered in luscious green grass. It's easier to play on a good pitch as the turf obeys you, the ball bounces less irregularly than it does elsewhere and there are no slopes that create an inescapable corner of the field like the infamous 'Hellfire Corner' at Redruth.

The lower the level, the worse the pitches tend to be, with divots and odd lumps in the field, patchy grass or the dreaded sand, used as a binding agent, resulting in raw legs and irritated cheeks. One day at Plymouth Albion we were called upon after lunch to shovel sand from the back of Graham Dawe's truck onto the playing surface at the Brickfields, feeling like we were digging our own grave, or at the very least, sowing the seeds of our future gritty discomfort.

The pitch isn't just a comfort measure. An irregular surface can lead to injury incidents that wouldn't occur otherwise. This isn't limited to random divots but your foot striking the ground in an irregular manner can cause you problems. Something as innocuous as that can cause absences from training and playing which at the more precarious lower level, can result in unemployment.

You end up relishing going to certain places to play, purely based on how nice their pitch is. Northampton Saints is commonly regarded as one of the finer playing surfaces while the preponderance of artificial turf has homogenised things somewhat, even if some players' bodies react extremely badly to playing on them.

Artificial turf is odd; playing on it sometimes has the feeling of a serious training session rather than a match and installing one doesn't always go well. Oyonnax, a team from a rather dull town nestled near the French Alps, were promoted from Pro D2 and caused a lot of problems in the Top 14 as the aristocrats of the division hated going to their parochial little ground and having to mix it with a big pack on an uninviting pitch.

They hated it so much that Oyonnax exceeded all expectations and qualified for the Champions Cup the next season, installing an artificial pitch so that their supporters could enjoy a more up-tempo style of rugby, even in the inclement weather that the town suffered through the winter. They did not foresee that the new surface made it easier for the previously uncomfortable bigger teams to come and play a style that was more suited to them and Oyonnax were relegated the next season. Tamper with a forbidding home ground at your peril.

You can imagine how the quality of playing surface varies drastically from place to place in the French lower divisions. Our home ground had a mostly flat but quite heavy playing surface whereas if we played at the Stade Diochon, on a pitch designed for football, the going was far easier and firmer, even if the grass wasn't necessarily so good.

Some of the grimmer teams around Paris had surprisingly great facilities. Domont had a brand new clubhouse, plentiful training fields, an athletics track and a great playing surface. They were awful but their *stade* was *fantastique*. Langon, where we spent a chastening afternoon somehow losing to a far worse resourced team than ourselves, had a horrific pitch, on a bit of a slope, dry and dusty, with numerous lumps and bumps on which to come a cropper and roll your ankle.

When you play at a better level, stadia are stadia. The atmosphere and the crowd tend to be what makes each place special. The inside of a sports stadium largely looks like any other. We played Lille, recently down from Pro D2, in the city's old football stadium, the top flight football team having decamped to a new facility. Playing in a smart ground without much of a crowd is a sad experience whereas away at Angoulême in a promotion decider, their small ground packed full to the brim and being assailed by the sound of brass bands and singing was great, even if we took a bit of a hiding.

We were embracing our Frenchness to such a degree that we contrived to lose to a little team from outside Bordeaux called St Médard en Jalles. St Médard seems like a lovely spot and the sun always shined when we played there. Unfortunately, the first time saw our forwards get absolutely outmanned by the St Médard pack and we lost the game, picking up 2 losing bonus points. The French bonus point system gives you a 'bonus offensif' for scoring 3 more tries than the opposition. We lost 30-27, scoring 3 tries to St Médard's zero.

Their kicker had a field day, largely off the back of scrum penalties awarded against us. It would be the obvious thing to blame a partisan home referee but St Médard is not an imposing place to play, nor are they especially ambitious. This was down to the absolute incompetence of our forwards and the dead eyed accuracy of their *buteur*[2].

Who was this miracle man? I can't remember his first name but he was a Botica, brother of current Bordeaux Bègles fly half Ben and son of the famous Frano Botica, a New Zealand rugby league legend. That day he played at fullback and did nothing but kick, showing little interest for any other aspect of the game. He absolutely dominated that match.

A good kicker can do this. Ruin the game for everyone else. He kicked 10 from 10 that day and defeated us by a thousand (10) cuts, knocking them over from all angles and distances.

Rugby relatives are fairly common in the sport. I'm one myself, albeit an older one. Once I matched up against Pale Nonu, older brother of Ma'a, in the RFU Championship and during the week was asked how I would deal with the threat he posed. I told the group that I'd sympathise with him as I also had a higher achieving brother and that I knew his pain, drawing a few laughs. This Botica must have felt similarly, traipsing around the fields of French lower division rugby, a curiosity to opponents who realised his status as a lower class sporting sibling.

If you're not ready to laugh about this then it can be an easy stick for your teammates to beat you with. Obviously if you're a reasonable person then you have pride in your siblings regardless of your own circumstances. Jealousy and envy are not the same thing; it's possible to admire their sporting situation and be supportive while still feeling a pang of 'if only'. I always felt that my brother deserved his success immensely; I've seen the hard work he put in from his early teens, his laser focus on achieving his goal of playing for Bath Rugby. I never had his monomania or his capacity for hard work. I'd consider myself a hard worker but he's someone who stands out, even in a Premiership environment, for his work ethic. I've seen senior Bath players follow him around the university gym, knowing that they'll work harder if they allow themselves to be led by him. He has a taste for the impractical, for finding and pushing beyond physical limits, far beyond anyone else I've met.

It's a common trope of youth rugby at age group trials where someone will whisper 'it's so and so's brother - apparently, he's better than him at the same age'. Most often, this would not come to pass but there's no doubt that a relative can smooth a path through the thicket of youth representative rugby even if just by having some name recognition or a coach vaguely knowing your family. Just to be clear, I was not able to do this for my brother.

This comes up countless times and applies across sports. Doubtless there are many times where someone has been over promoted due to their 'bloodline' and it's embarrassing. There are also guys like Owen Farrell who have gone on to become some of the best players in the world so maybe it's not a bad gamble for a selector to take.

Farrell and his mate George Ford are both sons of rugby league players, with Andy Farrell being an illustrious name in the 13 a side game, but maybe more pertinently, both their fathers are career coaches. Both players have grown up around elite sporting environments their whole lives, tagging along to sessions, fetching balls and soaking up wisdom from senior internationals from an early age. Perhaps this exposure was as important as their genetics for their development and neither are exactly good players because of their athleticism.

Being adjacent to the best in a field is perhaps the best route to success. You have proof, right in front of your eyes, that achieving these things is possible. You can see that these people are human and you can figure out how to get to where you want. Those two players are both great talents but I'd imagine that their adolescence in and around international sport has helped them immensely.

Perhaps my brother saw my academy rugby and realised that this was something that was eminently possible, that he could go beyond and represent his hometown team. I would never take credit for his success but proximity and circumstance are things that I believe aid someone immensely in pursuing their goals. There was an older guy at my school who, although much more talented than me, provided a day to day reminder that getting into the Bath academy and potentially on to the first team was a possibility.

Of course, these narratives around success and failure are mutable, subject to unreliable memories and your own self-mythologising. Becoming a professional is itself an achievement but I would never claim that my career went how I thought it would as a young player. Justifying and explaining your own successes and failures is fascinating and I stumbled across this quote:

> We all have a story that we tell about ourselves—about who we are, what our formative experiences were, and what our lives mean. But psychologists have shown that these stories aren't very trustworthy. They are based on distorted memories and wildly optimistic assessments of our own qualities. Yet, crafting these stories—and believing them—seems to preserve our mental health. People who don't overrate their own personal qualities tend to get depressed. So the little fictions we make up about ourselves are healthy, so long as they don't cross over into narcissistic travesty.

— Jonathan Gottschall

This is particularly true of lower level athletes, those that don't succeed. You can reevaluate, blame circumstance, situation, injury or teammates for your relative lack of success or why you never 'made it'. Without these qualifying stories, it could be easy to get depressed. On the flip side, stories also help guys at the top of the game to believe in themselves when things are going wrong, or to summon up reserves of strength and will to perform in front of a big crowd. If you have an origin story, a personal narrative that you firmly believe in, it can power you through tough times even if it can also be a double edged sword that cuts you. I like to think that I've maintained a healthy sense of perspective about my own career but again, this could just be something I've fabricated to protect myself.

24

SETTLED IN

THIS WAS MY THIRD SEASON AT THE CLUB AND I FELT WELL settled in the city. I'd discovered where I liked, where I didn't and now spoke a good level of French, augmented by extra sessions with Joe. I was also teaching English as a foreign language to French students in town and most importantly, coaching a local rugby club called Elbeuf where I had to keep my wits about me as they peppered me with questions and insults. My status as part of the furniture had been made official by being given the position of vice captain of the team; something I was quite proud of.

We had a good team environment, slightly split down national lines, well integrated in our social events while tending not to mix too much in the week. Now that there were more foreigners to hang out with in the day time, you would naturally stick together.

Hanging around in cafes is supposed to be a traditional French pastime; it's certainly a rugby players' pastime so the opportunity to combine two cultures couldn't have been better. The *flaneur* is a well-to-do gentleman who moves through the city observing everything around him. The rugby player is a sort of modern day *flaneur*, usually without the anonymity or sophistication. The similarities are that rugby players have a lot of free time and like to hang around in cafes.

French cafe culture is odd. The *salles* of Hemingway and his literary gang are the famous examples but the traditional tabac doesn't really cut it these days. The French labour under the misguided notion that their coffee is superior but it often comes as the result of a button being pressed rather than the complex artisanal processes that many of us are now accustomed to.

A flat white is relatively unheard of, especially outside of Paris, and service is not so often with a smile. A cappuccino can come topped with thick lashings of whipped cream and a latte will be extremely milky. Equivalents can vary between venues and there isn't really a unifying theory of coffee apart from that theirs is probably better than yours.

It's best to stick to black coffee to be honest and asking for un café will get you an espresso. A *café allongé* is a lengthened espresso so an americano or long black, my usual choice as you knew what would arrive, no calorific surprises attached beyond the bowl of sugars that they'd always bring.

Your pronunciation can get you in a spot of bother as I discovered on an away trip. The waitress asked who wanted coffee after our pregame meal and I requested *'un allongé s'il vous plait'* and heard sniggering behind me from Johanny Labitte. When I questioned our little winger as to what was so funny he did an impression of my *'a longer'* and gestured that I was asking her to lie down. He thought this was hilarious.

This sort of mishap can actually lead to romantic success. A different accent or origin can be as alluring to a French girl in France as, for instance, a travelling Australian can be to an English girl in the UK. Having a point of difference can make you interesting, even if you're not.

Rugby players in cafes are also very obvious. Someone might have some team kit on for a start but more tellingly, most of you are much bigger than the average *citoyen*. It's not hard to stand out but it helps to make you feel that you don't belong there as people are obviously looking at you. Citizen Coffee became our vendor of choice with its variety of breakfast items and inclusion of a flat white on the menu making it a rarity in France while the many tables outside enabled you to bask in the sunshine and watch Rouen's bourgeoisie take their afternoon promenades in front of you.

My favourite restaurant in Rouen is L'Espiguette. It takes up the corner of a building and has a small terrace with covered tables in a petit place back from the Rue de la République. It has the trappings of a classic French bistro with red beams, old school script and very waxy candles stuck in bottles everywhere.

Its French ambience is only heightened by their relaxed approach to service. There are no menus, just a chalkboard behind the bar. Reading the menu results in further havoc as then you're bang in the way of the only route for waiters to move from the kitchen to the tables. It teeters on the brink of anarchy but always comes through. Two old boys appear to run the place, one of whom never ventures out from behind the bar, peering at you from behind the tiny spectacles balanced on the end of his nose while tapping at a huge old metal till. The other is out on the floor and occasionally engages you in broken English but as my language skills improved he gave up on this.

L'Espiguette runs two servings; you book a table for a specific time but they will let you sit there for a few hours and then have another much later booking. You can luxuriate in your time there. You can tell this bothers the Tripadvisor crowd as the restaurant is not very highly rated and often criticised for its service.

To my mind, the clamour for immediacy misses the point. You'll get the food you ordered but why rush? You're there to relax and to enjoy an evening in good company, not to get something in your mouth as quickly as possible. This is why the second serving can run until 1am; if people are having a good time then they don't close.

The food is also great and although not cheap, represents excellent value. Many of the mains cost €24 euros or so but come in a small Le Creuset casserole dish, allowing you a couple of servings. You can of course share with your companions and I'd usually only get a terrine starter to share amongst us due to the volume of the main, with osso bucco being my favourite dish.

The large portions of l'Espiguette are an ideal entree into French food culture and how they eat meals. Over time I noticed a few fundamental differences in French and English eating habits. The French will eat until satisfied, not until they are full. I'm certainly guilty of the latter approach, having to compete with my brother for food when we were growing up and just generally always being hungry, I would try to stuff myself as if I didn't know when I would next get some food, Shrove Tuesday being the apogee of our competitive consumption. Even when eating out, it's quite common to see leftover food cleared from people's tables; they don't eat for the sake of eating and the lengthy time spent at the table allows for the proper enjoyment and digestion of each course.

The same approach goes for drinking alcohol. When we order wine in the UK we will pass around the bottle topping everyone up and making sure we finish it before leaving. It's not uncommon to see unfinished bottles or carafes of wine left on restaurant tables in France or they may take home what's left rather than demanding that everyone pitch in and finish it there and then. l'Espiguette wouldn't direct you to the most expensive bottles of wine either, advising you of what would go best with your meal, regardless of the price.

The only way they let me down was when I wanted to book a venue for my 30th birthday celebration and thought that if we could take the place for the second serving, we could all go to eat and drink in a relaxed and convivial environment. I asked the barman if this was possible. He cut me off.

'*Non - on a jamais fait ça.*' / 'No - we've never done that.'

I began to suggest that this could be the first time; I have a January birthday, a typically quiet and miserable time of the year.

'*Non - c'est impossible.*'

He was having none of it. Typically French. I left chastened. Later, I admired his stance. He didn't want to set a precedent of private hire in their restaurant. My Englishness probably had something to do with it too. He was a man sure of what he wanted from work and he would forgo some potential profit to keep it that way. The French tend to stand by their principles and work to live, not the other way around.

One of the other ways that we experienced French people was during events that were seen as attacks on their national character, almost on the idea of Frenchness. There were several incidents during my time there with the worst one being the Paris attacks.

As I've discussed, France is quite heavily divided along racial lines with racial commentary and difference both much more integrated and much more evident. People are there, next to each other and their difference is remarked upon.

Skin colours are used as signifiers or nicknames. When incidents arise in England involving foreign players and the use of phrases like 'negrito' (a Spanish word describing a small black guy) we are outraged. But in France '*le grand black*' or '*le grand noir*' are used every day by all sorts of people without comment.

Some things that would cause widespread condemnation are not necessarily remarked upon. The season after I left the team had a social where one of the French players blacked up and the photo was published on the website of the local paper without judgement until some commenters dissented. Some of the sensitivities that we in the UK have around race just aren't universal. That's not to say that I agree with blacking up. I thought what he did was offensive and knowing him, I know that he is someone who likes to cause offence.

I also see the sense in describing someone but this is obviously context dependent. If there is one white guy in a group of black guys, it makes sense to use his skin colour as a descriptor if he is the one you're talking about. Vice versa also applies. To avoid using an obvious signifier of difference in a descriptive context as a misguided expression of sensitivity seems silly to me.

One of the big opportunities for us to learn was in the diverse group of nationalities that we got to play with in France. In the UK squads tend to be more homogenous and largely composed of UK nationals. Not only do you get to meet other players but you then meet their families and partners, eat their food and watch them observe their religion. In this way sport is such a great bridge between cultures and religions.

Our time in France coincided with several racial and religiously motivated attacks on civilians. There was the truck attack in Nice, a spate of driving cars into busy shopping areas in various cities and of course, the Paris attacks.

These attacks were horrific and the sort of thing, that were they to be fictional, the creators would face some sort of opprobrium for suggesting that it could happen. I remember getting home after dinner and checking the news out of habit before remaining in front of the television late into the night, horrified by what I was seeing and listening to the testimonies of those who had survived.

The day after the attacks some of the guys had planned to go to the gym to work off our *côte de boeuf* from the previous evening. I went along to meet them when they were finished and get some lunch with them. Our new gym was based in a large commercial centre which kept typical French opening hours, meaning that the shops were usually closed on Sundays.

Nevertheless, it was incredibly disconcerting to drive there on empty roads, park my car in an empty car park and ascend the escalators in an eerily quiet shopping mall, no one else in sight.

One day there was an attack on a church to the south of the city in St Étienne de Rouvray, near where Fabien's parents lived. A man stabbed the old priest and kept hostages in the church. The story made the international news and we all received calls and texts from back home to check if we were ok. We were nowhere near there at the time and some members of the squad would probably burst into flames if they entered a church but it was odd to confront the proximity of such violence.

We were close to the violence and I'd grown close to the place and the people, feeling their pain when they felt under siege. They weren't truly my people, I felt too alien, too foreign to truly belong there, floating between the worlds of England and France, between professional and amateur sport. We were odd in that we were now part of the rugby club and I felt a kinship with the area but we would never be truly regarded as from there. My desire to play rugby and experience living in France had brought me to Rouen and I empathised with them, even if I still felt like more of an observer of French daily life rather than a participant.

The sense of dislocation was heightened when we were called upon to vote in the EU Referendum. More detailed arguments aside, I am for connectivity and togetherness, certainly for allowing other people to enjoy similar opportunities to the one that I was taking advantage of. The French guys were interested in how we voted on the matter and were quite shocked when the Brexit vote came out on top. It was embarrassing for us as mini ambassadors for Britain that we were essentially rejecting them en masse, withdrawing from them spiritually even if we would remain just the other side of the Channel. You can argue that there are good reasons, fiscal and political, but when you're stood opposite someone they will only ever see the emotional perspective.

One of the joys of our squad was its diversity and the result of the vote, at the simplest level, was a rejection of that as a future possibility, the essential belief that it's not a good thing. Not for the first time since moving to France, I saw my own country in a dimmer light than before.

I kept seeing vans labelled '*vigipirate*' driving around our neighbourhood, one of the less salubrious neighbourhoods in Rouen which so happens to contain a well-attended mosque. These vans held guys in full combat gear replete with large rifles. Upon looking up what *vigipirate* meant, I discovered that it denoted France's highest state of national emergency. The nation was on high alert, all the time.

Soldiers would often stroll through the historic centre of Rouen fully armed. If you were to go to Paris then these guys would be numerous, at attention amongst the areas thronged with tourists across the capital. If you're from the UK you tend not to be used to seeing weapons or armed soldiers and it feels alarming.

You can see how this exacerbates things. Our side of the river was widely known as 'not good' or not safe. We met some Irish Erasmus students in the pub one night and they were shocked that we lived over in Rive Gauche, telling us that they'd been warned not to go over the river.

Our side of the river was much blacker than Rive Droite, the historic centre of Rouen. That side was for the wealthy and for tourists, Rive Gauche was for the poor and the ethnic minorities. Rive Gauche was certainly grubbier, the streets dirtier and the shops more dilapidated. There wasn't much life among the residential areas and you'd have to head for the centre commercial to find cafes and shops for the most part.

Our flat in the first year, on a street corner above a tabac had a small newsagent just around the corner. We didn't tend to shop there often but they were open until the early hours and a steady stream of customers would come in and out. Whether the shop was merely selling Haribo and the odd pint of milk or something stronger was certainly up for debate.

Pepper spray is something I've seen in films and heard of being used in confronting large crowds of rioters. In Rouen, it appeared to be *de rigueur* among doormen and shopkeepers. One night we heard an argument drift up from the street through our window and leaned out to look; the shopkeeper was pursuing a man away from his shop, holding what looked like a small fire extinguisher.

The pursued turned to confront him after a short argument and was sprayed in the face, the man dropping to the pavement and yelling, holding his hands over his face. He'd been pepper sprayed.

We were amazed that this was happening downstairs and carried on watching until the spray wafted up on the warm night air and into our own throats, burning slightly and causing us some minor discomfort. Served us right for observing this other guy's misery.

Another time the police were called in the daytime to the tabac downstairs to arrest a man who'd got violent. It took 7 of them to get him in the van and take him away, causing quite a commotion. It was incidents like this that made me think that the unassuming newsagent could be serving a broader range of products.

One evening we'd been out in town at some of the bars, nothing too wild and were walking back to get our bikes and cycle home when we walked past a large, roiling crowd in the Place de Vieux Marché, the main tourist hub of the city. Something was going on so we paused to watch at a safe distance when one man broke from the crowd, walking away angrily, his girlfriend in pursuit. He reached his car, pulled something out from his driver's door and came back, brandishing what appeared to be a gun, upon which we quickly made ourselves scarce.

Cycling bikes around late at night seems idiotic and maybe it was, but our bike crew was one of the great joys of living in Rouen. I love riding bikes. Not in a strenuous way, not in a thrilling way, I just love to use them to get from A to B, to see a city from a different perspective.

Rouen is not a car friendly city. It is divided by the river, meaning that there are obvious choke points for traffic to get into town and when you take into account the French propensity for erratic driving, a simple 10-minute drive can become a white knuckle, death in the face, thrill ride. The amount of accidents I've narrowly avoided has been quite astronomical. It's one stereotype that you can count on being true.

The French are not car proud. To drive and park is to risk it being used as an aid by others. Our French teacher would park his car by reversing into a space, saying 'wait for the bump', knocking into the car behind and then easing his way forward. Bumpers are for bumping; red lights are a 'suggestion' and lane discipline is poorly named.

Rouen has a well-maintained metro system that can run you into town very quickly from wherever you are south of the river. It's cheap and easy to use. To begin with we didn't bother to buy tickets and it seemed that it was something that no one did. Believing this sounds ridiculous but anyone who has witnessed the barrier hoppers in the Parisian metro system can attest to this being a prevailing attitude.

This was proven to be a foolish belief when one of the players was stopped with his girlfriend and their infant child; he was fortunate to only be fined for one person without a ticket. After that we considered other methods of transport.

The metro didn't run towards or stop near training and driving there every time seemed unnecessary as it was such a short distance. We asked some of the other players about bikes and one of the French guys showed us his citibike.

It was a big robust battler of a bike, like a Velib or Boris bike and would stand up to quite a battering. Jérémy took us down to the office and after signing up with a deposit, it cost us 5 euros a month to keep the bikes with a lock and have them serviced at least every two months. They even had a basket on the front.

This discovery unleashed us on the streets of Rouen, suddenly able to cruise over to the centre and bring our own drinks, pick up shopping on the way home or just generally have our run of the place. If you diverted off to the left on your way to the centre, you could ride along the quayside, oddly underdeveloped for such an obvious place for bars and restaurants, and join the many families who would promenade along there on a Sunday.

We'd go out for dinner with visiting parents after games and when it was time to call it a night, we'd take one parent each on the back of our bikes, ferrying them through the deserted streets of the historic centre, buildings lit up and beautiful, bike battling the cobbles back to their hotels. My mum would stay right by the cathedral, strolling out to the market on Sunday mornings and filling up on fresh produce to take back home with her. It was a carefree way of living. We'd become insouciance personified. We'd certainly gotten Frencher.

25

VANNES

I'D NEVER HEARD OF VANNES PRIOR TO MY THIRD SEASON IN France but they were a team with designs on Pro D2 and were the best team in our pool. We headed to Brittany for our last away game before the Christmas break.

Vannes is a small but beautiful town of about 50,000 inhabitants, built around the old city ramparts and with some well-maintained gardens and waterways wending their way into the centre. Their ground is small but being a small town, the team are well supported and attract a pretty full house for matches, usually held on Saturday nights.

The majority of our games in France were played on Sundays and so any opportunity to play on a Saturday night was gold dust. A night game meant that we would usually leave on the same day rather than the day before and the previous season, we'd beaten Nantes in a similar scenario before staying over afterwards, enjoying the various watering holes of that Breton city. Obviously, we were all excited for this to happen again, even if Vannes was probably not as lively. Something that they did have over Nantes was the choice of animal as their city mascot; while Nantes has an elephant, Vannes has a weasel. Make of that what you will.

Instead, Hilly decided to refuse their invitation to play on Saturday night, as was our right as the away team, claiming that it would throw them off their game and disrupt their usual preparation. This dismayed our team and probably only angered them, leaving us worse off than if we had just assented to the Saturday evening. His attitude towards us drinking was beginning to turn as before, he'd been content to let us all socialise and indulge in team bonding after games. This was part of prepping the team for the eventual big push to Pro D2, even if that wasn't to be on the cards during this season.

We travelled to Vannes on the Saturday and spent a pleasant time strolling around the town, admiring the centre and imagining what it would be like to live there. The next day we could walk from the hotel to the ground, right through the city centre. Although there were no fans, this is part of French rugby in city centre stadia, most notably at Toulon where supporters throng the streets and create a tunnel for players of both teams to walk down to reach the ground.

It was a grey Sunday afternoon with not much in the way of support present in the stands. Hilly had listened to Semi and PJ, both of whom were percussive players rather than handlers, changing our strategy for this game to focus on hitting the ball up near the ruck rather than playing our usual expansive game.

It did not work. The game was close until before halftime where Bolty was hurried into a clearing box kick. The kick wasn't bad but we were not set up to chase properly, being very short handed in the inside channel. Luke made the well-intentioned but misguided decision to work his way to the end of the line rather than pushing the rest of us out from the inside and he was roasted by their fullback on the outside, leaving them to score on the far side of the field and go into the changing rooms with a bit of a lead.

We took a bollocking inside as Hilly pontificated out loud on how incompetent this one piece of play was for a few minutes. Eventually, feeling the temperature rise in the room as the possibility of a temper explosion from our halfbacks increased, I asked him:

'We get that you're annoyed about that but it's happened now. What do you want us to do for the rest of the game?'

He looked at me in a bemused fashion but it seemed to do the trick and we got on with discussing what to do. We were to carry on with what we'd been doing as it hadn't been going too badly. We'd not done anything with the ball but we had by and large repelled what they'd thrown at us, even if it had felt a bit relentless.

Constantly defending and nicking a win is possible but the longer you go without the ball, the more demoralising it gets. If you hold them out heroically then you feel buoyed by every mistake, cheering every knock on and redoubling your efforts. If you've got to chase the game a bit and you know that this way of playing can't last for the rest of the game, you can begin to tire in body and mind. This is usually fine if it's limited to one person but once it becomes a prevailing feeling in the group, it's probably curtains.

We were too fatigued to do anything and even with the arrival of some fresh substitutes, the confusion caused by the complete change of our usual game plan meant that it felt like we were throwing mud at a brick wall. Whatever we did seemed to go nowhere and Vannes brought on their own substitutes, scoring some more tries. We ended up losing 41-13 and deserving it.

Changing your game like this is an admission of inferiority. If the plan is in response to a common tactic of theirs then great but this seemed to not be based on any available data or any reason. This was one of the points where paying too much heed to the opinion of a few players made for an awful day out. I said afterwards that perhaps the strategy could work as a way of setting up a drop goal attempt but to play that way for a whole match was not only dull, it was more tiring than our usual game.

We closed out the year with an easy but not comfortable win over Tulle, shipping more points than was acceptable. Despite our mixed run of results, we were well placed in the table, aided by a few bonus points and now knew what to expect from our opponents before the second half of the season. All in all, not too bad.

26

CAPTAIN HINDSIGHT

Captain Hindsight is a superhero featured in South Park. He flies into a situation where a tall building is burning, people are trapped upstairs and the emergency services are earthbound, unable to do anything.

People cheer and whoop as he arrives to take command of the situation. He lands and dispenses his wisdom, courtesy of his powers of incredible hindsight, telling everyone what should have been done and why they can't save the people trapped in the tower block. He then leaves, the fire brigade pack up and head off and we assume that the people in the tower burn to death.

This is sometimes how video sessions feel.

The catastrophe has happened and everything is pointed out as if it's obvious. Certain people always have solutions post game but oddly never manage to implement them during it. Captain Hindsight has blessed them with his powers.

Video is obviously something that needs to be done to review and learn from previous mistakes. It's also potentially a vehicle for dick-headery from an overbearing coach or a player with a point to prove over someone else in the room. Some sessions can be incredibly tedious and drawn out and there are teams who insist on the whole squad sitting down and watching the game back all together as 'it'll be good for the boys'.

It is almost never good for the boys.

Every now and again a director of rugby will make an oblique point or obsess over something inconsequential or even invisible to anyone else in the room.

I've sat there at an English team, wondering why the coach kept rewinding the video, until he suddenly indicated our hooker on all fours with his hands holding the back of his head during general play and asked,

'What the fuck are you doing down there Clarky? Looking for buried treasure?'

I burst out laughing and had to pull a blank face very quickly as he turned around. It seemed that this wasn't an actual joke.

You can often discern the emotional dynamic of the squad from how they behave in a video session; at Stade Rouennais video sessions were conducted very differently between the backs and the forwards. Review for the backs would see someone make an error, apologise and analyse how they could do better. Frequently someone else would make a mitigating point, perhaps pointing out their own positioning and how it didn't aid their teammate, indirectly inducing the error. Taking collective responsibility for problems creates psychological safety and the greater likelihood of someone owning up to an error honestly and organically; a method far more likely to provoke growth and improvement in my opinion.

I once sat in on a forwards video session and witnessed an extreme degree of backbiting. Bouly the forwards coach would implement a new solution every week which would often not do the job, leading everyone to cover their own back or just remain silent when someone else was under the pump. It struck me as a very unhealthy learning environment and built up a lot of resentment between players and towards Bouly himself.

We learn quickly in life that mistakes are bad and to be avoided. Conversely the common approach to mistakes at some of the world's biggest companies are to get a Minimum Viable Product out into the world and learn from feedback, making changes and correcting errors on the fly. Sports teams are the same; you need material from which to learn and if you punish people too harshly for mistakes then the team will never grow or advance.

This seems a little simplistic and of course, there may come a point when a player is making so many mistakes that to keep playing him is almost a dereliction of duty, but the best teams take risks and look to new techniques or different sources to try and gain an edge on opponents. Not all of these attempts at growth are going to work.

I'd posit that a good team allows risk taking within parameters and makes clear where the boundaries lie. Review is not a time for blame but an opportunity for learning. If something is attempted that a coach does not agree with, he can say so, clearly and to everyone. This then becomes something that is part of your team DNA. Some things can be labelled as an experiment and reviewed as such. If it doesn't work, take the positives from it, discard the rest and move on.

The problem with review is that it feels personal and the tone needs to be correct, otherwise some players will interpret the whole exercise as an attack on them and their capabilities or, possibly even worse, take the perceived criticism lying down and stew over it in private, potentially affecting their confidence. You need to try to keep a healthy dissociation between what's happened on the screen and who you are moving forward, otherwise your self-esteem could take a real battering.

One obvious time to experiment in rugby is when there is an advantage, particularly for a penalty offence. You effectively get a shot to nothing and so might as well try something higher risk or more difficult to accomplish. If it doesn't come off then no problem. You have a penalty. If it does then you score. The most obvious example of this is to try attacking kicks and we scored quite often from this strategy through chips from the cultured boot of the Bean.

I certainly became more risk averse as I got older with my own play, thinking that certain things were not worth attempting. Now when I think back on when I played my best rugby, I realise that I was quite happy with the notion of risk and with trying things to be a difference maker. This development, from a risk taker to someone more conservative was probably partly down to the environments I was in, but certainly later was more of a failing on my part. I didn't want to put up with the opprobrium that would come my way if something went wrong, didn't want to waste the limited touches of the ball that I was getting, especially away from home, and settled for a more mediocre existence.

This is where review can be so fascinating if you approach it honestly and without judgement. Where in your life are you hindering yourself or holding back for fear of failure? At school, I put my hand in the air and answered all sorts of questions. If I got one wrong I wasn't too bothered. At least I'd found out the right answer and wouldn't get it wrong again. Later in my rugby career I was effectively remaining in my seat and keeping quiet, happy to try and optimise the team's systems and pattern rather than be myself; someone who could make a difference.

Video can be useful and even fun in the right hands. The best teams know what to highlight, what needs looking at and pointing out and, crucially, what needs celebrating. If you've done something right, something that's been practised in the week has manifested in a game or there's some relatively innocuous looking contribution that has resulted in a huge positive down the line, then it's good to point these things out. Positive reinforcement. It's like the well publicised story of the England team measuring time spent on the floor. It's not an obvious thing to measure and has no tangible impact on the score but it is a great barometer of how committed and interested the team are. A lazy side will spend longer getting up. A side ravenous for a victory and desperate to not let their teammates down will get up and get back into play.

A friend who'd been at Saracens said that boys basically sprint to video sessions as the coaches made such an effort to make each one a presentation, using humour and music to make them exciting. Crucially these sessions are also short.

In France, we were warned before an away game at Tyrosse that their crowd would be vocal and attempt to distract us, in particular a large man covered in badges and the like who wielded a large air horn. Given that these meetings were delivered in French, there is usually a ripple of comprehension flowing to the back of the room as the foreigners understand what's being said or have it translated for them by someone nearby.

We then watched a video of Tyrosse hunting for potential weak spots to be exploited when Hilly paused it and animatedly shouted 'Look!'

We all looked at an overweight, middle-aged man, covered in club badges and clothing with his trolley of curiosities including the dreaded air horn attached to the front.

The guys who have more recently come from a professional environment find this sort of insight really at odds with their previous experiences which tend to include more discussion of tactics or patterns of play rather than idiosyncratic supporters. Sometimes it's these previous experiences that are the problem as before our away game against Bergerac, the guys who had played for them in the past were asked what we should expect when we took the field down there. This time we received two exceptionally asinine answers.

The first was, 'They don't like to lose, especially at home.' Obviously true of any team anywhere, even more applicable to French teams with their away day disinterest.

The second was that 'they have a really knowledgeable rugby public', the implication being that the crowd could get on top of you even more than elsewhere due to their knowledge of the game. Bergerac were not good and their knowledgeable public can't have been pleased with conceding 41 points at home, even if they would have known exactly why it had happened.

There was something unusual that I really enjoyed when we'd review our games. We began something ironically that became a regular gesture of true appreciation. The team would applaud good pieces of play, literally clapping every time. This could be an individual exploit or a piece of team play, even a piece of ruck technique that had been perfected on the training ground, but something that was a bit of good natured piss-taking became a genuinely affectionate gesture of support among the group. Newly arrived guys from the UK would initially not know what to make of it but quite quickly come to enjoy it.

In my experience men are not good at giving or accepting compliments from each other. I had one former teammate who weirded out another by consistently complimenting him via text message and asking for tips on keeping in prime physical condition. The recipient of this admiration didn't know what to do with it.

This was a piss-take but highlights something; we are uncomfortable with actual recognition of our good attributes. It's an interesting thing in a team environment as difference or aptitude is both celebrated and mocked. It can be easier to stay out of the firing line all together. The clapping in the video sessions was a manifestation of this; originally mocking, it became celebratory and a way of enjoying our time together.

27

IT'S OK WE'VE GOT THIS NOW

WE RETURNED AFTER CHRISTMAS AND WENT ON A TEAR, BEATING everyone. Lille came to ours and were narrowly beaten 30-21, proving to us that we could compete with the better teams. It transpired that they were under severe financial strain and the club folded not long after, ceasing to exist, meaning that every team was granted victory from their Lille fixtures.

For every Rouen, Nevers or Angoulême; teams with designs on the upper reaches of French rugby with the means to get there; there are teams whose reach exceeds their grasp, usually on their finances. There are famous old names struggling in French rugby, teams like Biarritz and Dax, who exist in small markets without the on-field success that brought them sponsorship and players previously. Heritage counts for less and less in the modern game; it's a short career and players want to go where the rugby and the money is best. Playing for a struggling faded giant doesn't hold much appeal and playing a season where you lose your livelihood halfway through due to someone else's incompetence would be both stressful and galling. This had happened to Harry Spencer previously and he spent years in the courts trying to recover the lost thousands that his old club owed him.

We would have our own taste of financial problems the next season but for now, all was rosy on that front. I'd been fortunate to not have been at a club with these sorts of problems but there are numerous examples of rugby teams where something of this nature has occurred. Most recently London Welsh were victims of poor financial planning and have been slung to the bottom of the English rugby pyramid after their relegation from the Premiership. Bristol forced pay cuts on their players when they failed to regain promotion to the top flight and due to the time of year that these things occur, lacking any bargaining position and unable to find another gig elsewhere, many players just have to swallow a large reduction in their pay.[1]

We were sailing on, establishing ourselves as serious players in Fédérale 1, winning every game whether home or away. We struggled to a dull win away at St Nazaire and conceded too many points to poor teams, St Medard giving us a fright when they made up a large deficit at our place to gain a losing bonus point. Our firepower had been compromised early in the season when Marno, looking like our most dangerous player on the ball, did his knee ligaments, ruling him out for the whole season.

Injuries happen all the time and Marno was unfortunate that this was a serious one. Knee ligaments take a long time to recover but the procedure and recuperation are far more reliable than even ten years ago. Most people who sustain a ligament injury expect to be back playing and probably at a similar level of athletic capability if all goes well with their rehabilitation. Previously it was regarded as something of a career ender.

Marno's misfortune meant that there were opportunities in the first team for two of the *espoirs*, young players Simon Maillard and Gabin Villiere. Simon, a diminutive winger with a shock of blond hair, had a try scoring run in the team and managed to start most of the games in the second half of the season. Gabin was starring for the B team but lacked ball skills compared to his mate and was sporadically involved until the end of the year when further injuries gave him a couple of starts. Both were products of the B team and true sons of

Normandy, demonstrating that the coaching and community work that we'd been doing was bearing some fruit.

Neither were world beaters but Simon attracted the eye of Bayonne, then still in the Top 14, accepting a contract to sign for their *espoirs* and train with their first team. When you're a young player and you get an opportunity like this, you must take it in my book, and despite Rouen's efforts to keep him involved, he left at the end of the year. He didn't tear up any trees at Bayonne, making just a couple of appearances, but he still re-signed for Rouen the year after. You can always come back down the divisions but jumping up is something that doesn't come around so often. At least he gave it a go.

The best performance of our season was ironically the one post-Christmas game where we didn't come away with a win. Vannes came to our place, gearing up for their postseason and with eyes on Pro D2. They were organised up front with a USA international prop anchoring their scrum, and running threats from a powerful Fijian centre and some nippy back three players out wide. Their ten was a reliable player, kicking a lot of goals for them but also facilitating a more exciting handling game than most of the teams we came up against. They dominated the first period, racing out to a 21-0 lead and looked like making it into a drubbing. Then something funny happened.

During my time in France, much of the regular season was a jaunt around France playing against unheard of opponents of wildly variable quality in wildly variable venues, from almost a village green to a top-flight stadium. Although we were largely winning our games and it seemed very difficult to not qualify for the playoffs, every now and then even a minnow could have a storming afternoon where all their wild offloads and unusual choices will come off and you'd suddenly be looking at a 20-point swing.

Never fear, I have several examples. We had been hammering Arras at home the previous year, taking off a load of starters after half time, only to see them embark on a flairathon, score an inordinate amount of points very quickly and leaving us clinging to a very narrow win with very sheepish looks on our faces at the final whistle. St Médard had done much the same thing to us this year.

When the pressure is off and you have nothing to lose, you feel like you could do anything. Often this feeling will be quashed almost immediately as we had done to Gennevilliers in the Diochon but all it takes is for one miracle play, one offload, one chip ahead, to come off and it can precipitate an inspired surge from the rest of the team.

Although this is not only limited to French teams, there are historical examples at the highest level to point to. The All Blacks hate to play against the French, suffering at their hands in several World Cups. They famously lost to them in the 1999 semi-final, despite fielding a team including Lomu, Cullen, Umaga and Wilson in the same back-line, having no answers to the inspired comeback from the French, spearheaded by the silver fox Philippe Bernat-Salles on the wing and being cheered on by the Twickenham crowd who were stirred into life by the underdog spirit.

My hero Frédéric Michalak, the personification of the French trick-ster, came off the bench to set up the winning try in 2007, sending the All Blacks home at the quarter final stage, their supporters howling at the refereeing of Wayne Barnes and even in their victo-rious 2011 tournament, the French nearly did for them in the final despite having looked distinctly unimpressive the whole time, appar-ently banishing their own coach from the training field and marshalling themselves through the knockout stages.

You only need to give a French team a sniff and disinterest can turn to inspiration in a flash. Somehow this happened to us.

We scored a try and went back to playing. Suddenly we had the momentum and Vannes were under the pump. We scored again and now they were beginning to panic, trying to play territory but being constantly pushed back by our attack and cowed by our vociferous supporters. Then, late in the second half they pulled down a maul that was progressing towards their try line, giving us an advantage. Their centre rushed out to shut down our attack but the Bean chipped the ball, I caught it at full stretch out in front of me and angled my run inside the fullback, scoring under the posts, picking the ball up and tossing it to Luke who drop kicked the conversion. Suddenly we were level with a few minutes left to play.

Time was almost up when we got a penalty in our own half. Luke had landed all of his kicks but this was too far, even for him. Having subbed Fabien off, I was now in charge and we went for touch, intending to maul them and try to win a penalty. I gathered our pack and told them that if the maul went down, we were to pick and go open towards the centre of the field. This would mean that any penalty given would be in front of the posts and would also open up both sides of the field to stress their defence.

We set the maul which advanced briefly before going down. No penalty. Then Wilfrid, taking matters into his own hands, picked and went the other way, being pushed into touch and ending the game as a draw.

Wilfrid at the time was one of the biggest wastes of athletic potential I've ever seen. A 6"4, 135kg prop, as fast as some of the backs and incredibly strong, he has the physique of a top international. At the time, he had the game sense and resolve of a small child, without the endurance or mental toughness required to contribute deep into a match. To be fair, we often leaned on him to play for longer than most tight heads would have to but this was a lower level of competition where a man of his gifts should be dominant.

Not only is Wilfrid a phenomenal athlete but a great character. He's handsome and friendly, always ready to contribute towards charitable endeavours and loves working with kids. He did loads of fundraising for one particular boy, organising hospital visits and toy collections and with his charisma, could be a WWE star. He was somewhat selfish in his attitude towards the team but on balance, he was well liked and valued by the squad. After four years at Rouen, he's now signed with Castres, who won the Top 14 before he joined, and I hope that he can make the step up to the level that his physical capacity deserves.[2]

At that point, a draw with a team who were on their way up to Pro D2, the level that we coveted, felt like a loss. Our supporters were delighted and cheered us from the field for our heroic comeback but I felt that we could have done better and it was this lack of composure in crucial moments that limited us from being a really good team. Nevertheless, we had proven that we were not a team to be messed about and that we could mix it with the better teams on equal terms. It also demonstrated the folly of our limited approach when we had gone to their place earlier in the year and that we should have the courage of our convictions on the field.

One guy who possessed this courage was Kevin Milhorat, who had begun to round out the deficiencies in his game and become a big weapon in the team. He'd turned up the previous season, arriving from Massy, a famous club on the outskirts of Paris who were yo-yoing up and down between Pro D2 and Fédérale 1. He'd come down to us in Fédérale 2 to get regular rugby having not featured often for his home club. Kev was a quiet guy, very slim with a bouffant of curly hair and a complexion that earned him the nickname Malik from the other French guys. He was not only quiet but couldn't speak any English which made communicating with him initially quite difficult as, although we were much improved, we were nowhere near the near fluency that we achieved later.

Even though he didn't play too well to begin with, you could see that he was a talented rugby player. Despite his lack of size, he was extremely brave, both from a physical perspective and in terms of his sense of adventure. He was almost totally a non-kicking fullback and it was his aerial skills and kicking game that let him down initially as he ran everything back, even if it was not the best option to take.

When he did run though he looked spectacular. Fast without quite having the extreme top speed that some guys have, he had unbelievable footwork, his lack of weight allied with wide hips for his size helped him to be incredibly finely balanced and able to step both ways, several times, very quickly. He could slip through the smallest of gaps and could confuse defenders into making them miss effortlessly.

Despite seeming initially reluctant to engage with the foreign guys and keeping very quiet, Kev picked up a lot of English very quickly. Being a back three player meant that he was stood on the periphery of a lot of English speaking players and he assimilated a lot of vocabulary without anyone really noticing. Someone said something humorous in English one day that was relatively niche and I heard a chuckle from outside me. Turning around I realised that he'd understood quite a complex joke.

'*Tu as compris?*' / 'You understood?'

He nodded at me grinning.

I wasn't grinning when he did me in training, assuming that we had a bit of a Gentleman's Agreement during a touch game and making it obvious that I wasn't switched on. He beat me so casually that everyone laughed and I threatened him with violence as he chuckled off towards our line. He once scored an outrageous scissor kick volley during a casual game of training ground football, everyone going wild before being sad that no one had been videoing the session.

He became more English in his style of play too, becoming better under the high ball and a proficient kicker out of hand, without compromising his *joie de joue*. He was the Frenchest player in the team, the one that you'd most associate with the traditional image of French rugby and its inherent sense of style and elan. He was a bit greedy with the ball to begin with, sometimes making a break and failing to let it go but came to realise that he could give it and potentially get it back. He wasn't a prolific try scorer after his first year but he punctured the opposition line with regularity and alacrity, able to light up dull matches and dodgy surfaces with his play.

I thought he was brilliant.

He's still there, for some reason unwilling or unable to get a Pro D2 contract elsewhere and I think Rouen life suits him. He was refreshingly not bothered about stuff and we could often see him from our bedroom windows sitting on the floor of his apartment cross legged playing Playstation. He spent his off-seasons travelling, visiting the Caribbean one year and Japan the next, always returning as skinny as ever for preseason, working hard all year to gain 2 or 3 kilos before losing it all over again. He'll be a slim old boy that's for certain.

It's odd when a guy like that can't get a better contract but you don't know how hard he'd push for one. His talent seemed obvious to me but perhaps he's been playing at too low a level to make the step up now, no longer a young player and his best bet could be to remain at Rouen. Rugby has a lot of these guys who you think could have been very good. They just get lost along the way.

> To play with the best is very easy.'
>
> — NEYMAR

In our Bath youth and academy teams we had a winger who was extremely fast, fast enough to make the English Schools 100m sprint finals when we were 16. He was also an accomplished rugby player and I used to just half attract his marker and then immediately give him the ball. He'd then charge off extremely quickly and by front running or giving myself a shorter distance by running straight up the pitch rather than following him, I would often get an easy try as he would commit the fullback and give me the ball back. I would enable him to use his extreme speed in the easiest way and he would repay the favour, making me look good. Playing with good players made me look like a better player.

Amusingly for my mates, whenever we've played a village game of rugby or I've turned out for their university halls team, I've usually been terrible. When you play with worse players and your strengths are as a line runner and ball carrier, it's harder to shine. You also won't recognise or understand some of the things they do or the choices that they make.

One time during a university holiday during which I'd remained in Newcastle to play club rugby, the university 4th team had made it to their BUSA final match and asked if I wanted to play as they were short of players. Being the captain of the university 1st XV I thought that this was somewhat unethical and offered to sit on the bench to not take a place away from someone who had spent the season in the team.

This would have been a better decision for them to make!

I played ok but with no great contributions, unable to make sense of what my teammates were up to as they were playing at a rhythm that I was completely unaccustomed to, doing things that I would never expect. The referee, former Premiership ref Dave Pearson who occasionally refereed our first team matches, recognised me before kickoff and asked, 'Have you got nothing better to do on a Wednesday?' The truth was that I should have found something better to do for my own good as well as the team's.

As far as I can tell and partly to save my own ego, there is not that much difference between a lot of professional players. There are plenty of Championship players who could do a job in the top division and there are Premiership players who have made the reverse journey and not seemed unusually able in the second division. We had guys come to Rouen from the Premiership or Pro D2 who you wouldn't say were necessarily 'better' players than some of the guys who were already there. There are however, some people who are just better than everyone else.

Nick Abendanon turned up to Bath academy preseason training relatively unheralded. He had played age group England rugby but wasn't known by the rest of us when he wandered in. We trained for a week and then went to play in the Maidenhead 7s. Not the most glamorous occasion that he ever graced.

We played the first game, won and then wandered over to our little base to stretch out and recover. He proceeded to take his top off, put his designer sunglasses on and lie down on his towel with his hands behind his head to soak up some rays. This seemed like a slightly odd thing to do and could have led to some negative opinions forming about his character.

He spent the rest of the day shredding defences and was presented with the player of the tournament trophy after we won the final. The next weekend he played for the u19s and scored 17 points. Then on the Monday he was chucked on the wing in the A League and scored 2 tries. He was never seen in academy training again and went on to be named European Player of the Year later in his career.

Some players don't even need this run up of academy rugby and proving themselves in the second team. Guys like George Ford and Ben Youngs, players whose game doesn't rely on size or even necessarily on speed, have turned out in the Premiership aged 16 and gone on to represent their country multiple times. Some people are just obviously more talented than everyone else.

An old teammate had played with a young Jonny Wilkinson at Newcastle and said that initially he didn't see what the great fuss was about. It was when he stopped playing with him that he realised that Wilkinson spent the whole game making him look good by making his job easier. Every pass hit his hands, every decision was about empowering the team and those around him. There are lots of good, talented players but the truly excellent ones make others look better. Extreme outliers will usually rise to the top.

If there are so many capable players then what will get you a job as a professional? If you're not appreciably better than everyone else, I'd venture that there are only a few things that will guarantee that someone takes a chance on you. Those are being big, being fast (or both), or being an excellent kicker. Beyond those things, you need a bit of luck, a good performance at the right time or the faith of a coach who can hire you. That was the reason we were all in France; we were known to the coach.

You also need to be mentally tough and able to deal with rejection. Some very good players breeze through junior rugby but struggle when they hit the seniors. Others are great club players but can't handle the absolute ruthlessness of international competition. Being able to deal with failure, with setbacks or with injury is a critical part of being a professional and there are many talented players who aren't able to do this.

This is odd as getting good at a sport is the result of many failures, each one providing a small lesson; I should have passed that time or I'll get melted if I run in like that again.

Learning from feedback is how you improve as a player, so it stands to reason that mental toughness develops as a result of experiencing setbacks. This may be why the really talented can struggle; they have no experience of failing or finding things difficult and so give up once they hit a block on their progress.

What does it feel like to be good at a sport? When you consider your best moments on a field you sometimes remember how it seemed so slow, the ball arrived in your hands languorously and what to do seemed obvious in that instant. Then you were away, breaking the line and streaking up the field.

Elite sportsmen describe this feeling. Dan Carter is 'the coach on the field', Wayne Rooney sometimes pictures himself 'seeing the field from above' like he's playing Sensible Soccer and Roger Federer plays like the racket is unbelievably large, leaving him able to manipulate the ball any way he wants. Achieving this state of slowness and clarity is where the elite athletes truly reside while the rest of us get to tap into it a few times, when everything is just right. John Keats talked about 'Negative Capability', being able to inhabit a state of 'uncertainties, mysteries, doubts, without any irritable reaching after fact and reason'; the ability of an artist to rest in a state of not knowing.

This sounds a little bit much but bear with me. An athlete is effectively a problem solver, especially if you're the playmaker type player, constructing a passage of play where you have to think several phases ahead of where you are without losing the ability to adapt to changing circumstances in a moment. By being able to rest in a state of uncertainty, marked by calm, when the moment comes you discover the solution without the irritation of analysis or planning. You get it right and it seems so easy.

You don't only have to be a playmaker to experience this feeling. I'm more of a ball runner and when you feel right, you can sense that a gap will open up or when a defender has lost concentration. You rely on a teammate to get you the ball and sometimes, the solution seems so obvious to you that you scream silently to begin with, not wanting to let the defence realise what you've spotted. In this respect, rugby is also a game of deception, disguising your intentions until the last possible second in order to gain an advantage or break the opposition line.

This state requires a level of technical proficiency; what if the solution that presents itself requires a chip over the head of an opposition player, regathering the ball one handed and scoring with an acrobatic dive to the corner? You need to have the requisite technical ability to pull these things off. A great player has a quiver of skills that they can deploy at the right moment, consistently, amid the sound and the fury of a match.

I would never claim to be a technical master of the game but I can recall instances where the game seemed slow and easy to me. Chipping the ball over and catching it one handed, sidestepping someone and haring upfield, running between two players and flipping the ball out the back of my hand to a support player. Times where I didn't predetermine what I was doing but came to a solution without struggle, without 'irritable reaching'. Often, forcing a solution on a situation is what causes a problem; the opposition can read your intentions as they are so nakedly broadcast by your posture or your manner. Shoehorning a solution into a situation often results in a bad outcome.

This state is also one of pattern recognition. You practice situations, problem solving and coming up with solutions, so that when they arise on the field, you have a range of answers to the matter at hand that you know can work. It's just a matter of picking the right one. This awareness, allied with your practice of the technical skills of the game, allows for the automatisms to take over; a state of easy grace or relaxed brilliance. The best players can do this consistently, making good choices and executing technically over and over again.

A lot of people can get things right sometimes; the best players get things right almost all the time, so that it looks easy.

This doesn't mean that it's not exciting. It's thrilling to do these things well, to pull off a beautiful (or violent) piece of play. The shouts of the crowd and of your teammates tell you in the moment but you can feel when you've managed something special. That's why you play sport. Getting paid for it merely allows you to continue to try for these moments where you experience mastery. No one begins playing sport for money; they do it because of how it makes them feel.

28

THE BATTLE OF BAGNÈRES

BAGNÈRES-DE-BIGORRE IS A FUNNY LITTLE TOWN UP IN THE Pyrenees, not far from Pau and Lourdes. We were drawn against them in the first round of the playoffs and were immediately informed that this *déplacement* was likely to involve a lot of fighting.

Bagnères had a reputation for roughhousing, their pack containing some former Pau players and their coach made some combative statements in the press before we travelled down. The first leg was away which was a good thing. If we were to get roughed up then we could at least exact some revenge in the return fixture.

Our trip down to the Pyrenees was long and arduous so we left two days before the game, sitting on the coach all the way down through France, passing the time spotting deer in the fields, chatting shit with each other and watching snatched snippets of rugby streamed on various devices up and down the aisle.

Lourdes is a site of pilgrimage for Christians across the world, nestled in the Pyrenees and is known for the holy water which flows out of the rocks into the grotto, supposedly able to cure you of your ailments. This is not my thing but it was interesting to see the place, stuffed with nuns, Christian tat and travelling tourist groups. The large church there is basically an enormous underground car park, serviced by ramps to accommodate vehicles and the large numbers of disabled visitors who come to seek succour and solutions from a higher power.

The millions of visitors each year who come to anoint themselves with the water have ailments ranging from the minor to serious disability. It's distressing to see people hope so blindly that they will be miraculously cured by some ordinary water, the lines of carers pushing wheelchairs and the widespread availability of members of the various holy orders that station themselves in and around the town, feeding this delusion. It bothered some members of the team too, but not enough for any of our balding players to slap a bit on their exposed scalps, just in case there was something to it. Is it any different from another type of placebo cure? Athletes will try a variety of therapies to recover from injury, even if the science is sketchy so you can't necessarily blame people for taking a punt on this sort of thing.

What you can take umbrage at is the profiteering, the materialism and monetisation of religion taking advantage of peoples' struggles and inevitably, Lourdes stocks a range of tat to capitalise on the throngs of tourists with faux relics and tasteless statuettes stocked in the boutiques lining the hilly streets of the town. As a group, our have-a-go approach to the healing properties of the town of Lourdes didn't extend to buying any of this rubbish.

Before visiting Lourdes, we held a team run at Lourdes rugby club. The stadium is on the outskirts of the town and is stunningly beautiful, the mountain backdrop adding to the grandeur of the scene. I was amused to learn that the stadium is actually named le Stade Jean Prat, the man who also lent his name to the competition we were disputing. The beautiful, desolate place that his statue occupied was to become the perfect metaphor for our existence the following season; a formerly heralded rugby player standing alone and forgotten, his name representing a competition that we wanted no part of and hoped to leave behind as he had been.

We trained well and headed to the ground on match day to face our opponent, a test for which we were going to need a bit of courage under fire and the patience to ignore their shithousery. With away games in extremely partisan environments, you're unlikely to receive much help from the referee and know that you might have to take a punch or two on the chin without hope of sanction for the offender.

When we arrived to a relatively empty ground I was surprised. Then we walked past the hospitality tent and were assailed with booing and hollering from the assembled patrons, glaring out at us with manic looks on their faces. If these were the more well-to-do supporters, ensconced as they were in the hospitality tent, then I wasn't too keen to see the more typical punter later on.

The game kicked off and it very quickly became clear how the afternoon was going to go. There was an absolute devotion to kicking everything and no ambition shown by them whatsoever. In the scrum, they had obviously decided to go after Wilfrid by any means necessary and collapsed the first engagement before attacking him on the floor. When you're regarded as a threat for whatever reason, you're going to get targeted and they decided they were going to administer some old-school treatment to a young, athletically gifted but green prop forward.

It was unsavoury but they were right to go about him this way. Wilfrid was quite a sensitive guy and they hit him, hurt him and called him names while our forwards, unable to really retaliate in kind due to fear of receiving a card, could do little to help him. Amusingly Joe told us well after the fact that we should all have piled in to help him, even though he'd been bound on the bloke and stood there while Wilf got kicked about. Wilf had to help himself and he didn't really figure out how to in this game.

I obviously can't be too clear on the specifics of the scrum but part of watching a prop forward develop is that you can get too carried away by their numbers. 'He weighs this much, he benches this much,' sounds impressive but often falls apart under the scrutiny of a battered, gnarled old prop who can be far behind his young competition in physical gifts but streets ahead in technique, nous and knowing how to gain the upper hand through fair means or foul.

Young, strong props, and other players who have an early athletic advantage need to develop their skills as youngsters otherwise they suddenly find that they are behind their peers when everyone catches up in size. The problem with being a prop is that until you scrummage against older, more experienced guys, you can get away with relying on athleticism for the most part. There isn't much substitute for grim experience in the middle of a live, competitive scrum. This is where potential becomes reality. Or not. Wilf was finding this out that afternoon if he hadn't already.

The fullback for Bagnères was the most painful opponent I've ever played against, spending his time kicking every ball that came his way, avoiding any sort of physical contact and verbally abusing any opposition player within earshot. He really was a cretinous piece of work. Marno had played with this guy in a preseason game at another famous old French club, Tarbes. Tarbes had a preseason friendly against Toulon and this guy had done something to one of the Toulon players. He was chased down by All Black legend Jerry Collins and a couple of others who apparently exacted some rough justice. To keep up the abuse after a hiding from people like that shows great strength of character and I commend him for his iron will.

On pitch abuse or sledging is a big part of competitive sport. Some people are well known for their propensity for trash talk and what was previously relatively confined to the field of play can now go viral on social media. This is why when you watch football, where millions of eyes from all around the world are watching the big games, players and sometimes coaches cover their mouths to talk to each other in order to avoid being lipread.

This might seem paranoid but it's certainly the case. It only takes one slip of the tongue to be deciphered or caught by a nearby microphone to cause an incident and give a rabid press material for their various publications. A substituted player caught in a moment of annoyance can spark a story about unrest between them and the coach or even about ructions in the squad. It's these possibilities that cause players to be so guarded around the media.

Living in France insulates you somewhat from the threat of being overheard. Or at least it gives you the impression that no one will understand you. Normandy is a traditional area where not many people speak good English, as opposed to Paris where English is widely spoken and understood to the point that people will interrupt you when you're speaking French to speak back to you in English. This sense of general incomprehension gave you an air of invincibility as you walked around Rouen, able to swear in public or say things that you would never dream of saying in the same context in England.

It's quite a shock when someone understands you in public, let alone on the field. Our team had a reputation for having a lot of foreigners; we had a foreign coach and many English speakers; and other teams would have certainly framed the matches as a true 'us against them'.

As our French developed we would often hear or understand abuse for being English coming from the other team. This was not particularly bothersome but when our language skills improved further and we could understand some of the other things that were said, we realised that some of it was pretty borderline, even if it was also sometimes quite amusing.

Trash talk is not uncommon. There are numerous examples from within rugby at the top level and players have been known to give each other stick. Cricket is a leader in this regard as the psychological demands on a batsman are quite harsh and the bowling team will do almost anything to put someone off their game. There are some good examples on social media from basketball, where the pick-up culture can spill over into the pros as they wind each other up. Some of the greatest athletes in those sports were renowned trash talkers; Michael Jordan and Shane Warne come to mind.

That day, their trash talking fullback kicked well to begin with and it was clear that we were in for a tough game; the ball was at a premium, no set piece passed without a fight or a penalty and they were slowing the game down to make sure we couldn't run them off their feet.

Despite this we were narrowly ahead at halftime due to Luke having a good day out. This was until the final minute of the first half where we were forced into a rushed box kick clearance that was poorly set up and not well chased. The Bagnères winger made a big break back towards our line and they ended up scoring a try to put us narrowly behind at the interval.

We received a classic bollocking for this ineptitude before Semi brought up our kicking strategy, despite it having gone fairly well. It was awkward for a second as he and Luke were essentially at logger-heads, the prearranged strategy being to kick for distance rather than kick off the field to avoid them throwing into the line out. We smoothed it over in the unit meetings that we'd break into during the halftime break, an opportunity to discuss the strategy for the second half without input from the forwards and with the benefit of a sip of water.

The second half saw a swing in momentum towards us and we scored a good try in the corner after an 8-9-15 move, Bolty slinging a miss pass to Gabin who used his enormous hands to finish well in the corner. Moments like this are big for a young player; scoring in a midseason game is good but making decisive interventions in playoff games will garner you more respect and Gabin was now beginning to look like a better player at this level than his mate Simon, who did lack size. The Bean knocked over some drop goals, taking them early to offset the defence, helping us to win the game 22-27 away from home.

Once they felt that the game was getting away from them they stepped up their fighting efforts further and there were several post-scrum skirmishes. These don't often involve any actual violence but if they continue beyond the standard handbags, the outside backs are left with a choice. Run in from miles away to join in or stay put and awkwardly chuckle at what's going on. My opposite number, a friend of Leo's from the Chile national team, was frustrated that his team just wanted to fight rather than play so he and I mimed boxing each other while stood ten metres apart. I would only have run in as a peacemaker otherwise.

We almost had to scarper off the field as we were vociferously abused by the supporters for winning. Wilfrid felt that he was the subject of some racial abuse and threatened one of their players in the post-game meal while Hilly was barracked by some supporters who threw some water down from the stands. He gave them some mouth back which we all found very amusing. All in all, a good win and we managed to get out of the Pyrenees without sustaining any real damage.

They had to take on the mammoth journey to our place the following week and you could tell that they had no expectations of winning the game at all. We jogged together around half of the pitch as was customary before our team warm up and Semi stopped us away from the coaches to give us a 'one in all in' type of speech. It didn't really need saying but you could see that he was up for it.

He was too up for it as it turns out because although Bagnères weren't expecting to win, they were happy to try and take us down to their level through the same sort of behaviour they'd employed the week before. One of them snuck a punch in on PJ when he was lying on the floor in a ruck but he can't have been expecting the almighty around the corner thump to the head that PJ subsequently gave him having got up off the floor and jogged after him as he was making his escape in a leisurely fashion.

All hell broke loose and one of them landed one on Semi, sending him into a whirling rage which I'm delighted was not aimed at me. They were wild swings but catching one of them would be enough to put you in a spot of bother. Brawls were more common in France, tending to break out in the forwards or when a flanker makes it his prerogative to hit your 10 late after he's kicked the ball. Fighting then occurs at close quarters, with little real likelihood of being hurt or sanctioned due to the number of combatants and the lack of space with which to swing a punch or catch someone unawares. In the outside backs, fighting would involve covering 10 or 15 metres to commence or to join in an existing fight, making participation calculated and therefore ridiculously stupid.

One uniquely French phenomenon to beware of is the lairy little winger. This chippy chap is normally outwardly agitated, looking for a reason to scrap and will hare in at the slightest opportunity. We saw a few of these little fellows flying in to blindside someone during our time there and Gabin was one of them in this game, coming in late with a flying boot that he later claimed was a joke.

The upshot was that Semi and their scrapper were sent off with straight red cards, their fighting too egregious to avoid sanction even by French standards, so we continued with reduced numbers. We were racking the points up, Bagnères seemingly unable to tackle, even as they kept up their attempts to annoy or injure us. Our friend the fullback spent the whole game abusing everyone, even as the deficit on the scoreboard got larger and larger and I ended up quite respecting his persistence as he kept up his flow of invective throughout the matches without ever really backing up anything on the field. If someone gives you shit and they beat you then that's infuriating. If you give people shit and get beaten then you look like an idiot; this guy just seemed to have no shame whatsoever.

I'm fairly certain that he tried to stick his fingers in my eyes when I was stuck at the bottom of a ruck so I made a grab at them and attempted to bend them back on themselves. *La forchette* is a traditional part of French rugby, not being regarded as seriously as it is elsewhere where it's seen as one of the lowest acts you can perpetrate in a brutal game.

France was a throwback in this regard and due to the lower level that we were playing, video footage was amateurish and quite often inconclusive regarding such incidents, the camera being deliberately turned away from any outbreak of violence in order not to incriminate anyone. Having never really been eye gouged outside of Wales, where one particularly moronic opponent said 'Why eye' to me after he'd attempted to ferret around my eye socket, I found that the French were rather more eager to indulge in a spot of retina related jiggery pokery. Eye gouging usually occurs when you're trapped at the bottom of a ruck, unable to move or see where the offending finger is coming from. I'm a contact lens wearer so even if a *forchette* doesn't cause any damage, it may prevent me from being able to see for the rest of the game. I'm adamant that the best course of action is to try and grab the finger and that attempting to break it is not foul play. They are endangering your sight after all and it will certainly dissuade them from trying again later in the game, whoever they are.

We ran out comfortable victors 64-24 and were through to the next round of the playoffs against Chambéry. We were however, now light on players as a few injuries and a one match ban for Semi meant that we would face Chambéry at well below full strength.

29

NOT THERE YET

IN OUR FIRST SEASON IN FÉDÉRALE 1 WE WERE IN THE PLAYOFFS, through the first round and into the quarter finals. The caveat was that after the group stages, teams that could fulfil the criteria to go up to Pro D2 were placed in a separate promotion pool and would play off to decide who would go up. We were playing merely for the glory of the Trophée Jean-Prat.

Chambéry would go on to win the trophy, beating us reasonably comfortably over the two legs. Our injuries got to us and they were a good team, defeating us at home for the first time all season and then beating us at their place where our depleted side wasn't up to it. Semi came back from his ban and was having a great game with ball in hand before pulling his hamstring making a break and the back division was shored up by Thomas, Gabin and Polo, most of our big hitters being missing.

Gabin had been playing on the wing in his few run-outs for the first team and he played this game at inside centre. He was a nightmare to play with, not knowing the calls, running in to established plays late cutting everyone up and being generally uncommunicative. This sounds harsh but it only makes his future progress more impressive.

This sort of play did not make for great viewing but we did put some good phases together and only lost by five points. If we'd had our full lineup we could have probably gone all the way.

Despite the loss, the club were pleased with the season and we really looked to have the measure of the division. The next year was to be the year where we went for it, realising the goal of the project and bringing proper professional rugby to Normandy. Running teams like Chambéry close proved that we had the requisite quality and with a bit more depth would be able to sustain a level of performance. The regular season was not a problem; there were ample rest weekends and opportunities for recovery but the playoff matches came thick and fast, meaning that one ill-timed injury or off day could really cost the whole club dear. How the club recruited for the next year could make or break our prospects of getting promoted.

Towards the end of this third season in Rouen, we all were summoned for contract negotiation. I'd not used an agent for years and had been happy with my salary previously as it was commensurate with the others in the team. The next season heralded 'the big push' for promotion to Pro D2 and the French big leagues and you could tell that everyone was going to go and jockey for a pay rise.

We'd always been there to work and had negotiated contracts previously but this was the first time that the atmosphere in the team began to feel a bit mercenary. The French lads were always speculating about contracts but they all tended to be on much lower salaries than the foreigners and they dealt with Olivier rather than with Hilly. We had had an 'all in this together' sort of vibe but with some of the newer players going in to renegotiate and with rumours of some decent signings, everyone was beginning to consider exactly where they stood.

Contract negotiations are quite funny as you can see the busybodies in the squad running around gossiping about who said what to who and who gets paid what. Others complain about how everyone should mind their own business but you can tell that they secretly want to know too. At a lower level, rugby can be a stressful career path as most deals tend to run for one season, making it hard to put down roots anywhere in case you're back on the move at the end of the year, hence the big palaver around contract time.

Rugby differs from American sports in that salaries are not necessarily public. Across the pond, you know the exact details of every contract which seems appropriate considering the American love of 'the market' and its ways. I do think though that it could save a lot of bullshit and heartache in the game at the lower level where there are fewer agents involved. It means you know exactly where you stand and everything must be justified. We do have an aversion to talking about money in this country though so I can see why it won't take.

I'd stopped using an agent some time ago having not had many positive experiences with them, apart from perhaps the guy who got me my first professional deal. I'd spoken to a couple of French agents and had an approach from a Pro D2 team one season but I was unfortunately injured at the time. They thanked me 'for being honest' when I informed them of my physical condition which made me think I should have accepted their offer and been dishonest about how injured I was until I got down there and could go down in training.

We met a French agent in a Parisian bar during the 6 Nations one year but the encounter seemed so ridiculously unprofessional that I wasn't moved to sign with him. One of the lads did sign with an agent and negotiated his Rouen deal himself; this turned out to be a mistake as he then had to pay the agent a decent percentage of his salary for work that he didn't do. This was galling for him and amusing for the rest of us.

There certainly are agents who can do a good job and move you along but it was partly that I'd become unambitious for my rugby and was happy with my situation in Rouen, partly that I felt that I could handle my own negotiations. The one thing an agent does reliably do is remove the awkwardness from this transaction by handling it for you. Going in yourself can lead to some personal pain if you hear bad news straight to your face rather than delivered by a third party over the phone.

I went in for my negotiation and actually had some information about salary. I'd helped one of the newer players to deposit his cheque one month, therefore seeing his salary compared to mine. It wasn't much different but it was different. I was the vice-captain of the team, my ability with the language making me key for the group socially (so I thought) and one of the better athletes, in the gym and on the pitch. Hilly and I also went back a long way and had always been up front with each other. This would be the fourth deal I'd discuss with Rouen and they had always gone smoothly before.

We sat down and talked around the subject for a bit. I asked what the spread of salaries were amongst the foreigners.

'Basically, it's all much of a muchness and there are two of you who get paid more than everyone else.'

I looked at him, obviously wanting more detail.

'You can probably guess who they are.'

He was talking about Luke and Semisi. This was not a surprise but it says a lot about what he valued in the team. Those two were two of the worst conditioned players in the squad, as well as being two of the worse French speakers. Semisi was very popular in the club while Luke was less so, often rubbing up against some of the French guys when talking rugby. On the field their performances were generally good; Luke was our main points scorer and an excellent kicker while Semisi was almost unstoppable near the tryline and held a lot of sway with the other forwards who needed a unifying figure due to their relatively young average age and lack of consistency in their coaching.

It was clear that my extracurricular achievements probably weren't going to amount to much here.

I think that this is a mistake. A player needs to be considered as a whole package and these two were actually quite a hindrance at times. Luke was not much of a listener while both were quite lazy which set a poor example to the other players in the squad; a bit of a dereliction of duty when part of our remit was to instil a professional environment. Semisi was brilliant near the try lines and was respected by our forwards who were a mutinous bunch but he could have made more impact in the other areas of the field if he'd been a bit fitter. He'd also missed most of the previous year with injury, which although not at all his fault, is often used as a reason to withhold a bit of salary.

He probably wasn't bothered though as another team would take a man of his size without much hesitation. The French love a big player and during one sponsors evening, Semi was summoned to the front while the president was speaking, assuming that he was there for a reason. It turned out he was placed there as window dressing, an expression of the president's might in being able to employ a man of such stature. It was an insight into how we were regarded by the presidents and this would become even clearer the following season.

Anyway, I'd guessed who the two best remunerated players were.

I outlined my reasons for a salary bump. I'd also been coaching a local club team and was open to the idea of coaching a better one with Dieppe being mooted as a choice. They had a lovely ground and were apparently keen to improve.

'How much do you want then?'

I pitched myself at a similar level to the teammate whose salary I was privy to. This seemed fair to me and I could augment it with some coaching.

'OK great.'

Hilly acquiesced very easily and I was first pleased, secondly rueful that I'd not asked for more and then pleased again that he valued me and my contribution.

I trotted outside all aglow with my successful negotiation. People waiting around outside the clubhouse asked how it went and I replied very positively; I'd not been in there long and had come out with a positive result. Once they had the papers together then I'd sign and look forward to playing for promotion the following year.

If only it was so simple.

When the contract was ready after a week or so, I went upstairs to look them over and sign. There was some discrepancy between what we'd agreed before and the salary presented to me on the page.

'This isn't what we agreed.'

'Isn't it?'

'No.'

We looked at each other awkwardly, sat side on around a round table upstairs in the clubhouse.

'I'm not signing this.'

I was not in a good position here and it was partly of my own making. I'd counted on his honesty and not followed up with an email summarising what we'd said. When it's your own fault it's even more annoying. Like getting sunburned.

'Oh ok. I'll go back and see what I can do.'

This was very spurious as he was basically a law unto himself as far as contracts were concerned. I was not hopeful and the delay meant that I was even less likely to find a comparable deal elsewhere. It also made me begin to not trust him.

30

YEAR FOUR - THE LAST CRUSADE - PRE-PRESEASON

THE LAST CRUSADE IS A SLIGHTLY TONGUE IN CHEEK WAY OF describing what we all knew to be the end of an era.

Signing in France had been an opportunity to get out there - a gateway year more than anything. We'd been sold the opportunity to hitch ourselves to the Richard Hill bandwagon, do a good deed in Rouen, then ride on down to the south of France to a better team with more sunshine and a bigger pay packet. It seemed like a great idea at the time and although it hadn't quite worked out like that, it had been a lot of fun.

Victims of our own success and of Richard's enormous popularity in the city, we had stuck it out at Rouen and achieved one promotion. The next one to Pro D2 would put Rouen on the map as a proper destination for serious rugby. It had become an exciting project in its own right and this year was to be the year of 'the big push'.

This had been apparent during our contract negotiations where my own discussions had taken a turn and I'd had to sign what he had offered me. It wasn't a huge amount less than we'd negotiated but it showed that they were penny pinching, trying to juggle the finances to put together the best team possible on a budget. Others felt the sting as they were refused even slight pay rises, one of our foreigners unable to get even an extra €50 per week.

The problem was that Richard knew that we all wanted to be there for that season. I had spent three years grinding away as had Luke and Joe. Others had spent two seasons and this year was the reason we had stayed. To not sign a contract over a couple of hundred euros a month and deny yourself the chance to be a part of something you'd worked hard for seemed silly. He knew this and took advantage of it.

The offseason saw us all scatter for our various forms of rest and relaxation before congregating for a big preseason. The club had made some signings, some of whom we'd had to speak to and help convince the previous year, meaning that there would be more competition for places. I'd worked hard but smart and was in good shape as I met Luke and Bolty to head back across the Channel.

During the final days of our offseason, the Fédération Française de Rugby (FFR) had released the pools for our upcoming season. They had changed the league structure to 3 pools rather than 4, with a *poule élite* consisting of teams who wanted to play for promotion making effectively a Pro D3. This pool contained our main rivals in Fédérale 1 and would be a better standard of rugby than the previous season. Winning this pool would mean promotion to Pro D2 to play against luminaries of French rugby like Biarritz and Perpignan.

The French league structure can be confusing. What was also confusing was that we were not in this pool. Without playing in the *poule élite*, promotion to the next tier was impossible.

Naturally we were all annoyed and speculating as to what would happen. Assured that it was a mere administrative error, we were told to get back to preseason and it would all be cleared up as the club would appeal and get us reinstated. This seemed unlikely and there was a mutinous feeling amongst the group. We'd see how everyone reacted collectively when we got back there and reunited with the whole team.

I got back and deposited my stuff in our flat before going out for a wander around the *résidence* to catch up with some of the others. I bumped into Semisi and had a chat with him. He seemed himself but a bit distant in some way. I thought he was just super relaxed after his break from rugby. He was known as the Big Tranquil Man after all.

The next day I got a phone call from Nick and Joe asking me to come down to Semi's to give them a hand. I got there and found an empty house. He'd packed up his family and left in the night.

'What is happening?' The other two had moved some of their furniture in and were asking me for help with the rest.

'Semi's gone in the night bro!'

'Where?'

'Tarbes.'

Tarbes are a famous old club in the south of France who have fallen on harder times of late. Semi had evidently sorted another deal out with them to play in the *poule élite* and gone.

'Wow.'

The first mutiny had happened. We hadn't even met up as a team before one of our main players had jumped ship.

At that moment, our kitman Patrice, seeing action around Semi's house, entered the room. He was quite distressed when we told him the situation.

Now these things are routinely blown up by the boys, desperate for some gossip to liven up the routine of our usual existence. I don't think rugby players are alone in enjoying a good rumour or some speculation. This disappearance was quite contentious at the club, particularly as the support staff had done a lot for Semi and his family, but the players weren't bothered.

I thought fair play to him. The club had sold him something that wasn't real and he'd left as soon as he could. He wouldn't have to put up with the consequences either as he'd gone, leaving us with a preseason, some disgruntled new recruits and a prospective pointless season of rugby ahead of us. We went to go and meet Hilly before training began for him to explain what was going on.

We met for coffee around the corner from the ground and he explained the situation. At this point, considering my contract negotiation and now this, I was uncertain of how reliable he was but he seemed as annoyed as us. Not playing for promotion would be a waste of his year as well, even if he was substantially better remunerated than we were. He was initially sympathetic to our questions, assured us that the club were appealing for the right to play in the promotion pool before he told Nick and Joe to get their stuff out of Semi's vacant house (they'd attempted to plant their flag in there without asking anyone) and said that 'It's a job; you've just got to get on with it.'

He was right. It was a job and we didn't have much option but to get on with it. It just wasn't the job that we'd signed up for.

He repeated much the same stuff to the whole squad later, assuring everyone that the club and the presidents were doing everything that they could to turn this around. This meeting was also the first time that we were all together as a group and it always has the classic first day at school vibe with the new recruits there among everyone. That was when you realised that these guys had given up other opportunities and jobs to move to Rouen, sold on the dream of chasing promotion. Some of them had moved girlfriends or families with them, uprooting not just themselves but their dependents and partners. That made me more annoyed at the club's intransigence and suspicious of the amount of effort that would be put in moving forward.

Effort was not in question during our actual training sessions and this was the most professional that the setup had been in my whole time in Rouen. The popular jokers Remi and Leo had been moved on and there were now alternatives at each position. Big arrivals included Josh Drauniniu, a former England 7s international, Jorick Dastugue, a young, charismatic number 8 with flowing hair and great handling skills from Auch, Will Takai, a combative back row forward from Tonga, Wame Lewaravu, a Fijian international second row formerly of Sale and London Welsh, and Aurelien Diotallevi, an experienced and lithe back row player from Nevers. He would provide some leadership for our forwards, even more important now that Semi had gone and he exuded a warm, calm authority to go with his experiences of promotion chasing with Nevers. Marno was also recovered from his knee injury.

The conditioning had been overhauled with the outmoded and horribly outnumbered Olivier Barthaux becoming a quasi director of rugby while two young English conditioners arrived from Sale Sharks and Plymouth College. They were keen to seize what was a great opportunity to head up a professional team's program and were armed with more up to date knowledge than Olivier. We were immediately set upon with a battery of tests and quantified sessions that had been previously absent, although they had to make some early concessions to Hilly by including a series of maximal bodyweight exercise tests that I've never seen conducted by a professional team. This was just one way in which they would learn the amount of compromise that goes hand in hand with the conditioners' role.

In my experience, France is far behind elsewhere in terms of strength and conditioning. My final season was the most professional we had been in this regard, largely due to having the staff able to service the squad. Whatever his faults, Olivier had far too much other work to do to be able to deliver proper individualised sessions and when he did, some of the exercises were quite bizarre. There was some sort of science being applied as he would test us rigorously across most of the available gym equipment, using the results to figure out exactly what weights he would want us to lift for each set. He tested some odd exercises, I'd never before seen someone tested on a max bicep curl, and the whole thing seemed unnecessarily complex. However he figured out the percentages meant that each set was specified, allowing some guys to lift less than they could and coast through the sessions while creating even more work for him to do.

The French guys had a very mixed attitude towards the sessions themselves with some of them including Boya and Remi being extremely keen on weights while some of the others were ambivalent towards them. This was a shared attitude to be fair with Luke almost completely abstaining from any lower body exercises while Josh was a great practitioner of 'one, two, miss a few', finishing his sessions in record time and bringing Marno along with him.

Weights and conditioning is another area of professionalism that is quite opaque to the supporter and one where there is a lot of misconception around the subject. Some players who you would think set great store by it, barely do any and others may look like they don't but are extremely diligent. For many coaches, if you're performing on the pitch you can get away with doing what you want in the gym but as soon as your performance drops off, then that's when someone will have a word with you and strength and conditioning becomes a stick to beat you with.

Ironically, we were very strong in our first season as a combination of having not much scheduled training, living right down the road from the gym and not being able to speak to many people led us to go almost every day; this habit did continue into our other seasons somewhat with some weights sessions swapped out for swim club on our day off or merely a sauna and a stretch.

This final season saw the sessions become far more closely recorded and monitored. Often Olivier would just chat to you during sessions and with the session sheets being filled in already, there was no data to collect. He would maybe retest you later in the year to see if you'd made progress. The new guys were far more on it and we had to fill out each set that we completed on each exercise. Now this is somewhat ripe for manipulation and there's no doubt that there was some laziness in this regard, but most people were quite diligent about it.

What was disappointing was that these two guys had no authority with Hilly and would be routinely overruled when it came to workload or conditioning. Conditioning is now a real science at the top level with heart rate monitors and the like but at Stade Rouennais, we didn't have such luxuries. The old-school approach to conditioning is to just keep on running. Rugby has become more of a game of fits and starts, wrestles and sprints, although there is certainly a required level of aerobic fitness that needs to be the foundation of the modern rugby player.

The problem with the old-school approach is that it may reap initial rewards but it basically leverages the player's future health where wear and tear will result in injury further down the line. This is not necessarily apparent to head coaches who need to live in the here and now but managing the health of the squad is more important than ever as injury rates rise alongside the demands on the players.

The physical demands of rugby are so conflicting and so at odds with each other that athletic excellence is actually impossible. A rugby player would be physically better at any other endeavour. A prop would be stronger if he didn't have to run while a winger would be faster if he didn't have to cover all that ground. Everyone would be healthier and more athletic if they didn't have to tackle.

The demands of playing the game preclude true top line athletic excellence. Training for a marathon won't win you a sprint but rugby players must compete in both. There are some amazing athletes in rugby, we had some at Rouen, but their athleticism is tempered by the act of playing the sport. Part of the appeal of the game is that there are so many conflicting demands on the players; that a guy can be so fast and tackle, that he can be so big and run is incredibly impressive. It just needs respecting when talking about how to best train the players; too much of one thing and you neglect some other, equally important aspect.

I spoke to a former Olympic level swimmer who said that when you're fit, being underwater is an indescribable pleasure. You feel like you belong there and that every flick of a limb propels you, with no effort, exactly as far as you expect to go. Swimming is about knowing precisely how you move, how many strokes to the end, how many times you need to breathe. Most of them could close their eyes and swim their length. Michael Phelps won a gold medal with his goggles full of water, unable to see.

When you're running fit, your feet flick back up off the turf and you feel like you're in the air for a long time. You can hit a cruising speed and stay there, then stop, then go again. Over and over and over. The feeling of running fast and effectively is even more satisfying when you know you could do it again and again; you revel in your own capacity for work.

Sprinting speed is revealed by how quick your foot contact with the ground is. When your foot hits the ground and rolls through its motion quickly before springing back into the air you feel bouncy, light footed and fast. You know that you're being efficient with your movement and that you can keep it going.

We've all felt heavy legged at one point or like our feet are dragging on the floor. This is when you're fatigued. When you get in good condition you're able to stave this off for long enough to beat the session. In the season, you're already fit and there's no sense really tiring you out. The focus becomes more on completing good quality repetitions without getting unduly tired.

It's infuriating when people don't understand this. The old 'if everyone makes it in in this time we can stop' almost always leads to someone letting everyone down.

When you're fit, there's a pleasure in the monotony of running. You know you won't find it hard and you curiously push against your own limits, testing how fast you can run this one. Then the next one.

Sometimes coaches lose their rag and make you run. I've been in sessions where we didn't mind as we were so fit, what he could punish us with wasn't challenging enough and we were too close to a match or some other commitment that we needed to be fit for. Those threats became toothless.

When you're not fit it's another matter. Or when they don't need you that weekend. Or that month as is the case in preseason. There's a new breed of conditioner who subscribe to the just enough philoso- phy. Why tire the players, making them more susceptible to injury, for increasingly marginal gains in performance? Better to have them show up every day, than have them need every other day off. A more old-school conditioner won't stand for this and you'll feel every step. The feeling of being fit is mitigated by the horrible journey of getting there when you aren't.

We had a rowing test that summer, 1000 metres as fast as you could. The first baseline test I didn't go hard enough but the second time, I basically had to roll off the rower and remain foetal, sweating on the gym floor, legs pulsing with lactic acid and doing everything I could not to shit myself. You can remember times when you felt like this; once after a hill sprints session in the UK I couldn't even walk about after as I was so busy concentrating on not collapsing.

The skill demands of rugby are similarly complex and varied. As a winger, you can go up to catch a high ball, you've sprinted there, you're surrounded by other bodies, the lights are in your eyes and the rain is hammering down on you. You're not necessarily expected to catch it, it looks too difficult, but it's part of your game, it's your responsibility.

Then later, you're out on the wing alone, the other team are under pressure so are narrow in defence. There's no one opposite you. You get a penalty advantage meaning that you have a free play and your fly half realises what's on; you're there ready to take a cross kick and walk over for a try. If he gets the kick wrong it doesn't matter as there's an advantage being played.

He kicks it and it's perfectly judged, no need to jump, you just need to catch it and put it down. You're all alone, there's no pressure on you at all. You've practised this hundreds of times and you find it easy.

Being alone and catching that ball can be worse. There's no reason for you not to catch it so you should. That puts the pressure on you. The pressure demands are different, the skill requirements are differ- ent, you need to be able to do both, as different as they are similar.

Rugby is a sport for generalists, for people who have more than one athletic characteristic, but part of its appeal has always lain in its inclusivity. You can come from anywhere, be any shape or size and find a position. In this respect, rugby is an excellent vehicle for body positivity; you can be a tall, handsome winger, rippling with muscle, able to run tries in from all over the park and pick up all the girls on a night out, but if your squat, shaven headed, toothless prop (an enormous stereotype) doesn't do it for you up front, you'll never see the ball. You learn to see beauty in your rotund friends in the front row and recognise what everyone is physically capable of. You realise that different physical characteristics have utility and in this way, you learn the utility and value of different body types. Where this differs from the body positivity movement is that everyone is, more or less, in shape to do something, whether that be scrummage or sprint. They are physically capable. Body positivity appears to lionise physiques that have no physical capability whatsoever, a sad corruption of what should be an empowering message. This is an area where sport, and rugby in particular, is far ahead of general attitudes towards body composition.

Rugby clubs have always been like this too; anyone's welcome. Come, participate on or off the field and have a beer. This ethos still exists, even at the top level of the game where players, predisposed and encouraged to dislike each other, will battle each other voraciously for 80 minutes yet afterward, someone takes the initiative, knocks on the opposition changing room door and brings his jersey along with a couple of beers. If you peruse social media after an Antipodean international you'll usually see the players having drinks with their opponents in the changing rooms. In this way, rugby retains a sense of its amateur roots. Even the top level of the game hasn't left its past behind in the same way that other sports have.

We were similarly struggling between an amateur past and professional future, neither one nor the other, a team both in flux and in limbo, changing behind the scenes but not able to express these changes on the field due to the ruling from the FFR. We were discouraged from drinking beers after games and began to be treated more like employees where we had previously felt like partners in the project, professionalising our conduct without being able to prove ourselves against teams with similar ambitions. This created a sense of disconnect between players and management that would only increase over the course of the season.

31

KICKING OFF

Our preseason was somewhat underwhelming despite the hard physical work that we put in. When it became clear that we were not going to be included in the *poule élite*, the presidents cancelled plans to take a preseason training camp to Bath. This would have been ideal for us and for Richard as we could have a few extra days back at home but it was regarded as unnecessary seeing as there was nothing to prepare for. It was a swift and early example of them rowing back on the project as a whole.

We took our first preseason game on the road elsewhere in Normandy to spread the word about the project and, in the blazing heat, we defeated St Nazaire who were in our group. We also beat Bobigny, with our new signing in the centre Ivan going down with a ruptured anterior cruciate ligament, putting him out for the season, before rounding off with an insipid performance at home against Dorking, on tour and spearheaded by our former player Ed Carne. We won but without any credit, making a sharp contrast from the previous year where we'd demolished Ampthill, a much better side than Dorking. Spirits were commensurately not high going into the first league matches.

We were defeated at home in the season opener against Oloron before falling away in torrential rain away at Anglet. We looked a bit listless and lacking in motivation against Oloron whereas we were schooled by an experienced ex-Toulon fly half away at Anglet whose old school spiral kicking caused our back three all sorts of problems.

Rugby is a game of the collective and it's difficult to win a game on your own. One of the only ways that this can manifest is if a fly half is able to ruin a game for everyone else on the field with his kicking, marching his team down the field with seemingly no effort whatsoever. This old boy from Anglet was exactly like this.

He must have been knocking up to 40 years old but he had a rocket of a spiral kick as well as the insouciance that comes from years of playing, completely unconcerned about making mistakes. He was alive to small opportunities, catching us out with quickly taken kick-offs and chips kicks. We proved unable to hold onto the ball in the wet, our back three making some poor choices and our general lethargy meant we weren't alive to the chances he was taking.

To be fair we could usually rely on Luke for a similar kicking display and he also pulls out spiral kicks when he's feeling good, sending the ball sailing over the open side winger's head and rolling towards their corner. I once played an A League game as a 19-year-old against Harlequins against a late career Andrew Mehrtens and saw exactly what international class looked like. He ventured nowhere near the defensive line, instead spanking the ball downfield, finding grass every time and driving our forwards to despair. No one got near him all night and he controlled the game almost from start to finish. Playing the match was nearly as dispiriting as the bollocking we got afterwards for 'not putting him under any fucking pressure'.

Even in the return game at the Mermoz later in the year where we beat Anglet relatively comfortably, their ten recognised some poor defensive alignment and ran a specific play off a lineout that resulted in a try for them. There are some good players in the lower divisions and they know how to win games of rugby. Also, they feel no pressure, they don't really have anything to prove and everyone knows they're in it for an easy pay packet and a soft landing as they leave the professional game.

Two games, two losses and the atmosphere was souring quickly. We were looking difficult to motivate, our new signings hadn't settled, most people looked somewhat out of sorts and the relationship between the staff and the players was swiftly going south. The prospect of a long, pointless and crucially, a joyless season stretched out in front of us.

For the most part I'd played quite well, scoring some tries and assisting on a couple in the preseason games. For some reason this didn't convince Hilly and he told me I was fortunate to start the first game, despite the other centres not really offering anything in the matches and Josh Drauniniu still looking heavy on the wing. Marno was just finding his feet again after his long injury layoff and Gabin didn't look good in the centre, seemingly unable to pass the ball. It's all well and good being able to run with it but as our game plan was to play wide, he was a stopping block in the centre of the field and finding that tackles weren't so easy to break in the first team. I answered his criticisms with some decent performances and as the rest of the team was not offering anything, I felt personally vindicated, even if I wasn't enjoying the direction that we were heading in collectively.

Our next match was Tyrosse at home. Oloron and Tyrosse were probably going to be our main opponents at the head of the pool and another poor performance would probably see us chasing them for the rest of the year, trying to make up ground. After two losses, we changed our halfbacks, benching the old reliables Bean and Bolty for two new signings in Erwan Nicolas at halfback and Zack Henry at flyhalf.

These two were not as good technically as our usual starters but they were younger, quicker and hungry to make an impression. They also had little expected of them; they were new and young and the team wasn't doing well. We simplified what we were doing, allowed Zack to kick down the field rather than out to touch to avoid giving

Tyrosse opportunities to attack our maul and played an exciting game, scoring tries and finally looking like a good team. We ran out winners and had some fun on the field for the first time in a long time.

This game sparked life into our campaign and we went on a bit of a tear, winning the rest of the games before Christmas. We beat Langon, the site of a dismal performance the previous year, away from home before winning comfortably against Nantes at the Mermoz. I'd been dropped to the bench for this game to give Gabin a go in the centre where he didn't have much joy initially. In the second half, I came on in my usual spot at 13 and he pushed out to the wing. From a scrum, I got outside my man and set him away down the touchline where he managed to finish a good try in the corner. We then teed him up for another and he slipped away from a despairing defender, finishing with a brace. This was the beginning of something I've never really seen before.

32

THE RISE OF THE SUPER CABBAGE

GABIN VILLIÈRE WAS ONE OF THE WORST RUGBY PLAYERS I'D EVER seen.

He was a very young scrum half, skinny, covered in protective gear and unable to pass off the floor. We spent hours with him training, he had one of the world's experts in scrum half passing in our coach Richard Hill, yet still he was unable to improve.

His kicking was also terrible, his outsized feet making him seem incredibly clumsy and he'd developed the bad habit, of which I was certainly an offender, of throwing the ball up rather than dropping it onto his foot. By throwing the ball up you give the ball the opportunity to move and turn in the air before you strike it with your foot. As the ball basically follows the way that the point is pointing, you want to keep the ball position as static and consistent as possible for it to travel where you want it to go.

Very good kickers will deliberately point the ball in different directions to cause the ball to do different things. Sometimes it will even be done in order for the ball to bounce a certain way when it hits the floor. I'm sure the casual viewer will have seen the odd player point the ball sideways to do a 'banana kick'. These things are the preserve of the good kicker or the overconfident and do not apply to this young chap Gabin.

He and his friend Simon Maillard, another young player who was small but who initially seemed to have a bit more about him than Gabin, started to come to our gym sessions where they would lift in an incredibly unsafe manner but would refuse to listen to any advice or technical pointers. The sessions were largely unsupervised as Olivier preferred to chat and do admin on his phone rather than coach anyone and they were not regarded as important at all, seeming somewhat beyond help.

We played an away game at Arras for which I was injured. Gabin played for the B team and came on at scrum half. His passing and game management was poor as usual but when we ran an 8-9-15 off the base of a scrum, he suddenly came alive running with the ball in his hands. His decision making was still poor but he gained a bit of confidence and ran a couple more times, looking dangerous.

Now this was for the Stade Rouennais B team so was hardly a display of great quality in tough circumstances. It was a very low stakes environment. Having said that, we spoke to the coaches and said maybe Gabin would be better off elsewhere in the backs where he could run with the ball and wouldn't have to think about the other parts of the game that were clearly stressful for him.

He moved out into the centre and over the next season, began to develop. He has enormous hands to go with his clown feet, giving him the ability to deliver a big palming handoff, to hold the ball in one hand and to catch balls you wouldn't think he'd be able to. He got a bit quicker from the strength and conditioning work he was doing and began to develop his footwork, able to move side to side very easily. He was still raw and still struggled with knowing when to pass but was getting better at this too.

He then began to appear for the first team the season after that, making his bow off the bench. When Simon had a try scoring run in the middle of the season, he was regarded as a more likely first team player due to his better ball skills but he lacked Gabin's physicality and ability to wriggle out of a tackle. Gabin finished the year as a reserve player for the first team and started our last playoff game away at Chambéry due to injuries, being wildly inaccurate in everything he did but nevertheless scoring a try off of a loose ball at the end of the game as we went out of the competition.

The year after he was seen as someone who could potentially contribute from the beginning of the year. Simon had signed an academy contract at Bayonne, then in the Top 14 and had departed, leaving Gabin as the most likely *espoir* to make a breakthrough. He featured a bit in the centre at the beginning of the year but as he still struggled with his understanding, the ball would often stop with him as he would always look to run.

The Nantes game proved to be the turning point for him as he struggled to make any impact in the centre before moving out to the wing and scoring twice. Through this performance he had made an incontrovertible case to be considered as a serious winger whereas previously he had struggled to look like a proper option at centre.

The one thing you can't argue with is someone who scores. Even if the tries are essentially dot downs, the guy scoring is in the right place and can be relied upon. If you're scoring these and scoring efforts where you have to do something like beat a man, catch a cross kick or run it in from a long way out then you are really making a case for yourself.

Gabin went on an absolute tear the rest of that year. We were the dominant team in the competition but the games weren't all plain sailing and he scored over 20 tries, some of which were outrageous efforts from a long way out. His big hands meant he could finish in traffic, able to plant the ball over the line one handed in all sorts of circumstances and his speed and fitness meant that he could run in tries from all over the place at any time in the game.

One of the main reasons I believe he was successful is because of how bad he was in the first place. Never having been obviously coached as a school age player, he would make decisions and try things that, to a more seasoned player, looked impossible. Equally a defender would not expect them, giving him the element of surprise. The level of defence was largely not great but he broke tackles and made breaks so consistently, his confidence growing and growing every week.

Gabin had changed his attitude somewhat since we'd first met him and I'd spent a lot of time practising passing, chip kicks and one on one attacking with him. He was a pleasant guy, not super smart, but very eager to learn and he really put the hours in. He even learned a few words of English to better communicate with the foreigners in the team but his efforts were often hilariously bad. He also consistently expressed amazement at how often the word 'fuck' manifested in our day-to-day conversations.

By the end of the year he'd really cemented himself as the team's key player, always able to score a try. When it came to contract time the club were very keen to keep him, especially enamoured of him as he was a son of Normandy hailing from Vire about two hours or so away from Rouen. At the same time, he was fielding proposals from teams in Pro D2 and *espoir* contracts from the Top 14.

How true or concrete these proposals were is by the by. As a lower division player, you live waiting for a summons from the division above and have to seize it when it comes. He now had the luxury of choice. Rouen put a proposal together for him that involved training with France 7s alongside playing for the club in Fédérale 1 but 7s is no longer taken as seriously as it was as a pathway to 15s glory. The sports are so different in terms of their demands.

He asked me for some advice and I told him that he'd never have a season like this one again. He'd scored well over 20 tries and gone from pretty much a non-contributor to the team's homegrown star. To not move on would almost be insulting to other professionals who hope for an opportunity and would also not be a brave choice. If you're an ambitious player, you want to improve and to play in the better competitions. Also, he could always come back to Rouen; his mate Simon was after not making much of an impression at Bayonne.

He re-signed at Rouen and is still there, still playing in Fédérale 1. By not moving he'll have missed out on two years of playing at a better level and accelerating his development. I think he's made the wrong choice but my opinion of it is neither here nor there. It's his life and career and he can do with it what he likes. The thing with sport is that there is always someone else and you really need to make hay when the sun shines. A 22-year-old winger on the up is a more appealing prospect to the bigger teams than a 24 year old who has remained at the same level.

In the end Gabin is banking on the ability of Rouen to get up the divisions. As a winger, he is dedicating his athletic prime years to this endeavour and needs it to pay off. You can see it as a fear based decision on the one hand; he doesn't want to leave Normandy and his status as a local boy come good for the relative anonymity of a big traditional French club; or you can see it as part of his own hero's journey; he's actualised himself, become a good player through his own sheer hard work and he wants to make something unique happen by spearheading Rouen's charge into the upper echelons of French rugby.

Either way it depends on how you look at it. Whether it'll be a story worth telling or not is partly down to him but mostly down to Rouen. Rugby is not a one-man game and things don't always move so quickly. He could look back and regret not backing himself to make the step up elsewhere and how he justifies it to himself will largely depend on the choices of others.

Discussing Gabin's future and the season being pointless led me to reappraise exactly what I thought I was doing playing rugby. I had been keen for this year, a crack at promotion and maybe staying beyond that if we managed it. Now I'd sentenced myself to this interminable jaunt around France where the rugby had become less fun, even as my attachment to France had deepened and my life in Rouen had become more comfortable. I felt like I wasn't moving forward anymore and if you're not doing that, what are you doing?

When you begin playing rugby it's more than likely for the fun of it. And probably not even much fun for you but a sort of investment in your prospective fun by your parents. I didn't much enjoy the first time I played but when I got to school and played a match for the first time aged 7, I loved it.

You play for fun then and you play to win. I was a bad loser at most things growing up and couldn't stand to come second. This could have been rugby, football, swimming or another sport but it also included the PlayStation, board games and something called Jungle Jam, basically Snap with a totem that you had to snatch in the middle. That caused a few family holiday brawls.

I got into an academy almost by accident, just by doing my best at whatever rugby I was playing at school and in the Bath Rugby juniors until one day, a letter arrived in the post inviting me to be a part of it. Once you're on this track then you can see it's about getting better and later, that being an early stage professional is not necessarily even about winning. We would often be sent to the wolves on Monday nights in the A League against proper professional adult players and usually got soundly beaten. These games were about survival firstly, but mostly about improving and demonstrating that you personally could live with that level. It's like playing up a year at school but much harder.

Then you want to become a professional player and to do this, you take an academy contract. Even with one of these you don't really count, particularly at that point in time where the academy players were regarded as second class citizens. Loads of kids get to be academy players. But to get a proper first team professional contract? That's a win. And that's what some people forget when they hit the academy. They think they're on an inevitable track to success. But they're not.

I became a full time professional with Plymouth Albion after finishing my studies and I wanted to get to the Premiership. Plymouth had a reasonable track record of players moving up a league and I wanted to be one of them. Sure, I could have done more but you always can. I worked hard, played well and I didn't get to step up and was suddenly a bit bereft.

A few unlucky breaks with moves to other teams falling through meant that I was without a contract and considering what to do. It wasn't like my feelings later in France as I knew I wanted to play rugby and had recent evidence that I was a good player. I went to Sydney for an initial few months but stayed there for a whole season.

I didn't play great rugby there; the first place I was kept me in the lower grades believing I was leaving shortly after and never gave me a crack of the whip; but I loved living there and found some work. I would have stayed but I got contacted by the Cornish Pirates and I reignited my dreams of the top level.

Pirates had been a great recent success and I thought it would be a good launching pad for the resuscitation of my UK rugby career. I wasn't desperate to leave Australia by any step of the imagination and tried to see what I could organise. Eastern Suburbs were keen to keep me but were quite laissez faire about organising employment that would grant me a proper visa and save me a few months picking fruit on a farm, an apparently bleak endeavour that I was keen to avoid. I headed home to the delight of my family with excitement in my head and a new goal.

Pirates was an environment on the way down, having lost key personnel including the head coach and suffering from the accumulated fatigue of reaching the final the previous two years and losing. I overheard some of the senior guys saying,

'The best thing that could happen to us is to come 5th and miss the playoffs.'

We came 6th I think.

After that I was reconsidering my life choices. I'd hated that year in Cornwall and couldn't do that again. I decided not to compromise on where I was living. Basically, in the Championship I decided it was London or nowhere. If not there then I'd look for a job.

My rugby ambitions had ground to a halt and I'd had enough of the Championship bullshit. Existing as someone to play alongside the developing youth of the Premiership clubs, someone with similar skills and physique, taking similar risks, but with no security of salary or employment did not appeal to me. If I couldn't join the higher-level guys then I wouldn't bother.

Moving to France had been great fun and allowed me to carry on doing what I'd been doing without considering the future too hard. I was learning new skills and living somewhere interesting with a good opportunity to build something very special. A new club that would introduce a sport I loved to a whole region of France. It was a lofty goal and still is. It's just going slower than they expected and lost its lustre somewhat during my final year. Each year in France had felt like I was moving forward. Now it didn't and I didn't like what I'd settled for.

If you have any ambition and realise that you're on a road to nowhere then you have to consider what's happening. I had a realisation that this should be it for me. I was getting older, was unlikely to suddenly start commanding a higher salary and needed to do something else. The club was pushing me to the exit with their behaviour but I was now walking towards it quite willingly, feeling ready to put the rugby way of life behind me.

33

RUMOUR MILL RUMBLING

WE WERE ON A ROLL NOW AND WON ALL OUR GAMES UP UNTIL THE Christmas break. Zack and Erwan remained at the helm and we were scoring points, even if our defence still looked ropey at times. Despite our victories, we were not getting much credit and were being trained harder than ever. After matches we were sent home from the clubhouse, told to leave and go to bed with recovery sessions organised for first thing on Monday morning, usually a complete day off. Hilly seemed incredibly stressed and would often blow his top over quite inconsequential things, giving us less and less leeway while demanding more and more in training.

Then, at the end of one month, we didn't receive our pay on time. This had never happened in all my time at the club.

We'd missed a month's pay by losing to Strasbourg in our second season playoffs but we hadn't been contracted for that month. This was a different story. Along with signing a load of players to play a pointless season, the club were now reneging on their commitments to us as employees. This lack of respect, coupled with the increasing demands on our bodies and our time, engendered a growing sense of dissatisfaction amongst the players.

Wilf refused to train, having a massive shouting match with the coaches and storming out of the ground. You couldn't blame him and he received his pay, Olivier paying him from his own pocket, but I tried to explain to him how it wasn't fair that he received his pay and the rest of us didn't. He wasn't bothered and although I was annoyed at him at the time, I should have reserved my ire for the club. Wilf's attitude though, was an example of what happens when there is no shared goal. Whatever we were told, whatever was said in meetings about winning the Jean Prat Trophy didn't mean anything to us. It was an empty endeavour and people were now acting out of self-interest; Wilf getting his pay and not being bothered about everyone else was symptomatic of that.

Rumours began to abound that the club was struggling financially. This might sound obvious as we weren't being paid but, after the events of the summer where we were denied membership of the promotion chasing *poule élite*, it seemed that our presidents, usually so full of self-regard, had realised the true fiscal burden of chasing the upper echelons of French rugby as well as their relative lack of political clout. If they couldn't convince the Rouen métropole[1] and the sponsors to put more money in, they were not content to put their own cash down either. You can't blame them for not wanting to spend the money but now they had a whole squad of players' livelihoods on the line and they were considering pulling the plug.

We had an away fixture at Lombez Samatan, near Toulouse, for which we were told to pay for an extra day down there. The presidents were unwilling to pay for travel on the Friday as it would cost an extra night in the hotel. Hilly told us that we would have to pay for ourselves. Professional players paying to play their own fixtures was a new one and did not go down well at all. Hilly did himself no favours by remaining resolutely unsympathetic.

I saw the upside of going down the day before as it meant we could do some sightseeing in Toulouse. Dave Markham and I managed to scrounge some tickets to watch my favourites Stade Toulousain play a league game on the Saturday night too which was fun, even if the conditions didn't lend themselves to a good game. Paying for the privilege though was yet another instance of poor conduct from the club, instances that were racking up rather more quickly than I'd have liked.

Despite the off-field turmoil, our performances were improving and we managed to weather losing Zack to a knee ligament tweak away at Lombez Samatan with the Bean restating his credentials as the starting ten, coming back into the team and facilitating a sound beating of our old foes Bagnères who could not handle the rampant Gabin. The Bean was back and on his way to 1000 points for the club. He and Zack had contrasting styles; the Bean was a more considered, older style of player with a brilliant left foot while Zack was a more modern type of player, faster and with better footwork, even if he was more prone to error. They both got on very well and helped each other to improve throughout the year, not allowing competition for a starting spot to spoil their relationship.

This is usually the case; rugby players are competitive by nature but maintain a sense of respect and fraternity, even with starting shirts on the line. Quite often these guys will be your mates as well as your positional rivals and you will, by fulfilling similar roles, spend most of the training week together. If you don't get on, or at least make an effort, then life can get very awkward very quickly.

Ed Barnes had spent a whole year at Narbonne without exchanging a single word with his rival for the ten shirt, assuming from his detached manner that he couldn't speak English. Ed was learning French as it was his first season in France and resigned himself to spending a year not talking to his colleague. He was shocked at their end of season social when the guy offered him a beer in perfect English, meaning that he'd chosen to spend the entire season not communicating with him.

Until this final season in Rouen, I'd never had what I'd call a bad relationship with a teammate. Of course, there were some who I didn't get to know that well, or who I had little in common with. I'm sure there were probably one or two who thought I was a dick but at least they kept it to themselves. For this final year though we signed another centre, a French guy, who was insufferable.

The guy was patronising, a liar and would go out of his way to get one up on you at training. Now, training involves an element of competition and that's fine. This guy was a cheap shotter, dropping the shoulder on people in games of touch and using his knowledge of the calls to rush out of the line and spoil drills for the attacking team.

One aspect of being a professional is knowing what to let go in sessions. By all playing for the same club, you all know the calls and plays, or at least you should; we had a lot of players who never got to grips with our plays or structure, even after a couple of seasons and explaining the basics to them repeatedly was exhausting. Anyway, for a session to be worthwhile, sometimes you have to feign ignorance to the calls or to the pattern unfolding in front of you, otherwise you can just ruin every single play immediately. A good team trainer will usually make a deliberate choice, leaving the attack with a potential solution that they need to figure out in the moment. A bad team trainer or dickhead will just spoil the play in order not to 'lose', stopping anyone from doing any meaningful practice.

That was this guy's specialty and he combined it with a sense of entitlement, explaining extremely basic things to other players as if he was dispensing some sort of enlightened advice. He also had some odd mannerisms, speaking very curtly to everyone and demanding things all the time. I felt sorry for him when he did his ACL in preseason as injury is a long and lonesome road but I did not rue his absence from the training field. Not one bit.

What his absence did do though was increase the training load for me and PJ, the only two specialist centres now that Gabin had established himself as a winger. Lacking reserves meant that we were obliged to do almost every run through in practice and the lack of monitoring software like a GPS tracker or heart rate monitor meant that we were flying blind, probably covering far more ground than most of the other players. PJ was one of the oldest players in the squad while I was turning 30 that year. Probably not coincidentally, both of us succumbed to soft tissue muscle injuries later in the season; these could have been merely unfortunate but it's very possible that they were due to the accumulation of wear and tear; we were overworked, our conditioners not having the requisite data or authority to challenge our workload.

The rise of Gabin also coincided with the decline of Marno as he struggled to come back from his own ACL injury from the previous season. Where he had been a rampaging force of nature, he now looked timid and slow off the mark, even if his physical test scores and sprint times were just as good as the previous year. He had no help from the coaches and was castigated for any error, only making him more likely to commit another. He found himself playing in the B team, a hard place to find your form due to the vast discrepancy in skill level and the sheer alienness of their play. All of this made him miserable and seemed like a real waste of someone who could have been one of our best players.

Our last game before Christmas was away at St Médard, the site of an embarrassing away defeat the previous year. This time we ran out easy winners, Josh finally showing the quality that he had on the field with a couple of tries and we packed up to head back to Rouen. The bus was a boozy one and Hilly really pickled himself, taking himself off at a services to be sick before passing out for the rest of the journey back. You could tell that the stress had been getting to him as, although he regularly enjoyed some drinks with us in the previous seasons, he'd begun to distance himself and not do the same this year, a manifestation of our changing relationship as we became employees rather than the partners in the venture that we'd been previously. This was evidently a bit of a letting off of steam and he was left in peace to sleep at the front of the bus.

The problem with this was that it caused a power vacuum for the rest of the journey as there was no one to answer to in the event of bad behaviour. We had signed Siaosi Fono, a formidable number 8 from Massy who had run the ball back at us like a charging bull in a friendly the previous year and he was beginning to loosen up after a few drinks. Sia was something of a replacement for Semi and although he wasn't as big, being only slightly taller than me, he was built like a brick shithouse, bench pressing the heaviest dumbbells in the gym with contemptuous ease while his gold teeth and braided hair made him look like a cross between the Predator and a South Sea Island pirate.

Basically, if Sia fancied doing something, there wasn't going to be much you could do about it and as he got more inebriated, he began to rampage up and down the bus, slapping heads on his way past as even our biggest props in Boya and Wilf didn't fancy telling him to stop.

We would commandeer the back of the bus, by now being the old stagers of the side and Fono spied Luke, ensconced in the corner minding his own business. He had a bone to pick with Luke and started rumbling towards the back seat. Dave Markham, our mighty second row from St Helens, realised what was happening and slipped out of the way into one of the spare seats, cementing the nickname 'Brave Dave' as he ran away from trouble like Brave Sir Robin from Monty Python.

I saw him coming, although, thinking that Luke had seen him, I didn't move until he was right on top of him. The look of sheer terror on the Bean's face was quite something but fortunately, Fono didn't really go for him. I was there behind him in case he did but I doubt I could have done anything other than annoy him further. We eventually talked him down a bit, letting him stagger back down the bus to find some more beer and be distracted by someone else.

Fono was an odd character. When he arrived, it wasn't entirely clear if he could speak much English but he was equally unforthcoming in French, despite being married to a French girl. Drinking was a bit of a problem for him, making him more unintelligible than normal and he would often stay out till the early hours after games, no one able or willing to convince him to go home. He could be dangerous on the field, happy to run the ball back hard, but he could also stop before contact and offload the ball, neutralising the threat he posed when charging at full tilt. We got away with it this time as he ended up peacefully drinking away, the threat of violence having dissipated.

Violence between members of the team became more prevalent in this final season as frustration with our predicament and the increased competition for places led to the odd outbreak. It must be said that most of the violence occurred away from the training field where it would have been more acceptable, tending to happen under the influence of alcohol as grievances were aired, exceptions taken and peacemakers sought.

Our training had become more brutal though. It's fair to say that rugby is a rough old game and that's part of the appeal for players and supporters but it's amusing that older players lament the 'good old days' when tackles were lower, players were slimmer and big hits were rarer. These guys often neglect to mention that this 'ye olde rugby' was full of actual violence which if it happened next to the field rather than on it, would see you in a cell, barred or padded.

France is a little more connected with the past in this respect, an in-game brawl or *bagarre générale* being something that people look forward to, and their ideas about what constitutes effective training also take something from this approach. As his tenure continued, Hilly, a man who always enjoyed the brutal element of the game as a player, saw fit to include more and more contact work in training, to my mind visiting his frustrations on us players and enjoying the ensuing carnage.

Our forwards were often exempt from this by being so poor at set piece, their ineptitude working in their favour. They were dispatched to the other training field where the scrum machine was situated, moving their lax and ineffective sessions away from the keen eye and boiling temper of the Old Peanut as he was becoming known. He would instead visit his rage upon us little backs, making us do interminable tackling drills including the dreaded *plaquage offensif*.

Plaquage offensif was a horrible drill where you would make an arbitrary number of tackles, usually 10, at full impact, the padded-up ball carrier unable to choose a direction and obliged to take the tackle on the worst terms possible. This was carried out in an aggressive environment where we were exhorted to '*termine sa carrière*'[2], and were given extra reps if we tackled someone too softly. Phrases like this had once been tongue in cheek but his hostility towards us had increased markedly and now he seemed perpetually on the edge of getting angry about something or other.

This sort of drill is where a GA or Gentlemen's Agreement can come in. No one really wants to be doing this and the ball carrier can make himself as easy to tackle as possible while the tackler can put a big hit on without following through too hard, meaning that you end up on the ground quickly but with a smaller amount of force. Even this will lead to eventual pain and sometimes carrying the ball in softly is more likely to end badly for you, especially if the tackler is someone less 'gentlemanly' than yourself, perhaps someone keen to make a point or just someone who wants to exorcise some psychological demons. That's when laxity in the tackle can cost you and there were certainly players worth avoiding in these drills who would run into you in an awkward manner, perhaps presenting themselves hip first thereby inviting you to knock yourself out on them.

Marno was one of the most gentlemanly in the squad, managing to go down incredibly quickly upon being hit for someone of his size, looking like you must have used some force when he just had an incredible gift for simulation. A true Gentleman like him was someone worth seeking out for this particular drill.

Plaquage offensif was basically a sort of legalised assault which was also bad practice, involving not much relevance to a real match whatsoever. No ball carrier ever runs like that and the stakes are both higher and lower at the same time; it's pointless yet needs doing properly, both to make sure that it finishes and that you don't get hurt. When I explained this drill to some of my non-rugby playing friends, they were horrified, another instance of how you normalise the brutality of the game as a player.

If the mighty forwards deigned to join in, they would often go with some of the backs, making the drill far harder for their lightweight brethren and making their own practice essentially worthless. The drill removed the possibility of using your speed or footwork with the attacker running straight across a grid and waiting to be levelled by a defender. Skinny Kevin Milhorat was highly sought after, his 80kg frame coupled with the removal of his ability to step making him the ideal punching bag.

Most teams do little full contact work during the season and at the top level they probably can't really afford to, such are the rates of injury in the game. We had the luxury of fewer games and a couple of longer breaks in the season, meaning that contact could always be justified, even if nearly everyone thought it was a bad idea. In the run-up to Christmas where there were no matches, there was no excuse for avoiding contact and if we weren't running, we were now beating the shit out of each other.

We suffered through our training weeks before Christmas, trying to have as much fun as possible before heading home. The club Christmas party, always a great barometer of how we were valued as players, was the worst yet with us obliged to pay to attend a buffet meal in our own clubhouse, basically a slightly better version of our post-match feeds. It was a far cry from the fine dining we'd been treated to previously and no one was too interested in it, attending under sufferance and out of respect for the volunteers and *benevols* rather than to celebrate with management.

One of the presidents, when questioned about the late payment of our salaries, said 'They're my players, I'll pay them when I want.' More than ever we were regarded as property, something that stuck in the craw of most of the lads who were now at a real divorce from the higher ups at the club. Paying to attend a derisory Christmas party was just the latest sign of how little they valued us, further fuelling rumours of the club's financial trouble.

To try and engender some festive spirit I organised another team social with only players invited and we began at our flat. The Stade

Rouennais Santa Social involved everyone buying a cheap Santa suit from the supermarket and going on a drinking rampage into the city, stopping off at the Christmas market for some *vin chaud* before continuing on our merry way to the Panda Bar for some happy hour beers. Boya sang his song, a bizarre chant sung largely in gibberish with a smattering of French and our own team Franglais, and we all chanted it as we arrived at the cathedral where the market was based.

The Rouen Christmas market is not especially noteworthy, being a relatively modest collection of huts arranged in rows in front of the cathedral but it is, for some reason, listed as one of Europe's destination markets on the Eurostar site, a spurious attempt to get people to book all sorts of trains. Taking the train from London to Rouen is quite an endeavour as you arrive in Gare du Nord but must then negotiate the labyrinthine Paris underground network, not taking the metro but the RER one stop to Gare St Lazare and boarding a service to Rouen from there.

The Parisian underground is confusing as there are multiple metro lines, like the London Underground, but also the RER which is almost layered over the metro and travels further across the capital. Buying a ticket is not an easy process and even if you manage it, you'll see people vaulting the barriers with impunity, smoking weed in the train or even as happened to me one time, people holding the barriers closed and trying to take your ticket off you. Pleading ignorance through Englishness, something that we as a nation tend to be good at, is the best course of action here and rather than further harass someone who doesn't know what they're saying, most will just give up and leave you alone.

Anyway, do not take the train to Rouen merely for its Christmas market. The associated hassle just isn't worth it.

Back in Rouen with *vin chaud* in our beards and conviviality in our hearts, you could tell that morale between the players was high, even if we were feeling increasingly isolated. Boya tellingly omitted the lines about Hilly from the song, lines that had been tongue in cheek but with an element of sincerity. Leaving these lines out showed that he had now alienated a sizeable majority of the players with his increasingly standoffish approach.

34

LA REPRISE

THE NEW YEAR WAS TO SEE A LOT OF CHANGES OCCUR AT STADE Rouennais off the field but we had to get back on with our job, even if it was difficult to see the point of it. First up we were away at Oloron, attempting to avenge our defeat in the season opener.

Oloron did us again, showing a maniacal approach to defence and dominating our forwards. We were now almost completely a full time professional operation so this was embarrassing, defeated twice in one season by an amateur team. It can happen, witness the success of Richmond in the RFU Championship who have remained resolutely amateur even as they compete against teams like Leeds and London Irish, but it's galling when it happens to you.

My opposite number was something of a pain, talking rubbish all through the match. He was one of the opposition players we'd sometimes come across who regarded us as an affront, foreign intruders in the French game, our team a bunch of overpaid mercenaries from a no name rugby area. He wasn't necessarily wrong but his recidivism is quite a throwback given the growth of the game and the decline of traditional rugby teams in France. His lack of sportsmanship was more bothersome but easily deflected.

French people seem to react very badly to jokes about their mothers. In England, these became passé long ago as 'your mum' was often used as a nonsensical retort to almost anything. The French don't see it like this and I found that when an opposition player was insulting you, he would often invoke your mother thinking that you would find this offensive.

This guy fancied himself as a bit of a wind-up merchant and said something to me along the lines of how he would have intimate relations with my mother. This is obviously basic stuff and I don't think he was expecting a response in French so I told him he was nowhere near good looking enough for my mother and that he was a pigeon.

'Pigeon' is a relatively widely used insult in English, one ice hockey player was caught on camera calling an adversary a pigeon and cooing at him, meaning you're basic and rubbish. It goes well in French because it means you're gullible or an idiot making it a very useful cross cultural insult. He didn't like this one bit.

If you can muster a comeback insult in French then they generally find it quite a shock, especially if you don't take their familial insults seriously. Often their teammates will then give them stick that a foreigner has abused them back which is a lot of fun. All in all, I've found that on pitch conduct is a bit more respectful in England than in France and players don't usually engage in much of this sort of behaviour, although it certainly does occur from time to time.

Amongst our teammates, the banter that characterises rugby clubs did exist and grew stronger as everyone became *au fait* with each others' insults. The French guys came to the conclusion that 'fuck' was the most used word in the English language and had various other epithets explained to them but I enjoyed being taught the niche insults that weren't actually very offensive.

'Ta mère boit de la Kro' is a personal favourite of mine, meaning 'your mother drinks Kronenbourg'. I always considered a Kronenbourg a mid-tier, quite inoffensive choice as a beer but in France it's considered cheap. You could get 40 small bottles for about 15 euros in the supermarket so I suppose it was pretty cheap.

Anyway, it meant that so and so's mother was cheap and would usually raise a laugh coupled with an arched eyebrow that you knew such an insult. Another one is '*tu manges pneus*' meaning 'you eat tyres'. This insinuates that you're a gypsy which French people also find offensive; it was usually directed by the French guys at each other, often at the swarthier looking individuals like Thomas and Flo.

For our part, we tried to reciprocate in teaching some turns of phrase rather than straight up insults. 'When in Rome' went down very well, even more amusing as the lads struggled to pronounce the 'R', 'Sweet Jesus' was a popular one while my favourite was teaching one of our wingers to shout 'Yours!' when kickoffs sailed over the heads of our jumping forwards, their misjudged attempts making the tumbling *ballon* someone else's problem.

We couldn't keep our end of this knowledge exchange entirely PC though as Gabin one day asked me innocently what Hilly meant when he shouted, 'Fuck me dead' at someone's incompetence in a training session. When I explained to him, translating it word for word, I realised what an odd phrase it is. Gabin just looked genuinely a bit perturbed.

My opponent and I didn't have much to do beyond insult each other as the Oloron pack mauled ours into submission. It was a sorry day out, made worse by one of the worse injuries I've seen in my time.

Zack was making his injury comeback with an outing in the B team game before ours; full of youthful enthusiasm and brio, he was keen to get back out there. An opposition player ran between him and the hard tackling Yoann Merbouti, being sandwiched by the pair of them. Zack was not a gum shield wearer and his teeth came down on the side of Yoann's head, springing up into the air and glinting in the winter sunshine before scattering themselves over the grass. Play stopped while the players hunted for the ruined teeth and Zack tried to stymie the bleeding coming from his gums.

Scandalously, one of the support staff believed Zack not important enough to warrant driving to the hospital, claiming his presence was required at our match so Yoann drove him there himself, waiting as they attempted to reconstruct his mouth. The pitchside doctor had laughed at him when he asked if he should put his teeth in milk but on arrival at the hospital he was asked why he hadn't done so already. The injury resulted in several operations, a wire grill being placed over his teeth like a downmarket rapper and the adoption of wearing a gum shield while playing.

I've never been able to play without a gum shield and have seen so many incidents of people losing their teeth. One guy at university snapped his front tooth in half in an innocuous incident and upon seeing Zack's predicament, I know I've been making the right choice. Luckily he was insured, otherwise it would have cost him thousands.

Without the gum shield, what would have been a minor collision became quite a serious injury and could be seen as a dereliction of professional duty as you've put yourself in harm's way by not wearing one. I felt tremendously for Zack as not only was he a mate and a colleague but he'd worked hard to come back from his previous injury and was now facing something that could not only keep him off the field but could change his appearance for good. He ended up recovering relatively quickly and was fortunate to not have a recurrence, especially as he would sometimes report his teeth 'feeling loose' after the copious amount of metal wire holding them in place was removed. He showed a lot of mental fortitude to not let this bother him too much and get back to playing, with a shiny new gum shield, before too long.

We then avenged our defeat against Anglet before travelling to Tyrosse, one of the more exciting teams in the pool, to face their up tempo style based around their scrum half and their rabid crowd, including the gentleman with the trolley and air horn. This was looking like being an exciting game as we picked a quicker backline and prepared to run them around.

Unfortunately, as was the case with most of our games in the south of France that year, it hammered with rain during the warm up and we took the field in extreme conditions. A *tempête*[1] had hit the south of France and we were almost blown away down in Hossegor when we went for a beachside stroll on the morning of the game. Twice during the first half both teams sought the safety of the changing rooms as we were pelted by large hailstones and the game ended in a 7-3 defeat, the conditions far too severe to really do anything.

We then got back to winning ways with a run of victories, including a big win away at Nantes. I had not travelled to this game, being granted a rest and allowing for a first appearance for our fullback Théo Platon who had not been given a sniff of first team action all year, despite being a well-rounded player, big and fast with a good left boot and coming recommended by one of Hilly's French contacts. Théo had not excelled in the B team and when I was told I was being rested to let him have a game I ventured, 'He probably deserves a go anyway', being quite pleased for him but Hilly flatly responded, 'No, he doesn't.'

Théo had played against us the previous year for Vannes but had been recovering from his own ACL injury and was let go by them at the end of the year. He was a quiet, relaxed guy and popular amongst the boys but never got a go in the team. He was unfortunate in my book and sometimes it just doesn't work out at a team, even if the ability and will are there.

After Nantes, we were back to the southwest to face St Jean de Luz. St Jean is a beautiful town north of Biarritz and we snuck out for a quiet *demi bière* the night before the game with the French lads. The dissatisfaction with what we were doing and with the way that the club was being run had strengthened our resolve to enjoy the small moments we could snatch to relax together off the field, even with a game the next day.

On the field, we were doing ok when I entered the fray. Having not played for a couple of weeks I was eager to make an impression and I went to jackal the ball in a ruck. As I was hit by the clearing player I felt my hamstring pop. I've torn hamstrings before and this felt exactly the same. I tried to get back up off the turf, partly to get back into the defensive line but partly to test if this was actually what had happened and found that I couldn't bear any weight on it. I sat back down and hoped that the next tackle wouldn't happen on top of me.

I limped off to join PJ who had also suffered a muscular injury. This meant that we had no specialist centres left although Josh had had a couple of games there by now. We watched as we ground out a narrow victory and prepared ourselves for the monotony of rehabilitation. It was the beginning of February and it usually took 6 weeks or so for this sort of injury to recover so although I was disappointed to be unavailable, I'd be back well before the start of the playoffs. I was feeling like this would be my last season at the club and I wanted to finish it on my feet and contributing, but this turned out to be some of my last meaningful action in a Rouen shirt.

35

ACTING UP

By this point, everyone was pretty thoroughly fed up with what was going on. Although there was the prospect of a change of management on the horizon, we were being ridden harder and harder by the club, having to do more and more while our personal freedoms were being increasingly curtailed.

At the same time, some guys in the team felt like they were personae non gratae, having not really been considered for selection and consistently ignored. The rugby wasn't much fun either, we'd lost some games that we shouldn't have, with a lack of effort from everyone in both our physical and mental application. Some guys were constantly asking what was in it for them, demanding that we change certain plays or tailor things to suit them specifically. It made it all very boring as we circled back around the same problems, oscillating between the same solutions we'd all heard before.

At the same time, popular guys in the team were being mistreated. Marno had been ostracised to the B team while Wame was completely on the outer, his knee failing to recover sufficiently from the minor procedure that he'd had during the first half of the season.

In professional sport teams usually carry out a physical upon signing a player, the contract being contingent on them passing. Sometimes but not too often, a club will sign a player with a preexisting condition, making sure that their insurance covers them and perhaps excluding the player from any benefits in the event of a recurrence or inability to play due to not recovering.

Physicals are big business now and the biggest sides sometimes use them to attract eyeballs. Real Madrid filmed Cristiano Ronaldo's medical and pronounced him 'physically perfect' to watching supporters from around the world. It helps that physicals can look cool, a peak athlete wearing a mask running on a treadmill or performing feats of athleticism beyond normal people.

I've been through some physicals when signing rugby contracts but they have never been too stringent. Bristol Rugby put me through a more exacting procedure than most, partly to identify areas to work on with the conditioning team, but were more concerned that I was taking the odd diclofenac than any physical issue of mine.

I didn't realise some of the consequences of taking anti inflammatories and after hearing the surprise in the physio's voice, I considered them a bit more. Rugby players do tend to chuck them down and are therefore at a risk of some awful consequences like colitis. After that little bit of research, I stopped taking them and later even halted any sort of supplementation, preferring to keep things natural. At the top end of the game you might need that extra edge but that wasn't something that concerned me later and I began to resent mortgaging my long term health for decreasing rewards.

The burden of proof is on supplements and I don't think we have enough evidence of what extended use can do to you. People used to think that taking big doses of creatine was completely safe while many things added to our natural environment end up being bad in the long run. You only have to see the impact of pain killing medication on the population of the USA or the sudden focus on how awful plastic is for the environment; two things that were initially hailed as great breakthroughs.

Anyway, our physical in France was non-existent and we signed contracts on arrival. Later we had a cursory physical examination by a doctor for insurance purposes and he wasn't perturbed by anything that turned up apart from Luke's low blood pressure.

The French physicals seemed much laxer but they vary around the country. Toulouse signed Scotland centre Marcus Di Rollo with a pre-existing heart condition that Scottish Rugby had declared safe. On arrival in Toulouse, the French doctor disagreed and refused to sign him off to play rugby, meaning that he couldn't take the field for his new team. He never played professional rugby again.

There were some guys in the team who could have done with a physical on arrival. Every year there would be a gap year player, using Rouen as a nice soft landing for his retirement and completing some study while trying to avoid taking a field at all. We'd had Anthony Vigouroux, Romain Suster and now Wame.

Wame potentially arrived with a knee injury and had an operation relatively early in the season. How the club let this one happen was beyond me somewhat as he took a similar approach to Romain, even if he had looked like a good player in preseason, old but with the nous and ball skills of a 30-cap international. A French centre did the same thing the year after I left, not playing one single game before retiring. You would think they'd learn and would start physically examining the players better.

Wame was banished from the training ground, then the gym, but they couldn't keep him from cheekily turning up at each home game to sit in the sponsors' tent and have a free lunch in his team polo. The players thought this was hilarious as someone was getting one over the club, an entity now regarded as adversarial, while Hilly hated it. At the end of sessions in our team huddle, we'd put hands in and where we once shouted 'Rouen!' we now cried 'Wame!', another small bit of black humour to help the day ease on by. At the end of the day the club had signed him on those terms; it pleased everyone to see that there was one commitment that they had to honour and that it caused them so much pain to do so.

The problem is that when you treat adults like children, they begin to act like them and as our alcohol consumption was now a subject of scrutiny, there was a lot more sneaking out in midweek to indulge. There was one group, largely consisting of Pacific Islanders, who called it 'going to the cinema', tending to head to the pool hall and drink pints. There were the younger French lads who would seemingly drink most nights in their apartment on the other side of the city and there was us foreigners, who had largely kept a lid on things to this point.

Bolty's birthday saw a diplomatic incident erupt as a seemingly innocent trip to happy hour at the Berthom, a bar replete with heady Belgian beer options, turned into a rampage, the initial plan to go for a pint followed by a burger completely forgotten in the name of La Chouffe.

Chouffe is a devilishly strong beer, 8% strong, with a little gnome perched innocuously on the label. It doesn't necessarily taste strong but it will get you. That night it got the Bean early. I found him being sick in the urinal after two or three pints, him begging me to take him home. I did, leaving him with a variety of hangover aids by his bed, before returning to the bar just in time to catch our second row as he toppled backwards into another table, carrying him outside and depositing him on a bench.

He was so far gone that I had to take him to hospital. En route I received a furious text from Hilly; we'd been rumbled after someone had posted a picture of our mate in an unholy mess.

I had to do all the admin involved with leaving the stricken fellow at the hospital, giving them my number in case of emergency before holding him on his side so he fell asleep in a safe position.

I made it to the gym in the morning having had three hours sleep after sorting out my mate and making sure he got home. I did my weights session, only to see the Bean spend it lying on the floor, something that did not help Hilly's already aroused temper and he had a go at us when we were on our way out. I was angry as I'd not really had any fun or any beers, having spent my night running around getting everyone else home. Getting bollocked for no reason made me more determined to make up for it another night; childish but natural.

The club were constantly talking about how we needed to play well for the future of the project and that we had to remain professional, even as they acted in an increasingly adversarial and onerous manner towards us. The state of the project was sort of embodied by the current state of the Mermoz, halfway between a new training facility and a tired old municipal rugby ground.

Stade Rouennais wanted to redevelop the Mermoz and although this was underway, it had slowed, with the mooted artificial pitch being altered and delayed. Stadia in France are usually publicly owned which meant for us that every day would see local schools come to use the muddy athletics track for PE or the odd personal trainer making clients run up and down the stone steps. Buying or redeveloping a ground means that you must provide similar access for the public or purchase the whole site.

Another option would be to move to the football stadium which was a ready-made solution. Against this was that it was an old ground and although we'd sold out for a one-off occasion on a Saturday night, our usual attendance of about 1000 would make for a sorry atmosphere on a usual Sunday afternoon match.

This dilemma led to some odd negotiations where the club wanted public funding to cover the costs of redeveloping the ground while hanging the threat of moving to another publicly owned stadium if this wasn't complied with. To further complicate things, the president's company, who were heavily involved in the construction of public works around Rouen, would bid for the contract, meaning that he would be paid taxpayers money to refurbish the ground of his own rugby team.

In the end, some minor improvements were made to the ground and the president lost out in the bidding to one of his rivals, who took great delight in plastering his advertising around the place while work was going on. Most of the ground remained resolutely old hat, the stands undeveloped with stone benches ringing the field, the clubhouse and offices were still housed in Portakabins and there were no toilets apart from those in the dressing rooms, meaning spectators would either have to venture in there or go al fresco, something that to be fair, was common in France. Hospitality was conducted in a tent at one end of the pitch, just beyond the shale athletics track that skirted the pitch itself.

The new, full size 4G training pitch arrived around Christmas time in this final season, situated behind the main stand, with an enormous concrete wall along the far side and a new hotel under construction which would make up the clubhouse bar at the roadside end. Visiting teams would probably stay in this new hotel and there were meant to be some player apartments included there too.

Being told to try your hardest for something that you'll most likely never see the completion of is a bit rich; when it's coupled with late pay and general ill treatment it's unacceptable.

The personal conduct of various higher ups at the club, board members and the like, had previously been a source of mirth but now, as their bad behaviour extended to us, it became clear they weren't trustworthy people. Philandering was a problem for them and there was a big incident with one and his girlfriend's daughter at a home match, a community coach seeing them sat in a car together when he went behind the stand to relieve himself. Speaking candidly to one of the B team players, he swore him to secrecy, only to find that this guy went and told everyone, resulting in the girlfriend running away in tears and our senior official running after her up the road. It must have been awkward at the dinner table that evening.

Another was renowned for his taste for foreign prostitutes, despite being married. In preseason, he collared Joe and I to ask us about our holidays and we vaguely told him what we'd been up to while we were lacing up our boots. As he was describing some charitable work that he'd undertaken during the summer, we felt bad and that maybe we'd got him wrong before, until he went on to brag about his various assignations and how much fun he'd had. Joe was laughing hysterically while I tried to keep a straight face as one of my bosses told me how much he enjoyed the company of sex workers.

Sex workers are something that do seem far more socially acceptable in France than here. There are far more of them working on the street and they were often spoken about jocularly by the old boys at the club. Joe and I went to a concert in Brussels and were questioned on our return about how much fun we'd had with the prostitutes there. Pleading ignorance, they informed us that Brussels is one of Europe's finest destinations for that sort of thing and that we were surely liars. It's not my thing at all and our difference of opinion regarding this behaviour was quite stark.

Adultery itself isn't regarded as a big deal in France, the main thing being to avoid embarrassment rather than refraining from doing it in the first place. The President of France at the time, François Hollande, was caught commuting to his own extracurricular assignation and the problem wasn't that he was on his way to see his mistress but that he wouldn't even drive himself there, instead riding on the back of a scooter driven by one of his bodyguards. The French public regarded it as a weaselly way of conducting an affair, known colloquially as *le cinq à sept* or the hours of five to seven after work when it's possible to fit in a stop on the way home. Our management were also being caught with their trousers down, not having the cash or the inclination to carry on supporting the project they'd begun. It was beginning to look bleak for Stade Rouennais Rugby.

36

THE TAKEOVER

WITH THE RUMOURS OF THE PRESIDENTS PULLING THEIR MONEY out and a series of late salary payments, spirits had not been high and the future of Stade Rouennais Rugby had been in question. Semi had smartly got out of there right at the beginning of the year and now everyone else was considering their own position. Would the club carry on existing and if it did, would it even be able to challenge for promotion the next year? If either of those questions couldn't be answered then jumping ship was probably the best option.

I was continuing to question what I was doing playing rugby at all. The year had been ok prior to Christmas as we'd played some reasonable rugby but it was all for nothing; we were playing out a pointless year. I turned 30 in January and rugby had been a lot of fun but it wasn't going to earn me any more money and I could only have a few years left playing at the most. I'd see what happened over the next couple of months and revisit the question later in the year.

In terms of the club's situation, there were some huge developments. Olivier, our absentee conditioning coach, had been beavering away behind the scenes and had, with Hilly, been out hunting for potential investors to take over the club. This had been a discreetly conducted process but it began to emerge that they had found an interested party, a local businessman with a large enterprise supplying wooden pallets named Jean-Louis Louvel.

Jean-Louis had left school at sixteen and started his business. Now a middle-aged man, he was wildly successful and increasingly influential in Normandy, his business reputation and financial clout giving him the political influence in Rouen that our current presidents lacked.

He had taken some of the profits from his original business and created a funding vehicle for local entrepreneurs, with a purpose-built coworking and office space being built on the neglected side of the River Seine, not far from our Stade Mermoz. Here was a man who could pull off large projects, access public money, turn a profit and who supported positive local endeavours. The only problem was that he was not a rugby man and that he would need the approval of the club's members to depose the presidents in situ.

His disinterest in rugby was quickly overcome as he attended some of our sponsor events and watched a few games. Later he would even personally run the club's social media accounts, flying to distant away games on his private plane and most crucially, hanging on every one of Hilly's words.

The club had found their man and the presidents realised that a coup had taken place right under their noses. An election of sorts was called at the club AGM which for the first time we were told was compulsory to attend. We listened to some guff from the outgoing man about the healthy state of the club's accounts, him milking the stage for the final time, before being handed various pieces of paper to write our names on and sign. We didn't even have to fill in what we were voting for; that would be done for us afterwards. Jérémy filled in five or six forms to include his absent family members. It was a democratic process of which various totalitarian regimes would have been proud.

As players, the whole rigmarole was hilarious and while we all commented on the lack of democracy involved, we were happy to go

through with it. These guys had toyed with our livelihoods, threatening to pull our jobs and homes out from under us and shown a
consistent lack of humility in their dealings with everyone. This was
a deserved comeuppance.

Jean-Louis was swiftly installed as the new president of the club.
Marc-Antoine was kept on as a board member while Henchard was
cast out, leaving the tent in a hurry once his accounting presentation
was finished. The coup was swift and bloody but the future of the
club looked a lot brighter.

Immediately there was a better atmosphere. Our pay arrived on time
and in full and the new president would put money behind the bar
after each home game, much to the chagrin of the Peanut. There was
nothing he could do though as the players helped themselves liber-
ally, eager to show their appreciation to the new boss who would
hang around and drink with the team.

There was some residual bitterness from the outgoing men and
Philippe did not let sleeping dogs lie, posting a series of comments on
the club's official Facebook page. Jean-Louis, after a few post-match
bières, took him to task publicly about the parlous state of the club's
finances and saying that the players would like to scrummage him
due to the late payment of our wages. After that Philippe would
come to the home matches and didn't seem to hold much resentment
towards the club; whether this was the case or whether he was
making some sort of point I don't know but we were pleased to see
the back of him as our employer, if only for the more reliable cash
flow that we could now benefit from.

For the longer away games we would now leave two days in
advance, usually completing a light training session the morning
before the game and spending the afternoon either at leisure or doing
some sightseeing. One of the ways we'd been sold this diminished
season was with an email that said we could visit some 'interesting'
towns in the south west, something that wasn't too achievable if we
turned up at dinner time the night before the game, so at least this
promise had been belatedly fulfilled.

One of the great frustrations of playing in France was the sheer amount of travel that had to be done. In Fédérale 2 there were some longer trips but most of the games were within a few hours' drive, not dissimilar to playing in the UK. Once we were promoted to Fédérale 1, our previous longest journeys became the norm. Spending your whole Saturday sat on a bus to Bordeaux is not only boring, it's incredibly frustrating that you will arrive just in time for dinner and bed when one of France's most exciting cities is just there, tantalisingly out of your reach. We stayed in Bordeaux several times before having the opportunity to even go for a walk in the centre, particularly irritating when the French guys keep telling you how fun a place it is.

The bus is not a civilised way to travel when fifty men are cramped into small seats with not much in the way of entertainment. Jean-Louis was much happier to splash out for the train than the previous regime; we still had to take a coach to Gare Montparnasse which took about two hours but then we could have a leisurely breakfast and spend the train journey wandering around socialising if we so desired. Being able to walk up and down alleviates much of the stiffness that results from sitting on a bus for eight or nine hours and just feels like less of a chore, even if the whole journey would probably take a similar amount of time due to waiting, changing onto coaches and the associated delays that occur with public transport.

Jean-Louis is still the president now and is very serious about advancing the project. He doesn't necessarily conform to the French president stereotype as he acknowledges his lack of a rugby background; there are numerous examples of interventionist presidents who sign players no one has asked for or who come into the changing rooms during half time. Mourad Boudjellal, the Toulon president, sent the team back on the bus rather than on the plane that they had scheduled after a poor performance away from home. If you have one of these guys and benefit from their largesse then you should accept their vicissitudes and although the atmosphere with Jean-Louis was convivial, his business background meant that a lack of an immediate result was not acceptable or explicable to him.

He came into the training ground later in the year after the team had secured a place in the next round of the playoffs. The second leg performance had been very poor but the first leg had been an enormous win; we were through by virtue of our early excellence. He did not see it like this and upon being greeted with smiles by the squad, asked us why we were grinning having just lost a home game.

He had a point but it was the difference in attitude that was immediately apparent. One loss would see him looking for reasons why and a lack of rugby knowledge could mean repercussions for someone who fell afoul of this inclination, rightly or wrongly.

37

INJURY

Injury is unavoidable in rugby. Eventually you will get hurt. Somehow.

Even if it's not severe it can hurt. It might not stop you playing or even training but it can slow you down, affect your mood and become a problem.

Injury and pain is so subjective; what seems a problem to one person doesn't to another. You also can't gauge people's experience of pain and sometimes people are judged for refusing to do certain things or avoiding drills or exercises for reasons that aren't deemed sufficient.

During my time at Pirates I had a quad complaint that we couldn't get to the bottom of. It would lack power or be unable to fully contract sometimes, meaning that I felt it could 'go' at any point. It wouldn't 'go' in terms of a pull but it would stop being able to function properly. This sounds nebulous and it was; no one could decide what the problem was.

One day I said after the morning's sessions that it didn't feel right and that I'd like to not train that afternoon. Our physio, someone who is meant to look out for my interests, told me that there weren't enough players and that the coaches wanted me to train. To be fair, I should have told them to stuff it myself.

During training, I felt my quad 'go' and was sat on the floor as the physio ran over.

'I told you.'

They couldn't say anything. I had told them and this was the result.

In France, we were often told to train without much basis. An injury was diagnosed by the coach sometimes, 'it's just a bit of [insert problem]', and he would try to pressure you into training with an injury. This was quite inconsistent and subject to his changing moods. If he was relaxed he wouldn't be that bothered. If it was someone he didn't like at that point, someone who was underperforming or he was just in a bad mood then he'd pressure them to train.

Some injuries are worse than others and some you can suffer through. I played half a season with a dislocated a/c joint in my shoulder that hurt like hell. When I did the other shoulder, it didn't seem that bad. They both protrude now but don't really cause me any problems. They just look slightly unusual.

Some injuries end careers. Aurelien Diotallevi, our number 8 from Nevers was an obvious leader; he even looked like a benevolent Roman Emperor, handsome, tall and lean with a prominent nose and dark hair. He was a relaxed, experienced player who held sway with the French guys and had a refreshingly *laissez faire* approach to our structure and calls. In drills where you were meant to select a move, he would look outside to you and say quietly,

'Feelings.'

This is what you think of when you think about French rugby; playing by feel and off the cuff. Sadly, this is not necessarily true these days but Aurelien was someone who believed in his country's capacity for invention and flair. It was great to see this from someone who had experienced a lot of rugby but retained their basic joy of playing.

Unfortunately, he did his knee a couple of games into the season, rupturing his ACL. At his age, the length of the rehab meant he decided to retire with the injury and begin life after the game. He was a big loss to the team and to the squad off the field.

Everyone gets hurt at some point and I've been fortunate that I never sustained a really severe injury. You remember the near misses; when my boots got stuck in the turf during a university training session, managing to just whip my leg out from under me before something bad happened or when my jarred knee resulted in just a minor knee ligament tear rather than a major one.

The injury I sustained at St Jean de Luz was an odd one. Rather than being a muscle tear, the rehab for which I was quite well versed in, this was a tear of the fascia that bound the separate hamstring muscles to one another. The resultant gap between the previously bonded fascia had become a haematoma and I would have to avoid aggravating it or I could need an operation to remove the blood clot. For the meantime, I would have to do literally nothing.

Rehabbing an injury is boring but there is usually quite quickly something that you can do, however small. In this case though, I was told to remain immobile and even to avoid any upper body work to begin with, leaving me with absolutely nothing to do and days stretching out interminably in front of me.

An injury can make you feel utterly useless. Confined to the touch-line, not able to join in with the others and spending hours in the gym or in physio appointments makes for a solitary existence and it's easy to get down. If life isn't offering much in other respects then it can be a tough period for a player. I found during this last season that it only got tougher.

After weeks of inaction, followed by a few weeks of intense physical work involving swim fitness sessions without using my legs, upper body weights and lower body rehab, eventually making it back to running and changing direction, I was back and included for our first playoff game, a scheduling quirk meaning a trip away to St Jean de Luz where I'd sustained the original injury.

The day before we'd used our spare afternoon to take the minibus into San Sebastian and go for a walk. St Sebastian is beautiful, a city right on the beach with one sheltered by the natural harbour and another facing the ocean that attracts surfers. Apparently, it's got the highest concentration of Michelin star restaurants in the world but our tastes were simpler, instead getting some ice creams and heading for the harbour to people-watch.

Visiting these sorts of places was one of the great joys of playing rugby in France and I would always try to say yes to any sightseeing opportunity, no matter how tired or disinterested I was. I was rarely, if ever, regretful that I got out there and looked around. Indeed, I was usually the unofficial tour guide when we went somewhere new, planning a vague route around and leading a group of like minded wanderers through a European town. I'd been to St Sebastian before and remembered the claustrophobic streets of the old town, lined with pintxos bars where old boys leaning on tables chewed cocktail sticks and drank thin glasses of cold beer.

Too much walking around though did for me this time and my calf tightened up a bit. It seemed not too bad and having already taken up an inordinate amount of the physio's time, I didn't disturb him further. This was a mistake.

The next morning, I went for another walk, hoping it would loosen off. It didn't. Before the game, I had some treatment and some strapping, trying to go carefully in the warm up but not feeling right. I was on the bench as it was my first game for six weeks and although I was twitching to get involved, I felt like my calf was going to go.

When I was called to go on, I said that Zack should go on instead. It was one of our best performances of the season and although I really wanted to join in, I knew it was the right thing to do. Later in the game though, the Bean needed to go off with his own muscular complaint and I went on, hopeful that I'd last the final 15 minutes without mishap.

I pinched a turnover on our own line, pleased that my hamstring didn't go like the previous time, setting up a break by our replacement scrum half Erwan. I followed the break but felt my calf imme-diately, unable to run at any speed. Luckily, no one tested me for the rest of the game and I made it to the final whistle, applying some judicious effort to not break out of a jog.

I'd pulled my calf muscle and would not be available for the next game. It didn't seem too bad though and I was to begin treatment immediately. Hilly was encouraging, saying that he wanted me back and in the team for the final as we looked like going all the way. I was a bit down to get hurt again but had a target for my recovery; to get back and in the team for the semi-finals.

38

ATHLETIC CAPACITY

YOU KNOW AS A SPORTSPERSON THAT THERE WILL COME A DAY where you stop. When you're a young player you don't even consider it. You're fresh most days and can train and train. You certainly don't consider what you'll do when you finish which is a mistake. A very common mistake.

In my last year in France I felt my declining athleticism. It was partly due to the conditioning not being super dialled in and scientific. All the players largely did the same exercises and even the same rep ranges, despite our wildly differing personal and positional requirements, but now we didn't have the leeway to deviate from what we were being told to do like we did under the lax Olivier regime.

It wasn't just that though. I didn't have the same zip off the mark, despite being fit and strong. My hips felt stiff, even with all the stretching and sauna I was doing. There were certain bits of tightness I couldn't alleviate, even with therapy and extra work.

We did speed sessions later in the year and I would be in the fastest group. Previously I might have won a few races but now I would be lucky to win one or two. I got very fit while I was injured and felt like I could run quickly for a long time but in terms of top line, off the mark pace, I felt like I was getting worse.

It's quite dispiriting to be aware of your lessening capacity, knowing that you won't be as fast as before. You know you're over the hill and are in a battle with yourself, not for higher performance but to prevent too precipitous a deterioration.

My test scores weren't even bad. I was too tired to do the initial sprint tests but could do the change of direction ones later in the week and came out near the top of the class as I did in the strength tests. I could access some of my zip but not consistently and not without some preparation. You begin to envy the guys that can go straight onto the field and kick a ball, something you're always warned off doing even as an academy kid. I had begun to feel like I couldn't even kick a football without a warm up.

Older players do need different training loads with optimised schedules and programs to remain effective. Even guys like Cristiano Ronaldo are obviously slower, still able to access incredible reserves of power and spring but unable to access the repeatability that they had as younger players. LeBron James spends over a million dollars a year on his physical upkeep and is known for physically coasting over the gruelling 82 game NBA regular season.

Getting older makes you realise just how good the guys are who change their game as they age, remaining relevant and effective at the top level of competition. My playing idol as a young player, and as an adult really, was Brian O'Driscoll. This is an easy case to make as he was consistently brilliant throughout his career but what really set him apart was that he didn't remain brilliant for the same things. His hat trick against France and his try against Australia for the Lions were the acts of a young, fearless player with speed to burn. By the end of his career he had slowed down considerably but was much smarter, able to offload, had developed a kicking game and was rightly feared for his ability to pinch the ball in the breakdown. The sight of him sitting down after being substituted in his final Ireland match was fantastic, grinning at the reception he was receiving, a man seemingly completely content with his body of work and achievements in the game.

If these all time greats at the top of their sports aren't immune to the ravages of time then what chance did I have in the French third division with limited access to therapy or a moderated training load?

No chance.

Physical decline is something that's easy to rib someone about, speed being an obvious one as it's so visually apparent. You almost start to feel a bit defensive about it and second guess if you really did feel great all those years ago or if you've just forgotten the old tiredness and made out to yourself that this is new. I used to sleep in the afternoons and be stiff as a younger player but never doubted what I could do physically or if my body would hold up. Once this doubt creeps in, it's hard to shake it out of your head.

The fact that we were now even doing speed sessions was quite an advancement from where we were when we arrived. The French guys were far more engaged with their strength and conditioning, even if there were still some (hilarious) areas for improvement.

The new conditioners were full of beans, tracking everyone's scores and physical output as well as they could considering they lacked the equipment of top rugby environments where GPS tracking and heart rate monitors are the norm. We were tested intermittently throughout the season and gave RPE (Rate of Perceived Exertion) scores after each session. I'm certain that this data was largely ignored by Hilly who didn't set much store by data when it contradicted what he wanted to do.

Nevertheless, this was the most professional that the club had ever been and being motivated little fellows, our conditioners Owen and Nick were keen to keep improving the environment. In the kaizen spirit of continuous improvement, they came in one day with a piece of paper for everyone, divided into days of the week with boxes to record everything that you'd eaten over that period. Nothing too extreme or ridiculous, just asking some supposedly professional athletes what we were eating.

This initiative threw the squad through a loop. Guys who knew that their diet was subpar didn't want to do it and kicked up a fuss whilst the French guys, never having had to analyse what they were eating, were a bit confused as to what they were being asked to do.

Owen approached me in the gym with little Erwan Nicolas in tow. Erwan was a young, powerful scrum half, able to do a backflip from a standing start and a good player, even if he could have possibly been a bit fitter. He spoke little to no English and Owen's French wasn't up to explaining the concept of a food diary, hence the need for my involvement.

'*J'ai pas compris,*' Erwan told me, looking at the empty grids where his food intake would go.

Owen told me what he wanted; the grid was laid out to incorporate three main meals with three snacks in between. Not too tough to grasp. We told Erwan that we'd start that day and fill in the first box together.

'*Tu as mangé quoi pour ton petit déjeuner aujourd'hui Erwan?*' I asked innocently. He turned red, seeing that Owen was about to write down whatever his response was. I was excited now. Owen was getting annoyed at the delay and asked what it was again.

'*Un Kitkat.*'

Owen was incredulous, Erwan looked sheepish so I asked him if it was a Kitkat Chunky or Peanut Butter, just to get things completely clear.

News spread around the squad and when it became clear that some of the other breakfasts were less than ideal, Thomas was dunking cookies into a bowl of hot chocolate, the issue was addressed by Hilly in our team meeting before training.

'Now, make sure you all fill out your food diaries to help our conditioners out; this is important and needs doing properly.'

Fabien, our captain, patted his growing belly and said,

'*C'est nécessaire que je marque chaque bière que je bois aussi?*' / Do I need to write down each beer that I drink as well?

The room fell about laughing and this sent Hilly over the edge.

'You bunch of cunts! You're supposed to be professional athletes and I find out you're eating fucking Kitkats for breakfast [more laughs] Don't laugh! You're going to do this properly and from now on, you write down every fucking thing you put in your mouth!'

At this point our gay teammate, perfectly positioned on the front row of seats, put his hands behind his head and started laughing loudly. Everyone cottoned on and the room completely fell to pieces. Hilly realised what he'd inadvertently said and tried to recover,

'Jesus, not everything you put in there, everything you fucking eat!'

But it was too late. The tension was defused and we filed out for training. The food diary did get completed with Luke and I raising eyebrows with the variety of our meals. We didn't have much else to do so trying out different recipes was one way that we kept ourselves amused. It had turned out that other peoples' habits were amusing too, just for different reasons.

By this time, we knew the best places around the city to source a great variety of foodstuffs and so were eating like kings in our apartment. We'd eat our own healthier twist on *moules frites* on a Friday, availing ourselves of the fresh (and cheap) produce from the Normandy coastline and would often take a stroll around the markets on a Sunday morning before a game to stretch the legs and pick up any regional delights on offer.

We got to know the more industrial butcher, situated on the outskirts of the city, where you could purchase huge joints of belly pork or whole shoulders, boxes of chicken and trays and trays of eggs for very reasonable prices. We did tend to avoid the horse meat butchers as a matter of course but halal butchers would often have great deals and were very friendly, surprised to hear our English accents in their establishments.

These culinary escapades didn't always go well; I once walked into our flat and was assaulted by the smell of sewage and the sound of incredulous laughter. Joe and Luke had purchased a mixed selection from the butcher and had unknowingly set about cooking up some andouillette, a sausage like dish made with intestines which I never want to experience again. We couldn't believe that this was something people ate and needless to say, we did not eat it.

On a more pleasant gastronomic note, Normandy is a region of apples and dairy with a smattering of seafood and this would all come together once a year at la Fête du Ventre[1], a gourmands paradise where the city centre would be overrun with stands celebrating everything that the area had to offer from a culinary standpoint. Getting a vendor's attention could be difficult but we would see JP there and he would facilitate our tasting sessions.

Despite no longer receiving lessons from him, we were still close with JP and he would often invite us to his house for dinner, maybe helping him with some heavy lifting as payment, and we would also go to exhibitions of his paintings, mostly oils and watercolours of the Normandy landscape. These were often languorous evenings spent in his garden, drinking wine and chatting rugby and are some of my fonder memories of living in France.

Something that didn't fall by the wayside, even as our team morale plummeted through the floor, was that everyone would sit and eat together in the clubhouse at lunchtime. Lunch would be cooked up by volunteers or Bouly, who was a dab hand over a stove, and players and staff would sit down together and break bread over three courses. France really gets mealtimes right and this was a fine example, usually conducted with *bonhomie* and *savoir faire*[2].

In the interests of cultural exchange, we made English breakfast for some of the French guys. It went down a storm with Fabien who was a fan of the traditional fry up that we served him. He sent a picture to his dad, a big (and rotund) character at the club who called him straight back, jealous of the assortment of pork products, baked beans and fried bread that he had in front of him.

Our other communal gastronomic experience that I looked forward to were the team wine tasting sessions held in the vendor down on the quayside. We would spend an evening tasting solely reds or whites, a map of France indicating where each wine was from and JP would come and translate for the benefit of the foreigners, even if these insights were probably wasted on our less refined palates. We'd happily quaff good wine in good company though and usually would repair to the bar next door afterwards for a less refined drink to round out the evening.

39

RESPECT

ONE FUNDAMENTAL WAY THAT THE CULTURE OF THE TEAM changed was with the large influx of Pacific Islanders. The previous years had seen one or two guys from these famous rugby playing nations but in my final season, we suddenly had five and would have had another if Semisi hadn't scarpered.

I'll be speaking about these guys generally but they are just as different from each other culturally as an Englishman is from someone from the Celtic nations. Their cultures, traditions and languages are separate from each other but they have a lot in common too.

Rugby is a big employer for Pacific Islanders and due to their natural athleticism, they are prized in sports around the world, making up a disproportionate number of rugby union and league players, as well as there being a few guys playing in the NFL. Hollywood megastar and former wrestler Dwayne 'The Rock' Johnson has Samoan heritage too.

A scientific paper from 2013 presents evidence that "Polynesians are predisposed to possess physical characteristics potentially beneficial to rugby union performance". They are heavier, have more muscular limbs and smaller proportions of body fat, and can produce "greater force in explosive movements" than players of other ethnicities.[1]

A guy like me can do all the weights he wants but there will be guys of such natural ability from the Pacific Islands that it renders my efforts almost pointless. These guys are such natural movers that outrageous displays of athleticism seem easy and beautiful. This, allied with the sense of fun that imbues their existence, means they often seem to be simultaneously concentrating intently while laughing at themselves, or at you as they run around you. Top teams are now running academies in these places; Saracens have one in Tonga while Clermont have done very well from their Fiji branch; and it seems like a sensible enterprise.

In our first season at Rouen we had Fiji's record try scorer Fero Lasagavibau winding down his career with us, making a transition into coaching the B team while still playing. By our final year, he was no longer playing but retained seniority over the other guys because of his age. Fero was very warm and welcoming, often inviting us for dinner at his house where his wife Livia would cook up enormous pots of curry and chow mein, making us eat until we could no longer move.

Age is the usual signifier of seniority and determines the hierarchy between the Islander guys. The youngest ends up as a facilitator for the others; for us the youngest guy was a new arrival named Will Takai or 'Pila'.

Pila turned up in my third year at the club as a mid-season trialist during the two weeks of training before Christmas where we had no matches to prepare for. These two weeks are given over to a mini preseason, sometimes even involving an inter-squad game or if you're really unlucky, you play a 'friendly' against another team.

Pila was unfortunate to attend during a couple of days when we had a big weights and conditioning focus. We played touch games and did a lot of running, making him sick from exertion; not a great look during a trial.

This lack of conditioning was explicable due to him being in a bizarre but by no means unheard of situation in France. His previous team had folded midseason, owing him a not inconsiderable amount of money, but were still holding his registration as all the administration was sorted out, the possibility of a takeover meaning that he would not be released early. With a wife, one young child and another on the way he was not in an enviable position.

He stayed with the other Islander guys while he was on trial and I found myself alone with him at one point in Semisi's house and tried to make conversation. He was very quiet and it was not easy to get much out of him at all.

Pila signed with us for the next season and it turned out that this reticence was not really him. He is delightful, super relaxed and calm but hard working and conscientious. You would also not want to be tackled by the guy. He's about 6ft tall, not big for a back row forward, but he is stacked, with enormous calf muscles. I've seen him cause souls to leave their vessels as people don't see his stiff shoulder coming when they take short lines near the sides of rucks and although a back row, he had the skills and wherewithal to do a turn at inside centre in an emergency.

Pila was about my age, I think maybe a year or so younger. He hails from Tonga but had spent several years in France, possessing a coveted white licence, meaning that he could be selected as if he was a homegrown French player. He spoke some decent French too and was equally as respected by the French guys as he was by us.

Being the same age brings your differing backgrounds and priorities into focus; he had a family and was going to play rugby for as long as he could before taking his money back to Tonga. I had a girlfriend with no immediate plans to even live together, let alone start a family. Our worlds were so different; he seemed like so much more of an adult than me, unmoored as I was, living abroad and doing this for a living when I didn't have to. He was playing rugby as a necessity while I no longer really knew why I was playing. His world was linear and considered; mine was disconnected and vague. Discovering other perspectives is one of the beauties of rugby and Pila certainly made me consider what my place in the world was. He didn't mean to though; he was just trying to get on with his own business.

Jorick Dastugue, who hailed from the Pyrenees, was a similar character in some respects, with no higher aim in life but to retire to a small place in the mountains where he could play *pétanque* and live simply with his young family. Their quiet, modest goals jarred with what professional sport is supposed to be about and although Jorick was ambitious for his time at the club, you could see that both of them would be content to revert to a less complicated existence.

Pila was a respected guy in the squad for both his playing ability and personality. This was incongruous with his status amongst the Islanders where, as the youngest, he was effectively required to be of service to the older guys. When we socialised he would make sure everyone would have drinks to the point that it was ridiculous, topping you up or fetching you beers before you were empty to avoid sanction from his mates. It seems almost distasteful to have someone behave in such a deferential manner towards you but it's a cultural thing of theirs. To not observe this practice would seem offensive to them.

His tackling was the only thing I found offensive about him as I saw him hit a guy so hard that he basically handed the ball to him as he crumpled to the floor, certainly unconscious for a brief second or two. This was not unusual and I thought he was a spectacular player, unfairly overlooked for other back row players even though his form warranted inclusion. He wasn't the sort of guy to make a fuss and accepted this state of affairs with his customary good grace. It was probably this selfless attitude that precluded him from playing a better standard of rugby. That or the yellow cards that he received on occasion.

He objected to the violence that occasionally beset our group when we socialised too, annoyed and upset that people couldn't have a good time together without fighting and sometimes being moved to tears at the sight of people fighting each other. Drinking session fights are not uncommon at rugby clubs but they are usually totally unnecessary and monopolise the evening, being an extreme form of selfishness.

Fono and Leti were prone to these bouts of madness when drinking and due to their size, could be quite intimidating. It would usually be down to one of the other Islander guys to calm them down if this was the case but every now and again you'd just have to let them go and hope for the best.

How Islander culture reacts when combined with the western world is a fascinating thing to observe. These countries are very poor and often quite basic in terms of amenities and education so it must be jarring to end up on the other side of the world in a European country amongst all the temptations and distractions that become much more accessible.

Some of the cultural stuff is incredibly positive; the general respect for others, the fun-loving attitude to life and the reticence to give it the big I am but in other ways, it's an old culture that needs to adapt to its surroundings. If you live in another country, you need to adapt to where you are, not the other way around. Some of the respect stuff is not necessarily appropriate in the team environment and guys like Pila need not be quiet just due to being younger.

The seniority culture can be downright dangerous as upon arriving in Europe, some family members may regard them as having hit the big time, even if they are playing a lower level of rugby and aren't being paid much money. Succumbing to the pressure to help their relatives back at home can stress their day-to-day existence wherever they are, causing them problems that are difficult to broach due to their reserved nature and social isolation. There have been several suicides in France due to issues along these lines.

Respect was a value invoked not only by the islanders but by the management of the club. We were often told that we needed to respect the opportunity that we had, the club and the work that the higher ups were doing on our behalf. This respect seemed to only flow one way as we'd been almost fraudulently convinced to sign deals that weren't what we thought they were and were now being ridden harder and being paid later than ever.

Going to France means adapting to the French way. Imposing other norms or behaviours on a pre-existing environment is a recipe for rejection and disaster. We had seen this each year with guys arriving from more professional environments. Forcing professional values on the team would lead to a swift rejection. They had to be inculcated gradually. Similarly, with the better parts of what the islanders had to offer from their own culture; we could incorporate certain aspects of it into our environment and celebrate their unique ways but not at the cost of existing structures; this was something that one or two of them struggled to understand.

Coach Wayne Smith of the All Blacks describes the importance of 'connections' for performance:

> "A lot of your performance, I think, depends on the connections you have with people around you… connections with the game, but also connection with the fans of the game, connection with your family, and with each other. And generally those connections are stronger if you're a good bugger, and you do things the right way. That's where a lot of your resilience comes from, I reckon; is that you're playing for other people, as well as yourself."

I felt like this was something that had previously existed; the club had felt familial and we'd all been pulling in the same direction. It's certainly something that exists between Pacific Island players whether they are on the same team or merely in the same situation, far from home on a French rugby field. It's common to see these guys pray together before and after games and videos of their national squads performing ancestral warrior dances or singing hymns together often go viral. Fero and Pila would receive other Islanders to their houses and our away games were often attended by guys playing for clubs nearby, coming to catch up with other Pacific players.

Now that our goal had been taken away, we'd begun to separate, hang out more in our own groups and start to think 'what's in it for me?' There was nothing in it for the group so naturally, people began to play for themselves, using 'respect' as a sort of excuse to advance their own viewpoint. A selfish attitude led to the failure of some to absorb the existing team pattern and ethics; it's hard to satisfy both impulses if you feel underserved by what's happening. If you don't engage you can suit yourself at the expense of the collective. Strong environments don't do this.

We had become less resilient, prone to losing silly games and later in the year, sleepwalking through some playoff games and defending poorly. It didn't matter as we were going through anyway. Defence and kick chase tend to be good barometers of a team's attitude; when results are going well it's easy to slack off and that was the atmosphere at training; people were going through the motions, aware that this season didn't really matter and that they would probably be out of the club at the end of the season anyway.

Entropy is the continual degradation of things; if you're standing still then you're going backwards. Sport is full of such examples and the best environments are ones that keep questioning what they're doing, keep looking for new personnel to improve them and incorporate new ideas regularly. We were one of the best teams and were winning almost all the time but there were things left unaddressed as they didn't seem to matter, we were winning anyway.

It meant that playing rugby every day became joyless as people couldn't be bothered to commit to our style of play or even worse, would regularly petition to change the fundamentals of our structure. We would change it, sometimes game by game to fit certain individuals and part of this could be construed as a failure of recruitment. If you want to play a certain way then don't sign players who aren't suited to it. Square pegs in round holes and all that.

> "When you are consistent, people who work for you know who you are. When someone changes all the time, it creates a sort of confusion in the camp, people saying yesterday he was wanting to

go to the moon, now he wants to go to Mars. If you keep changing, I think it confuses your people."

— Alex Ferguson

If you're constantly flip flopping in your strategy due to the demands of players then it makes your authority as a coach seem questionable; changing because of considered feedback is a sign of strength but being constantly reactionary is the opposite.

Sometimes success can blind you to the inadequacy of your process and this was in operation here; good teams constantly concentrate on their processes, the old Bill Walsh philosophy of 'the score takes care of itself'. However, it was also a result of everyone being at loggerheads. Once everyone knew they wouldn't be sanctioned then all hell broke loose in terms of discipline. We were just riding out the season and it felt like the end of something.

40

GOODBYE ROUEN

BY THIS POINT IN THE SEASON I'D PRETTY MUCH MADE UP MY mind to leave Stade Rouennais. The year had been a nightmare, the feeling that the whole thing was a futile endeavour really bothering me and the general selfishness that now pervaded the club was something I could no longer endorse with my presence.

I was a leader in the team and had thought that a stoic response to adversity was the best approach in the first half of the season, getting on with my work, contributing to the wider life of the rugby club and playing hard on the field. Then, as the nights drew in and our pay arrived late, I became more and more dissatisfied with how we were being treated. Coupled with Hilly's changed demeanour towards us as a group and the advent of some new regulations regarding foreign players on the horizon, I thought I'd prepare myself to leave.

The new regulations meant that a team could only name six foreigners in the match day squad; currently the majority of the starting lineup was foreign, although there would be an exception for those who had been in France for a long time. Under the old white licence system, Luke, Joe and myself would have become valuable commodities the next year, able to demand a high salary to be an adaptable squad member, but these new rules made us a garden variety foreigner. Joe also made plans to leave while Luke thought he would stay another year.

Later in the season, I spoke to Hilly outside the clubhouse and he said that they would not be offering me a deal. I acted like this was disappointing, it was a bit, but I didn't want to hang around; the place was making me increasingly unhappy.

Being injured at that time of the year was a pain. The team were now embarking on the longer away trips, necessitating Friday morning departures, while anyone injured or not selected had conditioning work to do over the weekend. This led to several of us being left behind in Rouen, our only possible activities being to go to the gym, receive treatment and then drink. I was lucky that Dave Markham was injured too, he'd broken his hand punching someone in the St Jean match, and he and I embarked on various drinking sessions around the city, availing ourselves of the opportunity to go out on a few Saturday nights. I'd spend free afternoons on my bike, cycling *les quais* next to the river before catching up with local acquaintances in the various cafes and bars and exploring parts of the city that I'd previously neglected to visit.

The whole thing felt melancholic. Leaving somewhere behind is always strange and this was the longest I'd spent in one place since leaving university. I'd grown to love the city, beautiful and somewhat boring as it was, and had also been proud of the work that we'd done at the club, dragging it up from a bunch of chucklers in Fédérale 2 to the full time, promotion chasing outfit it was now. The progress we'd made and the experiences we'd shared were why this final season was so painful, why the naked self-interest from everyone was so hard to stomach and partly why I felt so sad. I'd be leaving behind not only the area and the club but all the people who'd become a big part of my life.

I looked into playing some more rugby and asked around some French teams. Foreigners were generally unappealing due to the new rules and their generally higher salaries and I only looked at teams in reasonable locations. My heart wasn't really in it and I felt that it was time to move on from rugby. How I was going to do that was less clear to me.

The best players tend to have their contracts sorted before Christmas and with their multi year deals, they don't have to confront their continued commitment to the sport each summer. At our level, contract negotiations were conducted later in the year; this is dangerous for a couple of reasons. One is that with the onset of better weather granting the ability to drive to the beach or lie on the grass stretching after training sessions, playing rugby for another year seems like a good idea. You easily forget the winter drudgery, the rolling in the snow or the misery of sessions in the driving rain. You sign on again, happy to not have to really consider what you're doing.

There's now a growing awareness about sporting retirement and I'd known it was something that I'd have to confront at some point. Questions of identity and self-worth bubble to the surface as you prepare to put something behind you that you've always loved doing but that doesn't quite do it for you anymore. I'd not achieved adulation and renown in the game, many of my ambitions had gone unfulfilled, but I'd had such a rich depth and breadth of experience, meeting so many diverse and interesting people and seeing the world, that I feared both the range of options open to me and the impending isolation that was staring me in the face. Some big choices were coming my way and I didn't feel like I knew what I was doing.

This interior turmoil isn't something that people associate with rugby players; you're often told how fortunate you are to be playing for a living while simultaneously being regarded with a bit of suspicion. Touring teams from the UK would discover our foreign enclave when they arrived and would pepper us with questions, our existence so aberrant and alien to them. What were we doing?

I'd always been happy being different and had wanted to be a good player. I'd not scaled the heights I'd hoped for but I'd had fun and been happy in France. Now I wasn't happy and I had to ask myself what I was doing. If it wasn't fun anymore then what was it? Why was it still happening? It felt more and more like I was wasting my time and that was difficult to confront.

Leaving the club also meant that I would be leaving France; somewhere that for all its imperfections I'd come to really enjoy. The rhythm of life, the quirks of the people, the general politeness of everyday life mixed with the surreptitious apathy towards order. Speaking the language, now something I could do with speed and nuance, would probably start to fall by the wayside. These were the sort of questions I pondered while cycling the banks of the Seine, looking at the enormous concrete bridge that crossed over to the new shopping centre and wondering exactly how on earth it lifted into the air every five years to let through the armada of tall ships that I'd heard about but would never see.

The problem with professional sport is that your job is so tied up with who you are. In the UK, we are all a little like this with 'so what do you do?' being the standard conversational opener, but sport can be all consuming. It dictates your life away from work as you keep up your healthy regime, or not as the case may be, and it completely dictates your life, day by day and week by week until the off-season.

Even during the off-season, I always found it difficult to completely switch off, taking maybe a week to do nothing, another week to do some light activity before working on whatever I wanted to work on for the remaining weeks. Obviously there would be holidays and the odd party in between but you're still thinking about what condition you'll be in when you get back to training.

Rugby is a masculine enterprise. You hang around with men, wrestle with men and then shower up with men. It's fair to say that it is a masculine environment, the only professional interactions with women coming either with support staff in terms of the physio and medical team or other roles in the club itself. Female rugby players contend with the traditional view that rugby is a 'man's game'.

What happens when the game stops? If all you've ever done for your work, a big part of your self-definition, is play a 'man's game' are you now less of a man? I don't think I've struggled to see myself as less of a man having found the overbearing masculinity associated with the game a bit ridiculous but I've certainly struggled with what to do next. When you've only ever done the one thing which you now have a slightly conflicted relationship with, it is tough to really make your way through what seems like an impenetrable forest of options.

The other thing that happens in a team is that you sublimate yourself to the team environment. It's hard to avoid talk of 'culture' and 'self-lessness' around professional sport. Rugby really lends itself to these messages; defensive technique is described as 'the links in a chain', 'backing up on the inside' and all the rest. You are supposed to become part of a collective and in doing so, if you're a good team-mate, you can lose a bit of yourself and what would be best for you. Sometimes you hold your tongue for the good of the group, even if you really think something. Sometimes you hold it because there could be repercussions down the line for you so it's not always entirely altruistic. Either way you're not being authentic and expressing what you really feel. I struggled with this dilemma during my final season in France.

I'd be putting all of this behind me and striking out for something new. Feeling nostalgic and perhaps searching for something authentic, I used my last months to revisit my favourite spots around the region, heading again to the beautiful village of Veules-les-Roses, where waterways snake between the buildings and cress grows in abundance on the outskirts of the village. I made a few pilgrimages to Pourville-sur-Mer to swim in the cool, clear water of the Channel, walking out gradually into the sea using the stone groynes that lurch out into the blue. Dave and I used a free weekend to visit Paris and les Marchés aux Puces, the chaotic Parisian flea markets where you can find trinkets and antiques, thrift stores and high end furniture dealers, eating a fine lunch in one of the arcades with steak and *vin rouge*. I even stopped in again at Étretat, where *les falaises* form huge arches in the white cliffs, framing the sea behind. I would miss all of this.

41

EN ROUTE TO THE FINAL

AFTER MY CALF PULL IN THE FIRST PLAYOFF GAME, THE AWAY LEG at St Jean de Luz, I was in a race against my twanging muscle to get available for the final. The team were in a pattern where, as the away legs were first, they would put in a good performance and win big away before coming back to the Mermoz, concede a lot of points and cling on to make it to the next round. After beating Nîmes away by a big margin, the team came home and sustained the worst loss that I'd seen in all my time at Rouen, losing 11-31.

The poor level of performance gave me confidence that I'd be back involved from a form perspective. The home performances were embarrassing and our supporters were disheartened by the loss against Nîmes, our defence still alarmingly porous. My problem was my calf.

What hadn't been a bad injury was proving difficult to shake. I'd spend the week rehabbing, doing weights and then running shuttles up and down the side of the field with Dave while the team trained next to us. Running felt fine, I even did some faster sprints and some change of direction, down ups and pushing tackle bags; there didn't seem to be any continued fallibility to be concerned about.

When I joined back in training, the lower speed but constant running would tighten up my calf immediately and I'd have to go and sit out before I tore the muscle properly. It was immensely frustrating as I was working hard, had gotten much fitter from all the running, even with my increased alcohol consumption, but as soon as I would try to get back properly involved my body would let me down.

I joked that my body was telling me to quit; Flo even agreed with me, shouting 'It's finish for you Ben' as I strolled off to sit on a tackle bag after one such episode. It was a classic bit of rugby humour; funny but true and therefore a little painful. I think there's something in this physical manifestation of inner turmoil, your body demonstrating that you're doing something that's inherently bad for you. A chronic problem means there's something underlying that needs addressing; even if it was just my more regular drinking, that was an expression of my inner dissatisfaction, brought on by my environment.

Some of the best jokes touch on something true. While I was injured, Hilly showed us a montage of the try scoring chances we'd squandered that season, demonstrating how many points we were leaving on the table, before boosting our morale with another montage of the tries we had scored, rounds of applause coming from the group with each effort. The highlights from the first half of the season featured me quite heavily and he mentioned my name as he talked through one of the tries.

'Who?' I shouted out, everyone creasing with laughter, looking around for the joke maker. It being me only made them laugh further but it also highlighted something true; I hadn't really been a part of the team in the second half of the year, spending most of my time off the field, and this was hurtful. I wanted to be playing with the rest of the boys, even if they were still being abused for poor performances or even for some of their good ones.

They'd come off the field after putting seventy points on one team and got told that they had been 'shameful'. By now everyone had stopped listening, going through the motions in training and doing the bare minimum to get through the week, getting smashed on the train on the way back after games and ignoring any request to stop. The coaches had lost their influence over the group and knew it; with so many leaving at the end of the year there was no need to keep them in line as long as the team won; they'd be gone at the end of the season and new recruits would come in who would be more malleable.

Pep Guardiola, when leaving his great Barcelona team, said that players stop listening after three seasons or so and once they have, it's time for the coach to leave. Jose Mourinho seems to have gone one better, having two initial seasons of success at each of his teams, signing a new contract and quickly getting himself sacked in the third season, pocketing a huge payout. In football, it's easier and cheaper to fire the manager; the players have too much power.

Rugby is becoming more like this but at our modest level where salaries are lower, Hilly had all the power. He'd selected his own boss, effectively firing the old presidents and was in the process of negotiating a new contract himself. He was the most valuable employee at the club and had the ear of the new president. Moving on some players wouldn't be a problem; plenty would want to come and join the project and would not be jaded from doing the same plays for the previous three or four seasons.

Despite the joyless atmosphere in the week, we qualified for the semi-finals and began away at Lavaur. I was ok for the bench and warmed up, full of trepidation that my calf would go again. I only got on for the last fifteen minutes but it felt like a personal win as I had no repercussions. Hopefully this tedious injury yo-yoing was over.

Again, the game wasn't great and we hung on to win, their spirit breaking before the end. What made this fixture memorable was that it was the last away trip we'd do as a group.

We stayed in a family run bed and breakfast with an attached restaurant. While the pregame meal is always chicken and pasta, we arrived on a Friday evening in May to sit down for a delightful meal of duck and potatoes, sleeping in the bucolic Tarn countryside. If somewhere epitomised the French rural idyll it was this unassuming little restaurant and after Saturday's breakfast, a couple of us borrowed some bikes and went cycling through the fields and villages nearby, enjoying the peace of the long grass and each other's company.

We bussed into Toulouse for the afternoon as a team and took over a corner of a local cafe to relax over coffees. When we got back we played in the pool like children, jumping in, wrestling and playing volleyball, howling with delight when someone messed up. It was idiotic and childish but joyful and somehow appropriate. We were lost boys, drifting around France, looking for meaning and not finding it in what we were doing but in where we were and who we were with.

We beat Lavaur at home the following week; I got some time off the bench and, not really caring what happened and having a penalty advantage, picked the ball off the floor at a ruck, ran sideways and launched a cross kick straight into Marno's hands. It stopped him dead unfortunately and I'll maintain that if he'd chipped ahead I could have scored but it was fun to do it; I'd never done one in a game before and this was the last time I'd run out at the Mermoz; I deserved to do something fun.

Our win meant that we had two weeks before the final, to be played at a neutral venue in the Oyonnax stadium. We were to face Mâcon, a team we hadn't come across but one who Harry and Marno had played for previously. They might be tough but we were the favourites.

42

THE FINAL

THERE WERE TWO WEEKS UNTIL THE FINAL; THE FIRST WAS SPENT training with a bit more intensity, including sessions on the free weekend that were probably designed to keep us off the piss. We reconvened the next week to make final preparations for the game.

After we'd completed the weekend session, a few of us were sitting in front of the cathedral, enjoying an ice cream in the summer sunshine when we began to receive phone calls from Hilly. He was phoning around with selection news.

Nick Seymour was sat next to me and found out that he was to be on the bench. Luke and Bolty were as well. I received my phone call, anticipating bad news.

My phone rang and I picked up. He told me I wouldn't be in the squad as Gabin needed specialist cover on the wing. All the hard work I'd put in all year was for nothing. All the extras I'd done, all the rehab, all the team meetings and conditioning, for something I already thought was a waste of time, had been for nothing and I wouldn't even get onto the field for the final.

I was furious and embarrassed.

He said that I was important in helping the team to prepare. This is true in the regular season when squad players are important for preparation but for this week, when we wouldn't do much training, it was absolute rubbish. A load of shit.

It's not like the others were even playing well; their knockout performances had been a minor disgrace but we'd won. To take me off the bench, after barely using me on the field, was incredibly insulting.

In this situation, I would never resent the other players or hold it against them; this was the coach's decision and something to take up with him. He could deal with the resulting awkwardness himself.

I'd not been picked for things before; as a young player or when trialling for representative teams. Once, when I was the team's top scorer, I wasn't selected for a playoff game away at Bristol. Then I was asked to come and run water. The Bristol lads asked me if I was hurt and when I replied in the negative, they told me that they'd wasted time analysing me that week. I thought the coach didn't want me to have a good game against them in case they offered me a contract but this could be really wishful thinking.

That didn't hurt like this though. This felt like a real betrayal, right at the end of the four years I'd spent at the club. I hadn't got to play for promotion, that had been denied us before we even turned up for preseason, and now I wouldn't even get to play in this final. The game was essentially pointless on a deeper level, winning the trophy wouldn't mean anything, but it was still the biggest match in the club's history and my last as a professional. It turned out I'd already played that game.

We came in at the beginning of the week to find that we had season review sessions with Hilly. This is unusual in my experience and quite brave of him; many of the guys being reviewed were either not selected for the game, on the bench or leaving the club and would have a bee in their bonnet and a perfect opportunity in which to unleash on him.

Many business organisations could learn some things from professional sport but I think it's rare that a sports team conducts exit interviews; guys who are leaving could be feeling bitter but are more likely to be honest, potentially providing some useful and actionable feedback. When you consider that sport is a constant search for an edge, a small improvement, or a 'marginal gain', conducting exit interviews seem like an easy way of making positive adjustments.

I was one of the first up and had seen that he had had an awkward conversation with the previous person. I had bitten my tongue for most of the year and wanted to finally give him a few home truths.

I sat down and received my review, on a piece of Stade Rouennais headed paper. It had positive and negative points about my year.

'We don't have to do the review if you don't want to,' he said, looking at me sideways.

'No, we can do it. Why not? I've got some things to say to you too.'

We went through it point by point. It was incredibly awkward, him squirming in his seat and me furious with him.

His review was obviously justifying why I hadn't been selected. I told him that since Christmas, when he'd reviewed us and been very pleased with my contribution, I'd been selected for two games, then been injured, rehabbed to get back on the field and been involved for the semi-finals before being binned for the final.

Due to white licence requirements, some of the guys knew that they wouldn't be playing or that they would be a substitute to accommodate a lower quality player. Both our foreign second rows had skipped training in the run-up to the final, knowing full well that the French guy would start regardless as he had a white licence. I told him that he'd mismanaged guys like Marno all year, making him feel worthless and denying the team of the value he could bring. His letting go of some poor personal behaviour from some guys and not others meant that he'd lost the trust of the other players and that his constant tinkering with our plays meant the team no longer engaged with training as he compromised what we did all the time.

The final point was that I was leaving; he had no reason to keep me happy and could go back on what he'd said to me previously about getting fit for the final. He said that wasn't the case.

'I know how you speak about us; I've heard you. You say you 'need so and so' and can't upset him. You don't 'need' me. That's how it is.'

I left after that, throwing my review in the bin on my way out. I already had enough useless paperwork from the club, the contract I'd signed for that final season among them.

In sport, you are useful until you're not. The NFL stands for 'Not For Long' as there is always someone else waiting for an opportunity when you get too old, too bad, too injured or too expensive.

The only thing you can do is stay available and play well. If you do that, all manner of sins are forgiven. Drinking, taking drugs, fighting your teammates; most places won't care if you produce on the field. Good team environments do care about how their people are, not just about how they perform; you only need to look at the success of Saracens and Exeter to figure that out. We were not a good team environment.

From his perspective, I'd not been available for months of the season and had no body of work to demonstrate why I should play. If you'd played well, he'd justify picking you somehow; if you hadn't then he wouldn't have to justify anything. I just hadn't really been a part of the team for a while now. Soon I wouldn't be at all.

We trained that week and really went through the motions. The guys not involved were resentful and felt like there was no point while the team, not playing well for a few weeks now, trained quite badly. Sometimes in the run up to a big game, training poorly is normal and can almost do you a favour; you know when it's going badly and so you approach the game with no complacency. If you train brilliantly all week you can go in under motivated, feeling like you all only need to show up to win. It's the flip-side of confidence.

The starters were showing a mix of confidence and fragility, trying ridiculous offloads but being cut apart by a demotivated group of reserves. You'll never see a darker group than the guys left out for a final and we were right down there. Being a reserve in the regular season is often greeted with black humour. Good environments convince the reserves that they are essential to the performance of the team that week and that their contribution matters. They also create an environment where there is the realistic possibility of moving between the two and getting to play. As soon as this mobility seems unrealistic, you start to lose the reserves psychologically. We were certainly lost psychologically by this point, given that there was no prospect of being selected again.

There's often a ridiculous charade early in the training week where a coach will select a team for an exercise, purporting it to be off the top of his head when it's obviously a starting team for the weekend. Dave Markham, often on the wrong end of this little play, used to turn around and say to whoever was there, 'Don't read anything into it.' Over my time, I've heard the reserves call themselves 'bin juice', 'the shags' and after my departure from Rouen and being told they had to *aide* the first team, they christened themselves 'Team Aids'. When we were shouted abuse at by a coach, we'd respond by shouting 'humiliate to motivate'. It was definitely time to leave.

That week went slowly but the team were leaving on Thursday to spend Friday and Saturday down near Oyonnax where they would train and prepare.

The unselected leftovers were going out.

We went to Delirium and really got after it. As Sia had thankfully stayed at home, it was just me and the French guys. The mood wasn't too melancholic considering but I realised that this was the first bit of extended time I'd spent alone with any of the French guys for quite a while. The professionalisation of the club had led to an increase in the size of the foreign contingent and a natural division in the squad. Here was a last chance for me to go back to how it had been in the first place, hanging out with French people on their terms.

I had a long chat with Bastien Le Picaut, Mr Pickles as he was known to everyone. He had arrived with Flo, used to a job share at loose head prop and had been left out himself. He was leaving to sign for Rennes and train as an orthodontist part time. He told me about his review and I thought I'd misunderstood his grammar; it sounded like he was saying that he gave Hilly a review.

He nodded at me and I burst out laughing.

Bastien had seen the reviews that had been given to the other players and had considered making one himself. He'd gone to bed but woken up unusually early, getting to work on his computer and making an identical version, complete with headed Stade Rouennais paper, that reviewed Hilly's performance over the past year. He'd basically taken my verbal approach, made it much funnier and been brazen enough to deliver it as if he was the senior party. He was a hero in the squad for doing this but he made a sad point at the end of the review; that season, Richard had made him hate playing rugby. There were more than a few in the squad who felt similarly.

We had a big night that passed without incident and travelled up to Oyonnax together to go and support the team. The final was to be held in the Oyonnax stadium and there would be a reasonable crowd with supporters having bussed over from Rouen, a pretty serious journey, and from Mâcon which was far closer.

The game kicked off, summer sun on an artificial surface makes the heat seem even greater, a haze almost hanging over the turf and the game was fast and error strewn. We were playing poorly, dropping the ball and unable to get into the Mâcon half. We missed some tackles and they broke our line, their ten having a field day carving through our defence. They scored some points and we didn't look up for it.

Then their ten made another break, racing up to our 22m line where he encountered the sweeping Gabin. He went to step him and fell over, spilling the ball. Gabin scooped it up and booted it roughly down the field, haring after it. As they'd been on the offence and streaming up the field in support of their playmaker, there was no one at home and Gabin, being especially fast on the artificial turf, had no problem picking the ball up and touching down for our first try.

We'd been poor but were now ahead and Mâcon's heads dropped.

We butchered a couple of opportunities and the game was still tight. Zack was growing into the game and kicked some penalties, giving us a bit of a cushion. Then in the second half, Gabin got on the outside of his marker and offloaded to Marno who had a clear run to the line. The game was basically over then.

We all came down onto the pitch to receive medals, involved on the day or not, and the team were celebrating. I was pleased for the boys but again, felt apart from it; the team doctor telling me to go and join in meant that my discomfort was palpable and I felt like an imposter. We'd won and played poorly with some of the points I'd raised in my meeting being evident but it was somewhat emblematic of our year. A load of effort, winning without putting our best on the field and sort of for nothing. The real final would be disputed in the *poule élite*, with promotion at stake. This was a sort of phoney war for the teams deemed not worthy of moving up the French rugby totem pole.

We had a big night drinking in Oyonnax with a nightclub visit in Bourg-en-Bresse. It wasn't a great night out, beginning with Hilly working his way around those not involved, despite being the very last person that any of us wanted to speak to. I wanted to tell him to fuck off but I'm not really brave enough for that.

We got back to the team hotel at about 6am and some of us sat up by the lake drinking. Fabien kept everyone amused by winging the Jean Prat Trophy, an enormous wooden shield, into the water. Apparently, people break it every year. We stayed awake all night and into the next day, still drinking when we got on the bus back to Rouen.

Carrying on drinking into the second day was surreal. We didn't feel tired but elated and oddly not that drunk. The bus was well stocked with beers and we were going to spend all day getting back to Rouen so we all pressed on, singing and talking as the French autoroute carried us home.

Social occasions had seen some fraught incidents over the course of the year and after Joe and I had had a well-deserved nap, our first sleep since Friday night, the beers available began to run low. This was the flashpoint.

One guy had some beers from the communal stock stored under his seat. Another went to take them only to be told that he couldn't as they were reserved. His sarcastic comment afterwards was over-heard by the hoarder himself who followed him up the bus and called him out on it. They were so drunk that the argument went nowhere until the hoarder threw a punch at the other before being pulled apart and separated by the rest of us.

He'd basically lost an argument over a couple of cans of beer and rather than accept it, had resorted to violence. He'd been embar-rassed and lashed out trying to regain some pride, wouldn't calm down and told the other guy that he'd see him on the field back at the club.

This was ridiculous and seemed unlikely but lo and behold, back at the club hours later, in front of supporters and volunteers, he went for him, stalking him up the field towards the club house, batting off any attempt at peacemaking to try and go for him again. It was embarrassing, unseemly and shameful.

This guy was a senior member of the team but he'd effectively committed a workplace assault. Not in training where it might be brushed off but in full team kit, in front of other employees, senior management and members of the public. You'd think that this would at least get him disciplined. Nothing was made of it, highlighting the double standards prevalent at the club; he probably would have been sacked elsewhere or in a normal line of work. A guy in Sydney did something similar when I was there and was banned for life from the rugby club. The ideals of the club, the respect that we were told to show each other, were obviously a load of rubbish. It's this sort of hypocrisy that I was pleased to be leaving behind.

43

CELEBRATE GOOD TIMES

Mad Monday was unknown as a phenomenon when we arrived and after our last game of the first season, away at Angoulême, we suffered through an outrageous bus journey back and signalled our intention to meet by the river with some beers the following afternoon.

Being a Monday, most of the squad were at work so it was sparsely attended, leaving mostly just the English contingent. This changed dramatically during my time there.

Mad Monday is a largely Antipodean invention and involves the squad meeting on the Monday after their season ends, usually in fancy dress, to go on a drinking rampage. Australian rugby league teams are blessed with even fewer brain cells than us and have a much higher profile, rugby league being the predominant sporting code in Sydney and other parts of Australia.

These events typically get out of hand and clubs have even taken to employing security teams to accompany their players out, knowing that they can't stop them partaking in the traditional outing.

These staff are to protect the players from punters, each other and themselves. Several have lost their contracts due to idiocy on Mad Monday, one incident standing out where a photo of a player with his dick in a dog's mouth appeared on Twitter.

So why instigate this sort of day? It acts as a last hurrah for the team before everyone goes away on holiday. People turn over a lot in professional sport and it becomes a send-off for those who are leaving, as well as drawing a line under the season as a whole. It is also, when done right, a bloody good time.

The second year we were knocked out in the quarter final against Strasbourg after having secured promotion. This was a bit unexpected but, after it emerged that we were not contracted beyond that round of games if we won, we had ended up losing and not playing well. With our season's goal achieved frankly, everyone just wanted to stop anyway.

This Mad Monday was well attended, although we were a little unclear on where to go later, ending up in a bar running a salsa dance class. Our little winger Johanny is an excellent dancer and he entertained some of the locals while the rest of us carried on drinking rather than lurch around treading on everyone's toes. Some of the lads went to Barcelona the day afterwards to carry on the rampage but I declined that year.

That was a big one but the next year saw an even greater escalation as the whole of the squad bought in. We set a bit of a route through the town, stopping at various spots before making our way to the park behind the Hotel de Ville. This place is slightly secluded, grassy and comfortable and not far from a shop to get refills as well as O'Kallaghan's and various fast food establishments for later in the evening.

For its association with our good times, this park became known as The Park of Dreams.

This time, more of the lads drew in to Barcelona and we were there for four days of frivolity. By the end, I was a broken man, my girlfriend being disgusted with my appearance at the airport, commenting that I 'didn't look like myself', I was sweating and that I stank. I needed a couple of days to get over it. The trip was regarded as a success and most of the next year was spent talking about the inevitable next one and trying to get the new president to pay for it if we won the trophy.

My final season was probably the greatest Mad Monday. Due to winning the final, it was held in the June sunshine and there was no team trip away afterwards; the season had gone on too long for another Barcelona jaunt, the president didn't want to pay and everyone just wanted to go home. It was all on this last big session.

The boys came out in force and I'd purchased my inflatable dinosaur costume months previously, managing to keep it a secret. I walked around the corner resplendent in my getup and was treated like a hero, the others creasing with laughter, until Polo and Robin came around the next corner with the exact same costumes about thirty seconds later.

I'd organised the route and we got the metro so Boya could lead us in his traditional nonsense song before we alighted on our side of the river to spend some time in the new park on the Left Bank. We then made our way to a sponsor restaurant who furnished us with more beer, ice and tables to stand on so that we could party in the town centre. Then we made our way to the cathedral, where a small garden with benches and stone walls is secreted round the side, Fono fell asleep dressed as 'Rastaman', a sort of ersatz Jamaican super-hero, and he was rudely awoken by the boys yelling at him. Amazingly he managed to keep his temper, seeing the funny side as the team headed to The Park of Dreams.

The Park of Dreams hosted an almighty bash with music, dancing, swimming in the fountain and copious beer drinking and, as the afternoon lengthened, the idea of going to the Mairie to receive our official congratulations from the mayor seemed less and less appealing. When Olivier arrived, he was greeted ecstatically before we realised that he'd only really come to make sure we turned up for the official reception. He was then booed mercilessly before we made our way there and performed the haka outside, led by Nick Seymour, our one real link to the ancient ritual being a New Zealander. We were officially received looking like an absolute shower, Fabien pulling his Adam West era Batman mask back on to his face to make his speech, sweating away in the opulent surroundings of the town's seat of power.

They'd never seen anything like it and we were covered quite comprehensively by the press, a load of idiots in costume eating canapés and drinking champagne when all we wanted was to be outside, away from these people, with each other drinking beers. Simple pleasures sometimes eclipse the trappings of success and we didn't want this recognition; we were pleased the season was over and we wanted to get on with celebrating.

After that it was the Irish Bar and *la continuation* late into the night.

44

WHAT HAPPENED NEXT?

No athlete ever ends his or her career the way you want to. We all
want to play forever. But it doesn't work that way. Accepting the
end gracefully is part of being a professional athlete.

— ALEX RODRIGUEZ

FIRSTLY, THERE WERE HANGOVERS TO NEGOTIATE. THEN, THE DAY
after the club didn't need us anymore, Nick and Joe were evicted
from their flat by the team, even though they were contractually entitled to be there until the end of the month. This surprised no one and
we let them store their stuff in our apartments and garages, the club's
behaviour towards us as a group now going beyond ridiculous.
These were two important players, Joe had spent four years there,
achieving promotion and a trophy with the club and they were told
to get everything out of their flat by the end of the day or pay for the
privilege.

The team recruited some Premiership players and went for promotion in 2017-18, playing in the *poule élite* and falling at the final hurdle
over two legs in the final. The guys who stayed didn't enjoy it much
and those Premiership recruits left after one season. They weren't

there long enough to build up an attachment to the place. The limit on foreign players meant that there would always be someone kicking their heels each weekend, unable to play due to regulation rather than any sort of selection policy.

The 2018-19 season saw them really go for it, the league reorganised into the old format, doing away with the *poule élite* and the rebranded Rouen Normandie Rugby steamrollered everyone in their group. The poor quality of the group stage meant that most of the season was a waiting room for the playoffs, each tie played over two legs with the two teams who reached the final being promoted into Pro D2 to compete with luminaries of French rugby such as Biarritz and Perpignan.

Rouen reached the semi finals, losing the first leg away from home by 11 points, meaning they had to win the home leg by 12 to reach the final and achieve promotion. The home tie at the Stade Diochon was a nail-biter but the Rouen kicker held his nerve to knock over a decisive penalty towards the end of the game, granting Rouen a victory on aggregate by 1 point. I would have liked to have gone to watch but I was away on a stag do, missing the celebrations in the home changing room afterwards. Luke returned to watch, kicking the ceremonial kickoff before taking his place in the *tribune* with the rest of the supporters. This season Rouen will be playing in Pro D2, a fantastic achievement.

Apparently, the outcome of the match wouldn't necessarily have mattered. Pro D2 have introduced a 'wildcard' promotion slot that will go to a team that:

•Must be located in northern France (with the dividing line running approximately from La Rochelle to Lyon)

•Have a long-term development plan

•Be located in an area that can demographically and economically support a fully professional club

Coincidentally, with the greater investment from Jean-Louis Louvel, Rouen Normandie Rugby fulfil these criteria, his political influence and financial clout coming to bear in ways that the previous presidents couldn't. The FFR had previously been petitioned by the club but had remained unmoved until Jean-Louis took over; these regulations appear to prioritise the expansion of French rugby in the non-traditional area of northern France over performance on the field. It's a moot point as the team have been promoted on their sporting merit but it seems that this was not necessarily a prerequisite for their ascension to the more rarefied levels of French rugby.

I don't have a problem with this. The game is in safe hands in the north of France with Rouen Normandie Rugby and now is an exciting time to join the project. It just shows how far the club has come, from an amateurish outfit where on field success was greeted with delight to a professional enterprise where on field success almost doesn't have any bearing on its immediate future. Sport is becoming ever more businesslike and Rouen can be a great asset to the French game as a whole.

This year's Pro D2 has 4 teams that Rouen have previously encountered or exchanged players with in Nevers, Vannes, Soyaux Angoulême and Valence Romans. These teams are not traditionally strong teams in the French rugby landscape; only Valence Romans have ever played in the top divisions; demonstrating that upward mobility is now very possible in rugby over the channel. The contrast between the vibrant French club rugby scene and that in the UK is somewhat damning where the Premiership want to close shop due to the vast disparities between them and the RFU Championship. How Rouen will do in Pro D2, contending with teams with bigger budgets for the first time, remains to be seen but I wish them all the best.

Another bit of upward mobility comes in the form of Gabin Villiere. The Super Cabbage became the toast of Normandy by helping Rouen achieve their promotion, while he overcame a tentative start to become one of the top performers on the World Sevens Series, garnering Player of the Tournament at the prestigious Hong Kong 7s in 2019. He clinched a move to Toulon in the Top 14 and will spend the 2019-20 season contending for a place in one of Europe's most storied teams, hoping to spearhead their revival. He's certainly proven me wrong and that his decision to remain at Rouen was a good one.

Richard is still there, his stock higher than ever with the president and the public as he's navigated the club into the promised land of Pro D2. His professional time at Rouen has certainly been a success. The turnover of staff and players during this period would perhaps paint another picture and there are not many that remain from my time at the club. Players, conditioners and physios turn over at a rapid clip and there has not been a consistent forwards coach for some time now. This could be framed as the cost of doing business as the club achieves a more rarefied level but I'd point to the lack of accountability and fairness when dealing with outlandish behaviour. You are what you walk past.

I was disappointed in him, with both his handling of me and of the other players and staff during my final year at the club. As I've alluded to, I can understand some of his decisions but others I found inexplicable. I felt a deep sense of relief when I arrived back in the UK and, now that I don't have to deal with the consequences of his decisions, I can view them with a sense of detachment that was previously impossible for me. We've spoken on the phone since and he's been supportive of this book. I hope he enjoys reading it and that I can make a Friday night game at Rouen to cheer the team on in Pro D2. Getting the club there, considering where we started, is a great achievement.

I gathered my things over the days following the final, not needing to move out immediately and prepared to go on holiday. The next stage of life awaited me but I wanted to enjoy my summer first. In some ways I'm still in the midst of this next stage, looking for my place, but think that writing might suit me. Now I've had time to reflect on my French adventure I look back on it fondly, even if there are things I would do differently. We can't get everything right and I loved my time in Normandy for the most part.

I miss the team environment; a load of guys like yourself, pulling in the same direction. I've been doing a lot of work alone, the polar opposite of my former working environment, and although I've always enjoyed a bit of my own company, I thrive on companionship and being part of a group. In my limited experience of 'normal' work, most workplaces don't foster much of a collective spirit and the bonds between you are far weaker. You don't hang out together on days off or stay up all night drinking. You don't push yourselves anywhere near a limit except that of your patience. Most people want to get things done and leave.

Rugby can be like this too and is losing some of its closeness as it professionalises, even as the best teams seem to retain the characteristics of camaraderie and brotherhood, of respect and honesty, regarding these qualities as key to their success. I hope that these values can remain, even as the body count stacks up and the wrangling over money continues. As a player, you are still more similar than you are different, even if you hail from all over the world. Running around and being fit is mostly a lot of fun, as is sipping coffee in various French pavement cafes watching the world go by.

I'd like to make another connection with France in the future, with its sheer size and beauty and its people's appetite to just be. I always felt like I was chasing something with my rugby that I was never clear about. The French are far more inclined to take things as they come. Quite often they don't ever arrive. And it turns out that that's fine.

My rugby story is at an end, something that I was, that I always wanted to be, is over but as time goes by, rugby will become just part of my story, something that I did once as a young man, that took me around the world and gave me immense joy, even if it also caused me some pain along the way.

It turns out it's true that *je suis un rugbyman*, but that's not all I am. My story will continue and I'll move forward, onto something else. I like to think though, that there will always be a little part of me in the clubhouse corner of the Mermoz field, even if like Jean Prat, it's there alone, looking out across the grass, reminiscing about simpler times.

NOTES

6. The Paris Suburbs

1. 'Great brutality' - a phrase that would enter our lexicon, being used to denote foul play, violence or harsh jokes.
2. Well worth a read if you're interested in French rugby - amusing to read about his then youthful teammates who are now at the end of their careers, including Louis Picamoles.
3. 'Away trip'.

7. Le Gros-Theil

1. Sadly not the Oasis one which would have been easier.

12. Saturday Night Fever

1. A fun phrase meaning 'to water the victory', usually with beers.

13. Race to the summit

1. 'Revenge' - they had evidently been stewing over their defeat earlier in the year.

14. YEAR TWO - Operation Promotion

1. The literal meaning is the slightly romantic 'hopes'; the *espoirs* are the academy players, treated as a separate entity from the main squad.

16. You can't win em all

1. This was correct at the time of writing but the 2019 edition has since eluded them…
2. 'They respect nothing!' This was also a common refrain from our teammates when French *politesse* was flouted by the foreigners during our day to day.

17. The big bigs

1. A *Star Wars* reference, referring to a Jedi's apprentice. Leo was insinuating that he was the Master to Ben Arous's Apprentice.

19. Back to the Diochon

1. A little jug or carafe. Probably the perfect amount of wine for a civilised lunch.

20. Off to the Playoffs

1. Essentially the Job Centre equivalent.

21. Being a Man

1. An infamous command levelled at LeBron James by a Fox News presenter in response to his comments on political and racial situations in the USA.
2. https://www.theatlantic.com/family/archive/2018/06/why-american-men-are-in-crisis/563807/

23. YEAR THREE - Fédérale 1 and becoming French

1. They have since been promoted to the Championship, making them a very serious outfit.
2. A fun word for kicker.

27. It's ok we've got this now

1. 1 Leeds have recently done something similar yet worse, cancelling everyone's contracts and leaving them on the hook for their previously covered medical bills.
2. 2 He's doing pretty well it turns out, often involved in their match day squads and turning out in the European Cup.

33. Rumour Mill Rumbling

1. 1 The greater urban area of the city of Rouen.
2. 2 'End his career.'

34. La Reprise

1. 1 'Tempest' - another bit of linguistic fun - we never have a tempest in the UK.

38. Athletic Capacity

1. Literally, 'The Festival of the Stomach'. Certainly accurate!
2. The French way of living politely and respectfully.

39. Respect

1. https://www.researchgate.net/publication/
270288637_Body_composition_characteristics_of_elite_Australian_rugby_unio
n_athletes_according_to_playing_position_and_ethnicity#pfa

ACKNOWLEDGMENTS

Writing this book has been a tough but wonderful experience.

I had been dabbling with it for a while before committing whole-heartedly to it, not quite certain about writing in general or the direction that I was going with the pieces I was putting together about rugby.

What I realised was that I had some aptitude, an alternative perspective that could be interesting to read and a desire to take on a creative project and stretch myself.

As you might have gathered from reading the book, I've been someone who was always keen to do unusual things, see new places and meet new people. I enjoyed physically testing myself during my rugby career but had latterly fallen into a bit of a rut, no longer looking for routes out of my comfort zone and having lost a bit of courage.

The book became a way to push on out of my own torpor and create something that I could be proud of. It's not taken that long in the grand scheme of things, about one year from beginning to end, but I've certainly held back from finishing it, getting it out there and getting on with my next stage of which this book is a key part. Saying goodbye to it is a big moment for me and hopefully the beginning of a new and exciting chapter of my story.

I have a lot of people to thank for enabling me to write this book. Firstly my family and friends who have been supportive throughout. Some of you have read passages, some have read the whole thing, some have just given me encouragement and advice. For all of that, I want to say thank you.

Maybe most importantly I need to thank my teammates. Not just my Rouen brothers but those who I've played with elsewhere, for one game or fifty. You've all shaped my worldview in some way, taught me things about other people and about myself that I would never have learned away from a rugby pitch.

I always knew that rugby's power lies in bringing together disparate people, it's part of the reason that France was mostly a wonderful experience, but since leaving the game I've realised quite how rare and extraordinary that is.

Most people carefully curate their immediate reality, rarely meeting or interacting with people who can challenge what they think they know. Your teammates will challenge you constantly, for better and worse and I wouldn't change it.

Rugby has given me friends all over the world whether they're former teammates or even adversaries. You don't need to be a professional player for this to be true but the shifting nature of employment at my less than rarefied level means that I have so many of you I can call on. Thank you for being there.

My Rouen teammates deserve particular credit - when I told them about my project, once I'd hit about 30,000 words and had some momentum, I messaged them for input, stories I may have forgotten and their own reminiscences. Not all of them have made it in, some of them are borderline to say the least, but that evening spent sitting in an armchair chuckling as the responses rolled in was one we've laughed about since. Reminiscing about past misdeeds is another way that rugby gives to you beyond the end of your time on the pitch.

I should also thank the various coaches I've come across. Some have taught me amazing things and made me think about the game and occasionally, who I am in a new way. Some have merely taught me how not to do things but those lessons are equally as valuable.

I should thank Richard Hill in particular for giving me the opportunity to go to France. He was a big part of my development as a young player and helped me have a great experience as an adult, even if we didn't see eye to eye by the end.

There are so many people I remember from rugby who deserve some credit. Any supporter who traversed the UK or France through hell or high water, or hail and no water, to follow a team I played for. Any parent who gave a teenage me a lift to a game in some backwater rugby club after a full day of work. Any club barman who slipped me a free drink. Thanks to all of you.

In terms of the book, this was largely a solo project in terms of the labour but there are a few people who need thanking. My friend James read a first draft and I was thrilled to hear from him that he thought it was good. He gave me actionable advice in his notes and the encouragement to press on and finish it.

I had some advice from experienced writers and creators who helped me with the process of shaping the book. Don McRae gave me pointers and contacts in the publishing game. Miranda West took the time to meet me and talk me through the publishing industry and some next steps. Cody Royle was incredibly generous with his advice and support over email regarding the content and the self publishing process.

My cover designer Adam McCarthy did a great job - when I received his first designs I was thrilled that he'd managed to interpret what I'd asked for in such a clever and striking way. If you want to get in touch with him then just ask me.

Lowri Pitcher has done a fantastic job with the proofread for the second edition. I only wish I'd got a hold of her when the book came out!

Helen Carr deserves a special mention - I bumped into her in the street and on hearing she was doing her own writing, we arranged to have a coffee. She gave me the confidence that my idea was a good one, a sense of possibility and the push over the edge to take it on. Thank you.

Mostly though I need to thank my editor Keziah Ford. She did a wonderful job of parsing through the book, correcting errors and suggesting improvements that were almost always obvious to her but not to me. When I received a file with over 1000 corrections, I realised the extent of her effort and expertise. She was indispensable, not only with her on page suggestions but also in pushing me to improve the text and finish the book. Thanks again.

Finally, thank you for reading this book, for sticking with me and for supporting my creative endeavour. The process of making this book has given me so much but if it's given you something too, then I'd love to hear about it.

À plus,

Ben

ABOUT THE AUTHOR

I'm a writer and former professional rugby player.

Fringes is my first book.

If you enjoyed reading then please leave a review.

To keep up with what I'm up to, visit my website at:

www.benmercer.me/now

Or even better, sign up to my email list to be first to hear when I'm working on something exciting or even to help shape it as it's being created:

https://www.benmercer.me/newsletter

For this book, my list received early draft material, samples of sections of the book and helped to design the cover. Who knows what they'll help me with moving forward!

Thanks for supporting my work,

Ben

OUR
RACE

THE UNTOLD STORY OF AN ALL-TIME SPORTING SHOCK
JASON GARDENER | DARREN CAMPBELL
MARLON DEVONISH | MARK LEWIS-FRANCIS
TRYSTAN BEVAN & BEN MERCER

How the Great Britain Men's 4x100m Relay Team shocked the world at
Athens 2004

OUR RACE - CHAPTER 1

2004 OLYMPIC GAMES ATHENS
10 MINUTES TO GO

The fastest men in the world stood in single file, the four of them waiting to show the world just how quickly a human could move.

The Athens air was tense with moisture and noise, the teams cramped in a small tunnel waiting to enter the arena. They whooped and called out the other teams, daring them to respond. They had won everything on offer individually so far at this games and now they were going to assert their dominance as a team. No one could touch them. If you did, all you would feel was tight, corded muscle and the iron self-belief of champions, straining beneath their red, white and blue vests.

They were Shawn Crawford, Justin Gatlin, Coby Miller and Maurice Greene. The fastest men in the world.

~

Prior to 2004, the United States of America's men's sprint relay team had been involved in a total of eighteen men's sprint final relays held at the Olympic Games going back to as far as 1920, winning gold in fifteen of them. They were utterly dominant. The event had not only become an exhibition of a track and field dynasty, but a final-event celebration of supremacy for Team USA. Winning was not only expected, it was expected to be fun. It was expected to be easy. It was their birthright.

Who were these unapproachable athletes, these men that no-one in the world could keep up with? They were sprint deities, picking up the mantles of men on the Mount Rushmore of sprinting. When your forebears belong in the sporting pantheon, figures like Carl Lewis and Jesse Owens, you arrive with a sense of destiny, a belief and entitlement to one day be spoken about in that company. To become a modern day myth.

Their lead out runner Shaun Crawford had recently become the first man in history to break 10 seconds for the 100m and 20 seconds for the 200m on the same day at an event in Pretoria, South Africa. Crowned Olympic 200m champion a few days earlier and finishing fourth in the 100m, Crawford had run sub-10 and sub-20 once again, albeit on seperate days. V-shaped, looking every inch the superhero, he ran with an implacable expression on his face, fully expecting to beat whoever opposed him, whether those were the rivals he beat to Olympic gold or the zebra he'd raced in a television special a few years earlier.

Justin Gatlin was the in-form athlete in the world. Crawford would pass the baton to a man who was not only the newly-crowned Olympic 100m champion but also a bronze medalist in the 200m. Gatlin would go on to be a five-time Olympic medallist, the fifth fastest of all time over 100 metres, a renowned drugs cheat and the man who ended the reign of Usain Bolt. Then at 6'1 and 23 years old, he had the world at his feet.

Gatlin would be taking the baton down the back straight and handing it to Coby Miller. Miller had recently written himself into the record books as the first ever American athlete to run sub-10 for the 100m in the USA Olympic trials and *fail* to qualify due to the standard of his contemporaries. He was the best of the rest for the Americans but would have strolled into any other nation's sprint team. He was in Athens with a point to prove.

Lying in wait on the last leg was Maurice Greene. The Kansas Cannonball was at 30 years of age the elder statesman of the quartet but in an alpha male lineup, he was still at the head of the pack. A 4-time Olympic medallist and 5-time world champion, he'd already equalled the records of two of America's greatest in Carl Lewis and Michael Johnson, his place on the mountain assured. Greene had been the fastest of all time, holding the 100m world record between 1999 and 2002, and despite all this, had his own point to prove. At these games, he'd been disappointed with his 100m bronze after losing out to team-mate Gatlin and was looking to supplant Team USA's all time greats with another Olympic gold. A man who had nothing to prove to anyone felt like he did.

Even those who didn't make the cut were a frightening prospect. Sydney 100m gold medallist Tim Montgomery, future world championship gold medallist Tyson Gay and Bernard Williams, a relay gold medallist in 2000 in Sydney and claiming 200m silver in Athens. The list went on but they weren't even here. This was the strength in depth of Team USA. How could anyone else hope to compete?